ALCATRAZ

MERRY-GO-ROUND

BY
LEON WHITEY THOMPSON

♣♣♣♣♣

To find out Leon Whitey Thompson's scheduled days to appear on Alcatraz, please call:
Alcatraz Books Stores
(415) 705-1046

WINTER BOOK PUBLISHER
LEON AND HELEN THOMPSON
P.O. BOX 219
FIDDLETOWN, CA 95629

i

DEDICATION

This book is dedicated to my wife Helen, she is a gem.

Also, to my beloved Wolf Hybrids, past and present. And to the Wolves of nature, and may they once again run free.

ACKNOWLEDGMENTS

I want to thank the following people for their encouragement. Ron and Ellen Strope who are a part of our family, and all their critters. Perky, Jeff, and Carol Perkins, Hank and Euona Rathjen. A special thank you to Dr. William Foote, also to Linda Nielsen, and Terry Tyler. I would also like to thank Terry Koenig and Frank Heaney for their trust and faith in me, and the rest of the staff of the Red and White Fleet for their friendship over the years. The three men I owe my life to, Dr. George Schilling, Dr. Alan S. Coulson, and Dr. Chen Liem. To Naomi Torres, Supervisory Park Ranger, and the National Park Service. To Nicki Phelps, Stan "the man" Zbikowski, and to the staff of the Golden Gate National Park Association.

And of course, my thanks to the Man Above.

AUTHOR'S NOTE

Writing my books, **ROCK HARD**, and the sequel **ALCATRAZ MERRY-GO-ROUND,** was a big challenge for me. I never went past the 6th grade, and I received no other formal education.

This book was previously titled **THE MERRY-GO-ROUND** and I have updated it, and it is now titled **ALCATRAZ MERRY-GO-ROUND.**

The writing of both books was the idea of my wife Helen. She encouraged me to write these books, so in 1980 we started this long project. **ROCK HARD** previously titled **LAST TRAIN TO ALCATRAZ** was completed in 1988. **ALCATRAZ MERRY-GO-ROUND** after many weeks of tedious work was finally completed in 1990. A total of ten years work on both books. Every word was written by me although Helen corrected the spelling and grammar. This is a true story, every incident actually occurred. All the characters are real, although some of the names have been changed.

Whitey is currently working on a novel titled, **DEADLY LITTER** which he hopes to publish soon.

Leon Whitey Thompson

FORWARD

DONNA MIDDLEMIST NPS
GOLDEN GATE NATIONAL PARK RECREATION AREA

ALCATRAZ MERRY-GO-ROUND is a deeply moving story of an incredible journey, taking one man, Leon Thompson, from fugitive on the run, to convict inside the walls, to the ultimate joy of realizing, with the gift of understanding, one's own self worth. It provides the reader a look into the very depths of a man's soul, with focused clarity sharply defining his weaknesses and his strengths, his emotions and his feelings, his fears and his joys, and always, the ever present desire to be free. Every word is a vivid color, flowing together on the canvas of life, creating a portrait of an experience one can only imagine—unless of course, one has lived it.

ALCATRAZ MERRY-GO-ROUND continues from **ROCK HARD** with the boy who wanted only to be loved, to the convict who wished only to be free, to the indescribable ecstasy of knowing freedom—only to once again lose it.

The turning point in Leon Thompson's life was born on the train ride from McNeil Island to San Francisco, slowly, almost imperceptibly nurtured on Alcatraz, and finally forged into realization many years later with the introduction of that for which he had searched his entire life—love, and it attendant faith and respect. The provider of this most precious gift was, of course, Leon's lovely Helen.

The people in this story are real people, each with an incredible contribution to this extraordinarily fascinating thing called life. Two of these people I am deeply privileged to call friend. They are warm and wonderful, charming and gracious. Leon and Helen Thompson are real.

In conclusion, I would ask that as the reader you focus on this one important fact: **ALCATRAZ MERRY-GO-ROUND** is the story of a human being—a human being who was Whitey Thompson, the convict, but is today what always he has been—Leon Thompson, the man.

ALCATRAZ

THE DESIRE TO BE FREE

Take a moment and listen - I've something to share
About some men for whom you may not care,
But they lived and that existance must be known
Because it's of importance - not just to their own.
You need to know of their thoughts and their mind,
For regardless of the journey, they were still humankind;
These men who rode the train and climbed the hill,
Whose voices in the cellhouse echo still.

Some of the men who came here were able to find
Alcatraz a prison just of the body, not of the mind,
And that their dreams could take them away
To another time, another place, another day;
Perhaps then to know and to understand the past
And maybe to realize prison doesn't have to last;
These soulless faces who rode the train and climbed the hill,
Whose voices in the cellhouse echo still.

Some of these men may have once been gentle and kind
And not the sort of man here one would expect to find,
But these were men of another place and another time,
Men for whom desire was really their only crime.
Men who were completely consumed by the unspeakable rage
Of having to face the non-existence of their world in a cage;
These long confined men who rode the train and climbed the hill,
Whose voices in the cellhouse echo still.

I feel the silence of their presence every day,
But with the passing of time it's in a soft and muted way
As I walk the blocks and out through the yard
With my thoughts running free, with no cares to guard.
It's then I wonder if just one night here you could be
Whether you might know the sound of their desire to be free;
The sound of the men who rode the train and climbed the hill.
Whose voices in the cellhouse echo still.

There is no brighter flame than from the kindled fire
Of a need which here can never be more than desire.
But it is just that, nothing else, don't you see?
It's the wish of these men - it is their desire to be free!
But this you must understand with love - not with fear,
In order to know it was *that* which brought them here;
These long ago men who rode the train and climbed the hill,
Whose voices in the cellhouse echo still.

DONNA MIDDLEMIST— MARCH 21, 1989.

ALCATRAZ, "THE DESIRE TO BE FREE," WAS WRITTEN IN MARCH 1989 BY ALCATRAZ RANGER DONNA MIDDLEMIST. DONNA HAS BEEN A PARK RANGER FOR A NUMBER OF YEARS, AND SHE TOO HAS WALKED THE CELLHOUSE FLOOR DURING DAILY DUTIES ON ALCATRAZ. SHE HAS ESCORTED HUNDREDS OF TOURISTS THROUGHOUT THE ISLAND. DURING THESE TOURS, ABOVE THE NOISE OF THE CROWD, SHE TOO COULD FEEL THE LONELINESS THE PRISONERS ONCE FELT, SHE TOO COULD HEAR THE ECHO OF THEIR VOICES THROUGHOUT THE CELLHOUSE STILL. THIS INSPIRED HER TO WRITE THE POEM, "THE DESIRE TO BE FREE." SHE CAME TO KNOW LEON WHITEY THOMPSON AND UNDERSTOOD HIS FEELINGS, AND IN DOING SO SHE DEDICATED THIS POEM TO WHITEY AND THE LONG FORGOTTEN PRISONERS OF ALCATRAZ.

Thank you Donna.
Leon Whitey Thompson.

PART 1.

ALCATRAZ TO FOLSOM

A NEW NUMBER A-92856

♣♣♣♣♣

PROLOGUE

♣ ♣ ♣

Alcatraz Island, (known as the Rock) was the most notorious and feared United States Federal Penitentiary this country has ever known. On October 25, 1962, Leon "Whitey" Thompson, after serving four years three months and six days was freed from this prison. In 1948, prior to his time on Alcatraz, Leon "Whitey" Thompson, convicted for bank robberies, and sentenced to fifteen years was incarcerated at McNeil Island Federal Penitentiary. This prison is in the State of Washington out in Puget Sound. On July 19, 1958, after serving ten years at McNeil Island, due to a disciplinary action for violence, Whitey was transferred to Alcatraz. There he served the remainder of his fifteen-year sentence.

When a prisoner nears completion of his sentence with only a few months to go before his release, he is usually transferred from Alcatraz to the penitentiary where he came from. Then he is discharged. The Federal Bureau of Prisons did not like to set anyone free directly from Alcatraz. For Leon "Whitey" Thompson, his fifteen-year sentence was almost completed. He had a few months to go and was waiting to be transferred back to McNeil Island for discharge.

On October 22, 1962, the cell house officer ordered Whitey to remain in his cell and not to come out for work call. "Well this is it," he thought, "I guess they're gonna get me ready for McNeil Island." But Whitey was wrong and was in for a big surprise that morning.

"Work call, Work call," the guards shouted. The moment the cell doors clanged open, the prison came alive with the thunderous sound of shuffling feet as the prisoners in single file marched off the tiers. In the wake of the noise, as ordered, Whitey remained in his cell. A few moments passed. Then suddenly with tremendous force, his cell door banged open and a guard shouted, "Okay Thompson, report over to A Block the Counselor wants a word with you."

Whitey reported to A Block and received word that he was being released from prison on a court order from Federal Judge Sherril Hallibert. When the release papers arrive he would be set free.

This was quite a surprise and a shock to Leon "Whitey" Thompson who never had a visit or a letter in fifteen years. Directly after

3

receiving the news Whitey was taken to the photo lab for a current mug shot. This photo was to be sent to all the police stations notifying them that Leon "Whitey" Thompson, AZ-1465 was being released directly from Alcatraz. After the mugshot photo was taken Whitey received his dress-out, and was returned to his cell B-204 to await his release.

Two days later, October 25, 1962, Whitey was set free after saying goodbye to a few close friends, Johnny House, Lou Peters, Big Longo to name a few. In the 29 years of Alcatraz prison history, Leon "Whitey" Thompson, AZ-1465 was one of 6 men to ever be released directly from Alcatraz to the free world. No one but Whitey, and the other five men will ever experience the feeling of being set free directly from Alcatraz. For Whitey, October 25, 1962, was a day to remember.

Whitey returned to Sacramento, the same city where fifteen years ago he was convicted of bank robberies, and sent to prison. After checking into a boarding house he quickly went about looking for work. Employment was hard to fine. Whitey had eighteen hundred dollars in his pocket that he had earned in prison industry. He used this money for a down payment on a used Kenworth truck. It was not long before he least his rig out to Senator Truck Service and started driving over the road. For Whitey it was a feeling of achievement, it was hard for him to believe that a few weeks earlier he was sitting in a cell on Alcatraz. Now he was sitting behind the wheel of a big rig.

Shortly after leasing out to Senator Truck Service, Whitey met Brenda who had two small children. She invited him to move in with her, and he accepted the offer. It was like a ready-made family and Whitey took over the responsibility of taking care of it.

The first year passed by quickly. Whitey devoted his life to his work Brenda and her children. The man from Alcatraz had found real love, and he was happy.

CHAPTER 1.

Whitey climbed up into the cab of his big Kenworth truck; the rig was parked close to Pier 41. He relaxed while he ate the hamburger and fries that he had bought from a concession stand on Fisherman's Wharf.

He had an hour to kill before he picked up his return load to Sacramento. As he munched on his hamburger, he thought about Brenda. Life with her had been good to him, they had been living together over two years now, and he thought it was time he asked her to marry him.

With thoughts of Brenda and her two children, he took a big bite of the hamburger. He was sure she would be surprised at his early arrival home twenty-four hours before she expected him.

Whitey sat there eating his lunch with his eyes focused on an island out in the Bay—Alcatraz. He remembered long ago just before pulling a bank job, he was parked in this very spot. He was looking at the Island and it reminded him of a grim battleship lying at anchor in the Bay. Alcatraz, the most notorious prison this country has ever known was closed now, and her dark secrets were hidden within her walls. It was just two years ago Whitey was a prisoner on this Island, and today it seemed like a dream, a haunting dream that would not let go.

The despair was painful thinking about Alcatraz and the few good friends he had left behind. Lou Peters, Johnny House, Big Longo, every friend he ever had on the Rock, like roll-call, their faces were flashing in front of him.

A screeching sea gull brought him back to reality. He looked at his watch—it was time to pick up his load.

After picking up his cargo he was on the road again making the short run to Sacramento. There he unloaded as quickly as possible, picked up his car, and drove directly home.

As he walked in the front door a strange voice called out, "Who's there?"

Without replying, Whitey walked into the kitchen and was surprised to see a young teenage girl sitting at the table. She sat

5

motionlessly with a sandwich in one hand and a glass of milk in the other. Her eyes were wide open, and in a fearful voice she said, "Who—who are you?"

Whitey replied in an angry voice, "I live here. Where's Brenda? And who the hell are you?"

"I'm the babysitter. Brenda's gone out on a date. Are you her brother?"

Thinking quickly Whitey replied, "Yeah—yeah, I'm her brother. How did you know that?"

"She told me, she told me her brother was staying here, but was seldom home because he was a truck driver, and always on the road."

"How long have you been Brenda's babysitter? And where do you live?"

"I live a couple of houses down the road, I've been babysitting for Brenda two three times a week for the past two and a half months. My name's Alice Corvel, I'm fourteen."

Whitey extracted a five-dollar bill from his wallet and handed it to her, "This is for your trouble Alice. I'll look after the kids; you might as well go home."

Her eyes opened wide at the amount of money he handed her, "I've only been here twenty minutes," she exclaimed, "Brenda only pays me fifty cents an hour."

"That's all right Alice, you've earned the extra. You can go home now."

Once the babysitter had departed Whitey looked in on the girls, both Mary and Jackie were sound asleep. He returned to the kitchen and got a beer from the refrigerator, lit a cigarette and sat at the table. He drank the beer and smoked one cigarette after another. He was not a jealous man, and it never occurred to him that Brenda might be cheating and he wanted to give her the benefit of the doubt. She might have gone to a show with a girlfriend, and if so everything would be all right. After drinking six cans of beer he thought it was time to go to bed.

He turned off the lights and in the darkness started for the bedroom, but stopped in his tracks when he heard a car pulling up in front of the house. Slightly parting the curtains he peeked out the window just in time to see the car door swing open. Automatically the dome cast a ray of light throughout the interior of the automobile. Sitting in the front seat was Brenda with her hand on the opened door. Next to her with his arm around her shoulder, sat a middle-aged man. The rays from the dome light were dim, making it impossible for Whitey to distinguish the man's features. Brenda released the door handle, and turned her attention to the stranger. She gave him a quick hug and a kiss before getting out of the car. She dashed up the front porch steps in such a hurry to enter the house, she did not notice Whitey's car

6

parked in the driveway.

She reached for the light switch by the front door, and as she did so she called out, "Alice—Alice I'm home."

When she switched on the light, she expected to see Alice asleep on the couch. Instead she saw Whitey sitting there. She was startled at the sight of him, her face paled and she cried, "My God what're you doing home? I wasn't expecting you. Where's the babysitter?"

"I sent her home," Whitey replied in a soft chilling voice.

Brenda regained her composure, color returned to her face, "What the hell are you doing home? I thought you were on your way to Nevada with a load."

"That was postponed. They gave me a load back here to Sacramento."

"Bullshit! You son of a bitch, there never was a load for Nevada, you're just trying to check up on me."

"I wasn't checking up on you. The Nevada trip was postponed. If I had a chick on the side, I wouldn't of came home so early."

"What the fuck do you mean by that?" Brenda shouted. "You saying I'm cheating on you?"

"I'm telling you the straight facts. I no sooner leave the house for work, and you're on the phone calling a babysitter. Why? Just tell me why."

"Because I felt like it goddamn it, I felt like it," she screamed at him, "and if you must know, I went to a movie—is that a fucking crime?"

Whitey jumped off the couch and grabbed Brenda by the shoulders and held her in a firm grip, "I don't give a damn if you go to a movie, it's who you go with that I care about. I just seen you out there kissing some dude in a car, deny it."

Tearing herself loose she screamed in a high-pitched voice, "No I won't deny it, why should I? I'm not married to you you bastard, I'll go out with anyone I please." She continued to cuss and scream, "Do you hear me you son of a bitch, I'll do as I please you dirty bastard you no good. . . ."

She didn't get a chance to finish. Whitey grabbed her and clamped a hand over her mouth. For a split second he was tempted to choke the life out of her, but he quickly restrained himself and said, "We no doubt woke the girls up with all this screaming, now just shut up and listen to me." He removed his hand from her mouth and continued, "For the past couple of years I've been breaking my ass trying to make a home for us, but you don't give a shit about anyone but Brenda. You're not even concerned about your kids, for if you were, then this argument wouldn't be taking place."

"What do you mean I'm not concerned about . . . ?"

"I told you to shut up, and don't interrupt me again."

7

Once again her face paled showing signs of fear.

"You ain't worth it Brenda, you're not worth the argument. So we'll end it right now, just as soon as I can pack my clothes, I'll get to hell out of here."

"That's right, gets the hell out of here, who needs you anymore? I certainly don't!"

It didn't take Whitey long to collect his things, and after he was packed, he went to the girl's room to say goodbye. Brenda was at their bedside trying to soothe the crying children.

"Get out of here your bastard! I don't want your kind round my children!" she screamed.

At the sound of her mother's voice Jackie began to cry louder, while Mary pleaded, "Please don't leave us Whitey, don't go."

With outstretched arms and fingers clawing, Brenda hurled herself at Whitey. He sidestepped the charging woman, and again getting her under control he shook her violently.

"That's it, that's enough Brenda. Just shut up now, I'll be out of here just as soon as I say goodbye to the kids. Now shut up." He released his grip on her, and turned to the children who were now crying profusely.

"Don't cry girls, everything will be all right," he assured them as he cuddled them both in his arms.

"You're not going to leave us is your Whitey? Please don't leave us."

He tried his best to comfort them and set their minds at ease, "Look girls I have to go away, but I want you to listen to your mother and does as she say, okay?" Whitey was cooing and tickling them until at last they began to giggle, "Okay Whitey, we'll mind Mamma, and do as you say."

Whitey hugged and kissed both children, and in a soft voice he said, "Okay girls, I love you, now go to sleep, everything will be just fine."

He picked up his suitcase and started for the front door, and as he reached for the knob he turned his head toward Brenda who was closing the door to the children's room. "I don't know what your gonna tells the girls in the morning, I know you won't tell the truth."

"It's none of your business what I tell them," she replied in a sarcastic voice.

"What're you going to tell them next time there's no food in the house, and they're hungry?"

"Get out of here damn you, get out!"

It was 12:30 A.M. when Whitey pulled up in front of the Raven Club. The bar was crowded and doing a roaring trade. He shouldered his way up to the brass rail and ordered a double shot of whiskey and a beer chaser. Once the drinks were poured, he

8

handed the bartender a ten-dollar bill, and before the man returned with the change, Whitey downed the drinks and ordered a refill.

I don't understand it, he thought to himself, for two and some half years I put a carpet under her feet and treated her like a lady. After everything I've done for her now she rejects me as if I were trash. Just about everything she has in that house I bought and paid for, from the furniture to the clothes on her back. The night I met her she didn't have so much as a slice of bread in the house. The dirty bitch, I should go back and kick her brains out. I just can't let her get away without doing something to her. I know what I'll do, she said she never had so much food in her home until I came along. I'll empty the freezer and throw away all the food. Yeah that's what I'll do. The son of a bitch!

It was ten minutes to two when Whitey staggered out of the bar and made his way to his car. With great difficulty he opened the door and crawled behind the wheel. Before trying to start the car he decided to light a cigarette. He fumbled for a match and in doing so he dropped the cigarette to the floorboard. He tried to retrieve it, but in the darkness he could not find it. He attempted to light another one; this time he succeeded. His next challenge was starting the engine, and after many tries he finally got the ignition key into the hole. The motor fired up, and luckily, without an accident he drove back to the house.

Once there he went directly to the garage where the freezer was kept. He started to empty the freezer out, and made trip after trip carrying the frozen food to his car where he stacked it in the trunk. He had removed over four hundred dollars worth of frozen meat, etc. On his final trip the kitchen lights suddenly came on casting a ray of light across the driveway. Startled, he tried to run, and in his drunken condition he dropped a package of meat. He did not realize it, nor did he see Brenda looking out the window as he scampered toward his car and drove away.

He headed straight for West Sacramento, and before he arrived at the Flying A Truck Stop, he pulled his car into a vacant lot. He opened the trunk and began to dispose of the frozen food. As he slammed each package of meat to the ground, he cussed Brenda out, "You won't eat any more of my food bitch!" Once the distasteful chore was completed, he continued to the Truck Stop. After parking the car, he climbed into the sleeping compartment of his truck, and fell asleep.

9

CHAPTER 2.

The following morning, shortly after nine, he was rudely awakened by a pounding on the cab door. He had very little sleep and was still feeling the effects of the night before. The pounding continued as a voice called out, "Thompson, Whitey Thompson this is the police. Are you in there?"

"Get away from here goddamn it, I want to sleep."

The pounding began again, only more vigorously, and the tone of the voice was louder, "Thompson, come out of that sleeper, unlock the door or we will bust it in!"

Pushing back the covers, Whitey turned his head toward the window to get a look at the intruders.

"Ah shit!" he cussed. He could not believe what his bleary eyes saw. Hanging onto the side of the cab and looking through the window was a policeman. Whitey unlocked the door, and as soon as it was opened the policeman ordered him out of the truck.

"What for? What the hell do you want with me?"

"You are Leon W. Thompson, also known as Whitey Thompson. I have a warrant for your arrest."

"A warrant for my arrest! Are you crazy? What the hell's the charge?"

"The charge is burglary. I'm sorry Thompson, I have to take you in."

"Burglary? What burglary?"

Whitey climbed down out of the truck as another officer appeared from the opposite side of the vehicle, and slipped handcuffs on him. "Is this your car parked here?" the policeman asked as he pointed to Whitey's Chevy. Without waiting for a reply he quickly shook Whitey down and found his car keys and opened the trunk, only to find it empty.

"What are you looking for? Who the hell am I supposed to have burglarized?" Whitey asked.

"The D.A. will answer your question's Thompson. Let's get into the patrol car"

Whitey was taken to the city jail and booked on suspicion of burglary. Later that morning, under guard, he was escorted to the District Attorney's office where he was confronted by an assistant

10

D.A.

"Well, I assume we have Mr. Thompson here?" The D.A. spoke with authority.

Whitey did not answer, but merely stood there glaring across the desk at the D.A.. The D. A. reminded him of a flat-faced Pekingese, with brown dog eyes, eager to pounce on a bone.

Still looking at Whitey, the D.A. spoke again, "All right Thompson, I'm sure you know why you are here."

"No, I don't know," he returned in a surly voice, "you tell me."

"All you punks are alike," the D.A. sneered, "you get yourself arrested, and then you don't know why. You're here on suspicion of burglary. You stole food from a woman with two children. How low can you get?"

"I didn't steal nothing from her."

"Deny it all you want Thompson, but she saw you at approximately 3:00 A.M. this morning running out of her driveway."

"Hey I don't deny being in her driveway this morning, and I don't deny taking the food, but I didn't steal it. I bought and paid for every piece of food that was in the freezer including the freezer itself, and besides I was living there."

"She says different Thompson, she says you never lived there. She admitted to me that she had gone out with you several times over the past two and a half years, but that's as far as it went. She also told me how you tried to win her favor by bringing her gifts of clothes, food, money, and furniture. Last night she told you she didn't want you coming around anymore. You got mad, and later on came back and broke into her garage and stole her food."

"That's a crock of shit! I supported and took care of her and her kids for over two years. I paid for everything including the rent."

"Can you prove you paid the rent?"

Whitey knew he was lost, he could not prove that he gave her money each week for all receipts including the rent, were in her name.

"No I have nothing in writing."

"That's what I thought. You paid for nothing Thompson, nothing."

"That's a damn lie! Why don't you ask her children? Or are you afraid they'll tell the truth?"

Giving Whitey a cold hard stare the D.A. replied, "I don't have to ask anyone about you Thompson. I know all I want to know. I checked you out for priors, and guess what I came up with? You're nothing but a hard-case, you don't belong on the streets. You were sentenced to fifteen years for bank robberies. You were incarcerated at McNeil Island Federal Prison. Even in prison you couldn't stay out of trouble so you were transferred to Alcatraz to finish your term. On October 25, 1962, you were released from Alcatraz. Isn't that so Thompson?"

11

"Yeah it's true, so what? I did my time"

"Let's see now," the D.A. continued, "you've been out over two years, what have you been doing all this time?"

Whitey was angry and shouted, "What the hell do you think I've been doing? I've been working."

"Besides working, what else have you been doing?"

"Nothing. I'm clean goddamn it"

"Bullshit! I'm sure you committed a few felonies since your release."

"You're a fucking liar?" Whitey hissed. "I haven't done a thing wrong and you know it."

"Except commit a burglary!" the D.A. snickered.

"That's a fucking lie too. That bitch is framing me, and you're helping her do it."

"Now why would I do a thing like that Thompson? Just tell me why?"

Whitey took a step forward, "Why? Because you're a no-good bastard, that's why!"

The D.A. was infuriated at Whitey's remark, "Take him back and lock him up," he ordered the officer, "take the suspicion off and book him on burglary."

With the guard at his side, Whitey called back, "You're nothing but a shyster, a mother fucking shyster!"

Whitey was returned to jail and placed in a holding tank. The cubicle was crowded with recently arrested men who were waiting to be assigned to cells. The smell of compressed bodies blended in with the stench of human waste and disinfectant, was more than one could bear. The sound of voices was deafening as the angry prisoners tried to talk above the noise of each other. Now and then someone would shout, "Hey you fucking coppers, let me out of here!"

Others would call out, "How about my phone call? I'm entitled to a call."

"I got your phone hanging between my legs, and it's yours to use!" Someone heckled.

"Hey, you some kind of wise-guy? I'll cave your fuckin' head in."

"Up your ass punk, cave this in!"

Shouting in each other's ears was enough to get on your nerves. To make matters worse, apart from two benches that ran alongside the walls, there was no place to sit. If a person chose to sit on the floor he would be trampled by many feet.

Whitey was standing near the end of one of the occupied benches. He reached into his pocket for a cigarette, and lit up.

"Hey can you spare one?" a gruff voice asked.

Whitey turned to the speaker. Sitting on the end of the bench was a rough-looking individual in dire need of a shave.

"No, I can't," Whitey replied, "but I'll tell you what. I'll give you a cigarette for your place on the bench, is it a deal?"

"Okay it's a deal," the man returned, "give me the smoke first, then you can have my seat."

"No way, when I sit in your spot, then I'll give the smoke, and not before."

"Suppose I just take the fucking smoke from you?"

Whitey was in no mood for threats, as it was he had enough on his mind. The man on the bench never saw the punch coming as Whitey drove a powerhouse right hitting him square on the jaw. Before the man could recover, he received another one to the mid-section. Doubling up, he fell off the bench onto the floor amid the many feet. Taking his place on the bench, Whitey sat and stared at the wide-eyed victim as he pulled himself off the floor. Reaching into his pocket Whitey retrieved another cigarette and handed it to the fallen man.

"This is for the seat, but don't ever threaten me again pal. Next time I'll stomp your head in!"

Immediately his thoughts returned to Brenda. He couldn't understand her actions. She had betrayed him. She had betrayed a man whose only ambition was to make life better for her and the children. He was saddened at the thought of them, for they too had become victims of their mother's stupidity.

His thoughts were interrupted when a guard called his name, "Quiet down in here, is there a Leon W. Thompson in this tank?"

"Yeah I'm here," Whitey answered.

"Come out of there," the guard ordered, "there's someone here to see you."

After being released from the tank, the guard led Whitey past the booking department to a doorway at the end of the corridor. The visiting area was divided by a thick pane of glass that extended from one end of the room to the other. On each side of the see-through panel was a row of stools, one side for visitors, the other for inmates. The only means of communication was by telephones that hung in their respective spots in front of each stool.

Whitey was astonished to see Brenda seated on the other side of the glass. Holding the phone to her ear she spoke first, "Whitey, the D.A. told me you served time on Alcatraz. If I had known that I would never of let you come near me."

"What're you trying to pull Brenda? That's the first thing I told you when you wanted me to move in with you."

"Let's get one thing straight Whitey Thompson, you never lived in my house, and you never told me anything about your past."

Whitey knew exactly why Brenda was here to visit him. The phones were tapped and no doubt the D.A. was listening in on the conversation.

"Bullshit! I told you all about myself, where I came from and what kind of work I did. It didn't make any difference to you where I came from, you was looking for a sucker. Well you found one in me. I never done you any harm, I treated you and the kids with love and respect, and you repay me by cheating, and then having me put in jail."

"That's a lie!" she screamed.

"A lie hell," he snapped back at her. "All you had to do was admit you cheated on me, and I would of forgiven you. But no, you preferred to lie, then have me put in jail, and to top it all off you lied to the D.A."

Again she screamed over the phone, "That's a lie, it's a goddamn lie!"

"It's no lie Brenda, you know that yourself, but I don't give a damn now. You do as you please. The only thing I ask of you is to drop the phony burglary charge. Then I'll go away, you'll never see me again."

"No, I won't drop the charges. I won't drop the charges because I'm afraid of you."

"Afraid of me! What have I ever done to you? I never laid a hand on you."

She sat there with the protection of the glass between them and stared coldly at Whitey. Finally she spoke, "I know, I know you never did, but I'm afraid of you now."

"Come off it Brenda, you have nothing to be afraid of, only the lies you told. It's not too late to clear them up. Just tell the D.A. the truth. Damn it girl, don't you realize what you're doing to me, if that phony burglary beef sticks, they'll hit me with fifteen years."

"Oh don't be silly! The D.A. told me you won't do a day over six months."

"Goddamn you woman, listen to me. He don't give a shit if I'm guilty or not, he wants to send me up because I'm an ex-con from the Rock, don't you understand that?"

Brenda sat there a moment staring at the glass while he waited patiently for her reply. She could not look at him, and finally in a soft voice she said, "I won't drop the charge." Not waiting for a reply she quickly hung up the phone and started for the door.

Whitey sat there in dismay, "Why? Why is all this happening to me?"

A guard interrupted his thoughts, "Don't get up Thompson, there's someone else to see you."

Whitey was not prepared for the next visitor, and was in disbelief when May Hanny walked through the outer door. Her pleasant smile was a spark of life.

Whitey's thoughts immediately went back to October 25, 1962, the day of his release from Alcatraz. It was on this date he returned to Sacramento, and met May Hanny who ran a boarding

14

house on G Street. May knew Whitey had been in prison, but it made no difference to her for she treated him with kindness and respect. The day he left her boarding house to move in with Brenda she told him, "You are always welcome in my home Whitey."

May was talking before she picked up the phone, "Whitey what in the world has happened to you? What's this burglary all about?"

In his excitement he ignored the questions, "May, I'm glad to see you! How did you know I was here?"

"You were on the Noon News, I couldn't believe it. Is it true Whitey?"

"No May, it's not like it sounds, it's not true."

"Well tell me exactly what it's all about."

Whitey told May everything that happened, from the moment he left her boarding house, right up to the present time. He left nothing out.

"Oh this is horrible, simply horrible. How could she do that to you? I just wish you had kept in touch with me Whitey, but no matter, I'm going to talk to the D.A.. Then I'll go see this Miss Brenda and see what I can do. Whitey this shouldn't be happening to you, it's not right."

"I know May, I keep telling myself that, but it sure as hell is happening."

"What are your feelings toward Brenda now?"

"I'm mad May, mad as hell at her, I could twist her fucking head off! But it's me I'm really pissed at for being suckered in by that bitch. Can you believe it, I fell in love with her."

"Are you still in love with her?" she asked.

"Are you kidding?" he replied with a bitter laugh. "I love the kids though, and I'm gonna miss them."

"Whitey, if you get out of this mess, will you do any harm to her? I don't care about her, but I am concerned about you."

"You don't have to worry May, if I met her on the street I'd walk right past her without saying a word. You know something, I thought I knew her, but I didn't. If I had really known her I wouldn't be here in jail. Dammit May, I should have my ass kicked, I wish I had stayed at the boarding house."

"So do I Whitey, I wish we could turn back the clock, but we can't. Look Whitey, I hate to rush, but I have to get back to the boarding house. But the first chance I get I will go see the D.A. and see what I can do. Then I will go see that Brenda girl, okay?"

Once the visit was over Whitey was returned to the holding tank.

He had lied to May Hanny about not wanting to harm Brenda. If the truth was known, he would cut her throat.

15

May kept her word. She went to see the D.A., and later that day she went to see Brenda, but it was all in vain. Brenda would not drop the charge. The D.A. had assured May that even if Brenda were to drop the charge, he would definitely press charges himself on behalf of the state. The situation looked hopeless for Whitey. This proved to be so, for on September 14, 1965, he was sentenced to fifteen years in state prison.

This must be a dream, Whitey thought, it can't be happening. Fifteen years for what? It has to be a mistake. But it was no mistake, he was going back to prison for fifteen more years. The following day he was taken to the Guidance Center at Vacaville, California, where he received a new prison number, A-92856.

After a short stay of ninety days at the Guidance Center, he was transferred to the penitentiary at Repressa, California, where they put him behind the cold gray granite walls of Folsom State Prison.

Whitey immediately went on the defense. He was churning with anger, and the old animal instinct of survival was within him once again.

CHAPTER 3.

Just outside the Folsom Prison main entrance gate, a huge gray ten wheeler bus came to a halt. To a passerby it looked like any ordinary tourist bus, but a closer inspection would reveal barred windows. Along its side exposed to view were the words, THE DEPARTMENT OF CORRECTIONS, STATE OF CALIFORNIA. The passengers aboard this bus were by no means tourists. Behind the shadowed windows like some hidden secret, bound and shackled together were forty-two desolate men. Of the forty-two convicts, twenty-one of them were being returned to Folsom for parole violation. Seventeen of the prisoners were two, three, and four time losers, having served a sentence in various other prisons. The remaining four men were first-termers.

The solid steel gate remained closed while a security check of the bus and its passengers was made. Once completed, a signal to the guard in the high tower set the gears in motion, and the half ton gate slowly opened. The bus moved forward, just enough to allow clearance for the movable barrier to close behind it. To the front of the bus was another movable structure, enclosing the vehicle between two heavy steel gates. Again a security check was conducted, only this time the prisoners were ordered off the vehicle for a complete search. When this was accomplished and the chain of men were safely back on the bus, the signal was given. The high tower guard was like a hawk on the wing observing the fowl below. No move went unnoticed, and when the signal was given for him to open the barrier, everything had to be to his satisfaction, for only he had the power to set the gate in motion.

Inside the walls the bus moved along a narrow asphalt road to the lower gate. Another security check was made before the vehicle went up the hill to the main yard where it came to a halt in front of R and R (Receiving and Release).

As each prisoner disembarked, his name and number were checked off, and at the same time his shackles and cuffs were removed. This was done under the watchful eyes of the yard gun towers. Then forming columns of two, the prisoners were escorted off the yard through a side door into Number Two Dining Hall.

Folsom consisted of five cell blocks accessible to each other by runways. Numbers One, Two, Three and Five buildings were the main Cell Blocks, whereas Four Building was the Segregation Unit (the hole). There were two dining halls, number One and Two where the population of twenty-eight hundred convicts were fed daily.

After receiving their food trays, the new arrivals, in an orderly fashion were seated. Once they were seated, they immediately began to consume their dinner. The food consisted of leftovers from the evening meal. The hour was 8:00 P.M. and the main population had long since eaten. Except for the scraping and clicking of silverware, the dining room was quiet, almost an eerie quietness. There was no laughter or talking from this group.

Besides the transfers, the only other occupants in the dining room were the guards and one Mess Hall worker who dished up the food. At the moment the worker was pouring coffee and announced, "If any of you men want another cup of coffee, set your cup to the edge of the table."

Whitey was sitting alone at the end table and was last to be served.

"Want some more coffee?" the worker asked. "If you do, slide your cup to the edge."

Whitey slid his cup to the edge where the worker refilled it.

"Where did you come in from?" the man asked.

Turning his head to look at him, he was greeted with a cheerful smile. Whitey was in no mood for talking, but there was something genuine about this man. He was surprised to hear his own voice reply, "I don't know about these other guys, I came from Vacaville."

"Vacaville huh? Is this your first time to Folsom?"

"Yeah this is my first time"

"Well, if you got to do time, this is the place to do it at. Most prisoners here are over forty. They've been around once or twice and know how to do time. If you ever need any. . . ."

"Let's go, let's go," a guard interrupted.

The majority of prisoners had finished eating, but those who hadn't began to hurry.

"There's no rush," the worker told Whitey, "the bull will try to make you hurry, but they always wait until the last man finishes eating, so take your time. By the way my name's McCulley, what's yours?"

"Thompson, Whitey Thompson."

McCulley held out his hand to Whitey, and as he accepted it, he asked McCulley where the Fish Tank was.

"That's in Two Building," he replied. "The fifth tier of Two Block is always reserved for new arrivals."

"Are they single or double cells?"

"They're all doubles unless you're some kind of a nut, then they jam you into a single cell."

"How long do they keep ya on Fish Row?"

"Let's see, today is Thursday, so you should get off Fish Row by next Tuesday or Wednesday. You see the day before you move they'll take you up for classification and job assignment. What kind of work did you do on the bricks?"

"It doesn't matter what I did, all's I know I won't make any license plates or work in any goddamn mills."

"About all that leaves is the Culinary Department. Culinary isn't bad, I've been working here over three years now."

It took about twenty minutes for the prisoners to eat. When the last man had finished eating, a guard ordered the transfers to rise with their trays and form a single line. Then they were ordered to move out toward the rear of the Dining Hall where the dirty trays and flatware were disposed of. The men remained in a single line as they marched out the door to the rear left side of the Dining Hall. They proceeded along a caged-in runway to a flight of stairs. At the head of the stairs was a security gate, and just to the right of the barrier on the wall, was a push-button. The escort officer pressed the button and a guard appeared from the inside; he opened the gate allowing the transfers to enter Number Two Block. Again the name and number of each prisoner were checked off a list before they were assigned to a cell on the fifth tier. Except for their meals in the Dining Hall and daily showers, the new arrivals were to remain in their cells for the consecutive six days.

On the following Monday morning Leon W. Thompson was taken before the Classification Committee, he was placed on medium close custody, and assigned to the Kitchen Culinary. That afternoon upon receiving his dress-in issue, he was given notice of a cell move for the following morning. He was to move into cell 755 on the second tier of Number One Building.

The next morning shortly after the 8:00 A.M. work call, Whitey moved to his new housing. He was accustomed to a single cell, and wondered if he could live with another person in such a confined space. He wasn't going to worry about it now, for he had to make up his bunk, store away his prison issue, and report to the kitchen for work.

On and off over the years, Whitey had done a certain amount of dinner cooking, and was considered by others quite good at the trade. At this particular time the kitchen was in dire need of a fry cook for one of its six grills. He was placed on the morning shift from 4:30 A.M. to 1:00 P.M. The prison population of Folsom was at a new high of 2,800 prisoners, thus making the grill hours long hard and sweaty work. The first day on the job was tiresome for Whitey. Shortly after 1:00 P.M. he finally returned to Number One Building where he climbed the stairs to the second tier.

A guard was standing at the control box, and in a gruff voice he asked "What cell are you in?"

Whitey walked by him, and in the same tone of voice he replied, "755."

The guard pulled the bar. When Whitey reached his cubicle the door was wide open for him to enter. As he stepped through the doorway, he did not expect a warm welcome from within the cell.

"Hey Thompson, how ya doing pal?"

It was the voice of Charlie McCulley, the worker he had met in the Dining Hall on the evening of his arrival. McCulley was stretched out on the bottom bunk, and as Whitey came through the door he rolled over dropping his feet to the floor, and held out his hand in greeting.

"So you're my new cell partner. How ya doing McCulley?" Whitey said as they shook hands.

"Okay pal. By the way, where you working at?"

"Grill cook."

"That's a good job. I know the Lead Cook, his name is Webb."

"Yeah I met him today."

"He's a good con boss, you'll like Webb. He's people."

"If he is, I'll find out," Whitey remarked coldly.

"You sound like you may have done a little time," McCulley stated.

"Yeah I've had a taste. I'm no cherry if that's what you mean."

McCulley smiled, "Well that goes for me too. Besides Folsom I done a little time myself at Granite, Oklahoma. Where did you do time at?"

"I did a jolt for the Feds."

"They tell me if you have to do time, you're better off doing if for the Feds. What joint was you in?"

"I was on the Rock."

"The Rock! You mean Alcatraz?" McCulley was startled.

"That's right, Alcatraz."

McCulley started to laugh, and in between bursts of laughter he said, "When they told me, a man's better off doing time for the Feds, I don't think they were including Alcatraz. How do you compare Folsom with Alcatraz?"

"You can't. In comparison Folsom is a country-club, a college campus. As for Alcatraz, it was just what the name implied, Alcatraz, the Rock, and that's just what it was, the end of the line."

"How do you figure Folsom is a country club?"

"Shit man, on the Rock us prisoners had nothing, absolutely nothing but time. We didn't have the luxury you have here. Hell man, we didn't even know what a canteen was!"

"There was no commissary on Alcatraz?"

"Hell no! We didn't have anything like you got in this play-

20

house," Whitey replied. "Like I said, on the Rock we had nothing but time. Here you can buy anything you want or need, such as cigarettes, candy, cookies, ice cream, pastries, coffee, toilet articles, or whatever. Shit, here you even got an education building with programs and classrooms. A big yard where you can play basketball, baseball, racquetball, handball, and a small yard for weight-lifting. You have the pleasure of TV. You also have Group Counseling along with AA meetings. Shit you got everything here, schools, art classes, visiting three times a week, movies every Saturday and Sunday, and above all you can go to the yard every fuckin' day if you want to."

"How about a library, did you have one?" McCulley asked.

"Yeah we had a library, but we were never allowed in there like you are here. I'm telling you on Alcatraz we had nothing. Shit you even have a real church chapel here that you can go to every day if you want. You have TV out in the yard man, what more could a guy want while in prison? If it weren't for the walls I'd swear I was free!"

McCulley went on to tell Whitey about the different groups of performers who came to Folsom to put on shows for the prisoners. A year after Whitey's arrival Johnny Cash with June Carter and family put on a show in Number Two Dining Hall. It was during this time Johnny Cash recorded "Graystone Chapel" for the inmate Glen Shirley, who had written the song. Along with the Carters and Johnny Cash were the Statler brothers who performed their old-favorites.

Whitey segregated himself from all yard activities. He seldom went to the weekly movies or viewed any of the stage shows. As always he was a loner with no correspondence or visitors. With the exception of a few acquaintances other than McCulley, he hardly ever talked to anyone. Whenever possible, his days were spent in silence, and he liked it that way. His daily routine would seldom alter. At 4:30 A.M. a guard would wake him up. At 4:40 A.M. he made the trek to the kitchen, and at 1:00 P.M. the trek back to his cell. At 5:00 P.M. the usual trek to dinner. Then the return to his cell where he was locked down for the night.

There were six standing counts a day. Each count was precisely on time commencing at 6:00 A.M., wake up. At this time Whitey was at work, and therefore counted in the kitchen. At 6:10 A.M., breakfast was served. The 8:00 A.M. count was work call for the general population. 11:45 A.M. the general population returned from work. 11:50 A.M., count. 12:00 P.M., lunch. 1:00 P.M., work call for the general population. 3:30 P.M., return from work. 3:45 P.M., dinner count. 6:00 P.M., last standing count of the day. All other counts were made on the spot. Lights out at 10:00 P.M.

It wasn't hard for Whitey to fall back into his old routine, see all, but see nothing, hear all, but hear nothing. As in his Federal prison days, upon entering his cell he would check it out for contraband, inspect his light bulb before turning it on, and made a point to always know who was around him. While incarcerated, he knew he must never let his guard down, and it would be wise for him to use these same tactics in society.

During the first few months of incarceration the thought of Brenda was always on his mind, her name was haunting him, and he despised her to the point where he began to plan her death. He couldn't get it out of his mind that because of her he lost his truck, car, the children who loved him, and above all, his freedom. God, he thought, what's wrong with me? I love the children, how can I think about destroying their mother? I mustn't think of Brenda anymore, I must control my mind, keep her out of my thoughts, and channel my thinking to other things.

CHAPTER 4.

Six months later Whitey was scheduled to make his first appearance before the California Adult Authority Parole Board. He felt it was a waste of time, but decided to make an appearance just to have a change in routine.

Midway down the corridor to the Board Room was a grilled barred gate, and sitting in front of the barrier was a line of inmates waiting their turn to make their appearances. Whitey was sitting just beyond the gate (termed the hot-seat), he was next in line to go before the Adult Board. A prison guard was standing between him and the Board Room. Whitey's attention was attracted by the Board Room door as it swung open and an inmate walked out.

Speaking to the inmate the guard said, "How did it go Frank? Did you make a good appearance?"

"I think so," Frank answered, "I'll know in a few days"

The guard unhooked a key ring from his belt, and after unlocking the gate he motioned Whitey in to wait his turn on the hot-seat. He did not have long to wait before the door opened and a gruff voice called out to the guard, "Do you have Thompson, A-92856 out there?"

"Yes sir."

"Send him in."

Seated behind a long table facing Whitey as he entered the room, were two gray-haired men dressed in dark business suits. The Classification Counselor, a dark brown complected middle-aged man sat alone at the end of the table. He was the first one to speak, "Have a seat Mr. Thompson. This is your first appearance before the Adult Authority Board hearing. These two gentlemen represent the California Parole Board; they are Mr. Morson, and Mr. Larkin, member and representative of the Adult Authority, and I'm your Counselor. Please have a seat."

Whitey stood there for a moment, and like a military man holding inspection, he carefully looked from one person to the other. There was no trace of warmth on their faces, just cold hard stares. Each one of them had the look of an executioner waiting to pull the switch.

"Please be seated," repeated the Counselor.

Directly in front of the panel was a single chair. Whitey took his seat facing the panel.

"Well Thompson," Larkin was the speaker, "how does it feel to be incarcerated again?"

Whitey did not reply, he merely sat there staring coldly at Larkin. What's wrong with this guy he thought, asking me how does it feel? He knows damn well how it feels.

"Come come Thompson," Larkin taunted, "cat got your tongue?"

For a brief moment the room was silent.

"You have quite a record Thompson," Larkin continued as his fingers leafed through a folder. "Hmm," he mumbled to himself. "What have we here? Hmmhmm, well now look at this, you even served fifteen years in a Federal penitentiary, McNeil Island, and in 1958 you were transferred to Alcatraz. You were discharged from there in 1962. Well what have you to say about all this?"

Whitey did not answer and stared coldly at the man.

"What have you to say about all this?" Larkin was shouting now.

In the same tone of voice, Whitey shouted, "Why the stupid questions? You got my records."

In an easier voice Larkin returned, "We just want to hear your version of it Thompson. Why were you sent to a Federal prison?"

"Bank robbery damnit! You got the records."

"Bank robbery? Or do you mean bank robberies Thompson? Your record states you committed many more." Larkin continued leafing through the folder. "Fifteen years for bank robberies, is that right Thompson?"

Whitey was furious as he looked at Larkin. From his face he tried to figure out why this type of questioning.

"What the hell is this?" he shouted, "Am I on trial?"

"On trial? What gives you the impression you are on trial Thompson? This is a parole hearing, not a trial."

"Bullshit, you people are trying me for the time I already served on Alcatraz."

"Nonsense Thompson," Morson cut in. "Mr. Larkin is only trying to understand you better, and to do that he must ask you questions of your past record."

"He's absolutely right," agreed Larkin. "Now let's see, you were also arrested in Seattle, Washington for robbery while at sea. The case against you was dismissed. Did you pull the robbery Thompson?"

"It was dismissed," Whitey replied.

"Come on Thompson, I know the case was dismissed, but between you and I, were you guilty?"

Whitey seemed to be losing control of his temper, "Hey I'm not copping out to nothing, the case was dismissed."

24

"I know it was dismissed, but I'm sure you were guilty of the charge, so why don't you admit it so we can get on with this hearing?"

"Admit shit! The charge was kicked out by a Federal judge. He found me not guilty for the lack of evidence. So what gives you people the right to sit there and pass judgment on me for a charge that was dismissed over twenty years ago? I thought I was here for a parole hearing."

"Do you actually believe you are ready for a parole Thompson?"

"Does a bear shit in the woods?" Whitey retorted.

"I don't think there is any need for further discussion with you Thompson," Morson hissed.

"Wait a minute, this is my hearing," Whitey shouted. "Your job is to judge my progress during the six months I've been in this prison. In fact I don't belong here and you know it. I'm not doing time for burglary, I'm doing time because I'm an ex-con from Alcatraz. I'm doing time for the time I've already served; I'm no longer the convicted, I'm a victim. I've become a victim of my own reputation."

"All right, all right Thompson, that's enough," Morson said. "Is there anything to discuss further with this man?"

Both the Counselor and Larkin replied with a no.

"This hearing is ended Thompson, we'll let you know."

"Yeah I'm sure you will," Whitey said as he walked out the door and returned to his cell.

He was disturbed as he lay on his bunk, the parole hearing hadn't gone the way he had anticipated. He didn't expect a parole date on his first appearance, but he had wanted to make a good impression. He had expected the Board members to question him about the Whitey Thompson of today, his plans for the future, and what progress he had made. Instead, their only interest was Alcatraz, and the sentence he had served.

When Whitey left Alcatraz he felt he was leaving the past behind him, the harsh bitterness, and above all the remorse he had suffered for past crimes. He had been guilty and felt he deserved to be sent to prison, but it should be over now. The book was closed, the debt was paid the day he was discharged from Alcatraz, or at least, that's what he thought.

"Hi Whitey, how did the Board meeting go?"

McCulley had just returned from work and was standing outside the cell bars. Whitey was about to answer him when the door slid open and his friend entered the cell.

"Not too good," Whitey replied ruefully.

"You didn't expect a date the first time you went before the Board did you?"

"Of course not, but I at least expected some kind of consideration, and not the bullshit they handed me."

Whitey told him about the interview.

"Well that's about all you can expect from them," McCulley said. "Did they mention anything about your crime?"

"What crime man? I didn't commit a crime! I don't belong in here." Whitey answered in a sarcastic voice.

"Yeah I don't belong in here either."

"Hey are you getting wise with me?" Whitey jumped off the top bunk. McCulley was taken aback at his sudden move.

"Hell no Whitey, I'm not getting wise with you. I meant what I said, I don't belong in here, or at least I've been here too long for what I did."

Whitey's expression turned from anger to sympathy. He placed his hand on McCulley's shoulder in a gesture of friendship.

"I'm sorry Okie. I was just thinking of myself, I forgot other people have problems too."

"Ah forget it Whitey, I'll tell you about it sometime, okay? Do you want to tell me what happened to you, why you're here. Sometimes it helps to talk about it."

"Sure why not? There's nothing else to do."

Whitey recounted the whole story, how he was released from Alcatraz, how he purchased the truck, how he met Brenda, the breakup with her, and the fifteen-year sentence.

"Boy that is cold," McCulley said sympathetically. "Hell if they gave you thirty days in the county jail it would of been too much time for what you did. You really didn't do nothing. You were good to that woman. You should break her ass when you get out, kill the bitch!"

"You know what," Whitey replied, "them are my exact thoughts, kill the bitch and the fucking D.A. too!"

"I wouldn't blame you if you did kill them Whitey, you're doing fifteen years for nothing."

Three days later the sergeant stopped in front of Whitey's cell and handed him his Board results. As expected he was denied parole. McCulley was sitting on his bunk watching as Whitey stared at the word denied on the result paper. DENIED, DENIED, he could see the word flashing like a neon sign, only the flashing was in his head.

"By the expression on your face Whitey there's no need to ask what the results are. How long they shoot you down for? When do you go back?"

"Just one year from now," Whitey answered. "Just three hundred and sixty-five days!"

"Hang tough man, don't let them get you down."

When Whitey was on Alcatraz he made a vow he would never die in prison, and he was still holding himself to the vow. At times it was difficult to keep a good attitude, but he knew he must if he expected to survive prison. He still had a lot to learn, his last birthday reminded him of that. He was forty-two years old, and was still maturing, but at least he was growing. He looked back on his childhood and the years of imprisonment as a school, of learning; it was a course he had to complete before he could learn the meaning of life.

The following morning Whitey was back on his job in the kitchen. To the eyes of his fellow workers they could not tell that he had just been denied parole. He was ready for work, and in a cheerful mood he picked up a spatula and turned to the grill.

As the morning progressed Mr. Prewitt, the Food Supervisor could not help noticing Whitey. He was amazed to see him with such vigorous energy, and at the end of the shift, he was pleased to see that the grill was left spotless and shining.

Prewitt was a pleasant man who spent the last ten of his thirty-five years with the Department of Corrections as a Food Supervisor. He was of medium build, black hair, dark eyes. He was an excellent cook who knew his way around the Culinary Department. The sole purpose of his job was supervision of the convict cooks. Almost at any given time he could be seen at the end of a row of huge stationary steam pots. He would be sitting on a high platform chair that enabled him at a glance, to view the overall kitchen and workers.

CHAPTER 5.

Six months later, September 1. Webb, the convict Lead Cook, had been granted a parole, and was due to leave in three days. He was a happy-go-lucky man of thirty-five, blond hair, blue eyes, fair complexion, and medium height. Whitey was at his grill flipping hot cakes when Webb stopped a moment to talk.

"How's it going Whitey? Everything okay?" he asked.

Turning his attention to the speaker Whitey replied, "Hey short-timer, you got a job lined up yet?"

"Yeah I got one with Kentucky Fried Chicken in Los Angeles."

"That's great Webb. It don't take much brains to fry chicken, any fool can do it!"

Webb laughed, "When do you go back up for parole Whitey?"

"Next year—March '67. Why do you ask?"

"I'll be leaving in three days. They're gonna need a new Lead Cook Whitey, it'll be a good job for you."

"Are you crazy man! Me a Lead Cook? Your ass is sucking wind!"

"Why not Whitey? Everybody likes and respects you, it pays nine dollars a month. Nine dollars a month is better than a kick in the ass on a cold windy day! I'm gonna tell Prewitt you're interested in the job."

Without waiting for Whitey's reply, Webb walked over to Prewitt who was sitting in his favorite chair at the end of the steam pots.

"Hey you fucker!" Whitey called after him. "Don't tell him that. I don't want the job."

It was too late, Webb was already talking to Prewitt and pointing in Whitey's direction.

"Damn that fuckin' Webb!" he exclaimed aloud. He slid the spatula under a hot cake and flipped it with such force that it splattered all over the grill! Out of the corner of his eye he watched the Supervisor walking toward him, while Webb moved around to the far side of the grills.

"Thompson, I'd like a word with you." Whitey nodded his head in acknowledgment as Prewitt continued, "You know Webb is leaving, I'll be needing a replacement and he just recommended you for the job."

"He did? Well I'm not your man, I don't think I can handle the job."

"Don't listen to him Mr. Prewitt," Webb called from behind the grills. "He's a good man, he can do it."

With an up and down motion Whitey gave Webb the finger. "Up your flunky ass wise-guy." Then turning his attention to the Supervisor he said, "Thanks Mr. Prewitt, but I don't want the responsibility."

"That's just what you need Thompson, and it will look good when you go back before the Board next year. Think it over."

"Do you really think I can handle the job?"

"Of course I do, I've been watching you Thompson. You're a good worker and Webb told me how you had done some dinner cooking over the years. So what do you say?"

"Okay Mr. Prewitt, I'll take the job on two conditions. First, the crew has to accept me as con boss. Also any replacements in the kitchen, I want to do the interviewing. It has to be up to me if he gets the job or not. I don't want anyone who resents taking orders from a con boss. Oh yes one more thing," Whitey added. "I run the crew. If there is any problem, I'll handle it my way with no interference from you."

"All right Thompson, we'll give it a fair try and see how it goes. How does that suit you?"

"Okay Mr. Prewitt I'm your man if the crew accepts me."

The morning crew consisted of sixteen men. Whitey spoke to each man asking if he objected to having him as a con boss. All of them seemed to like Whitey, and voiced no objections.

Establishing a good understanding, the kitchen ran smoothly. The work was hard and tedious preparing breakfast and lunch seven days a week with no time off. Being the Lead Cook, Whitey had to report to work an hour early each morning, and was the last one to leave when the shift was over. At days end his back, arms, and leg muscles were in pain. This was contributed to the long hours standing on the concrete floor where he constantly stirred food in the stationary steam pots. Four of these pots had the capacity of seventy gallons each, there also were two fifty-gallon pots, and one thirty-five. To stir these huge containers it required a six-foot wooden paddle. At times the working conditions were unbearable, the overhead air vents were so old that half of them didn't work. During the summer months the temperature at times would reach 130 degrees. At the end of each shift Whitey's body was constantly drained and on several occasions he felt as though he couldn't make it back to his cell.

Each month the Supervisor was required to turn in a progress report on each man's attitude and working habits. Prewitt always marked Whitey's report with Number Ones which stood for excellent. Number Two was good, Three fair, and four unsatisfactory.

CHAPTER 6.

Time moved right along and before Whitey realized it, the month was March '67, and he was ready to make his second appearance before the Adult Board. His record for the past year was excellent.

Whitey's Parole Board hearing was a repeat of the previous year. Sitting directly across from the panel he noticed that their faces still maintained the same stony expressions of executioners. Their line of questioning pertained to Alcatraz and what had gone before. There was no mention of his hard work or excellent record for the past twelve months. Sitting perfectly erect in his chair, with arms folded across his chest, looking straight ahead, Whitey took the abuse of each insult. They called him a misfit, a hard-core slob not fit for society. He simply sat there concealing his temper. These fools, he thought, they're trying so hard to get a rise out of me. I know the game they're playing. Try as they might they could not get him to show the slightest sign of anger.

"Okay Thompson, we'll let you know," Larkin said to conclude the hearing.

Looking at each member of the panel, Whitey rose from his chair, and with a somber face he said, "Thank your sir, thank you for your consideration." Then, like an honor guard soldier he performed a snappy about face, and marched out of the room!

The guard unlocked the gate, Whitey walked through and as he started the long trek back to his cell he had a beaming smile on his face.

He had known before he appeared in front of the Board that he would be denied parole. He was ready for the denial when he received his results, and was not disappointed. Three hundred and sixty-five days was a long time to wait for a five minute appearance before the Board.

Three weeks after his parole denial Prewitt asked Whitey if he would like to move into Five Building. This was known as the old prison for it was the first cell block built, and at the time it was all that consisted of Folsom. Each cell was constructed of granite rock, the blocks were two and a half feet thick weighing up to a ton or more. The entrances to these ten by ten foot cells were sealed off by a solid half inch thick steel door. As the years went by more men were being sent to the penitentiary, and Folsom Prison underwent an expansion with cell blocks being added on at random.

Whitey accepted the offer to move to Five Building. Two days later the request was approved, and he was placed in cell 27. It was a two-man cell, and as no one else was in there, Whitey asked McCulley if he would like to move in. The request was put in, and on the following day McCulley joined Whitey in Five Building.

It is difficult to serve time in a small cubicle with someone you don't like or can't get along with. McCulley and Whitey had developed an understanding friendship over the past year which seemed to grow stronger as the days went by. McCulley still held the job of coffee-maker in Number Two Dining Room, and his hours of work coincided with Whitey's.

Shortly after their move Whitey mentioned to McCulley how he used to oil paint while on Alcatraz, and decided to resume painting.

Before an inmate could do any hobby work in his cell he was required to put in a request for a hobby card. Whitey submitted the necessary request, but it was not until six months later that it was approved. Once he had received his hobby card he put in an order for art supplies. This request entailed another month of waiting. At last he was able to get back into oil painting, and it seemed to him as if it were only yesterday that he was painting on Alcatraz. His talent was still with him, and to look at his workmanship one would never know that it was five years since he had last picked up a brush. He would always treasure this talent, and every afternoon while in his cell he would escape from prison in his painting. He was totally engrossed in his art work, and found it soothing and relaxing after the long tedious hours of cooking.

He did a number of paintings for McCulley who sent them home to a sister. Whitey also kept himself in cigarettes and canteen supplies with the paintings he sold to other inmates; there was always someone wanting him to do a painting.

In March 1968 Whitey went back up for parole. Once again a good report was sent in on him. Work excellent, attitude excellent, gets along well with people, department head recommends parole, but it was not to be. Once more he was denied, and it would be 365 days before he would again appear before the Adult Board. Was he disappointed? No, because he knew their game, they wanted to suck him dry, they wanted to drain him until he was nothing more than a vegetable. He felt he was smarter than the Parole Board members gave him credit for; he knew their game and how it was played. He also knew the rules of the Adult Authority, and how it was supposed to work.

    1. The functional supervision and control of a diagnostic clinic.

2. Prescribing and supervising the training and treatment programs at the prisons, and classifying prisoners to decide what prison in which they shall serve their time.

3. Determining the nature, type and duration of punishment administered to prisoners, and awarding and forfeiting credits.

4. Setting and resetting terms of imprisonment.

5. Serving as the State Parole Board.

6. Directing the operations of the Bureau of Paroles.

7. Restoring civil rights forfeited by felons upon conviction.

8. Serving as an Advisory Pardon Board.

9. Serving as members of the Board of Corrections.

As one studies this list, it immediately becomes clear that the assignment is not workable, but is self-contradictory. How can rehabilitation and punishment go hand-in-hand? Besides there is no way the Board of Corrections could ever rehabilitate any one man. It can't be done, and it is a waste of taxpayers' money to have group therapy on rehabilitation.

How could seven men, no matter how qualified, be expected to go through thousands of prisoners' jackets (records), and accurately diagnose, classify, prescribe and supervise the training and treatment of inmates? Particularly when items' 1. and 2. are followed by item 3. which concerns meting out punishment. There is punishment, but no rehabilitation.

There is a small minority, very small, who do intend to follow a more virtuous form of life when they are once again in the free world. This minority rehabilitates itself, not because of what was learned inside the walls and steel bars of prison, but in spite of it. Group therapy is a joke, and it is looked on as a joke by the majority of convicts. No matter what is said to the contrary, the only reason most convicts go to therapy is that it looks good in their records to hit the Parole Board with.

For nearly twenty years, although he didn't realize it in the beginning, Whitey had been trying to rehabilitate himself. The functions of penal institutions are for the protection of society, and to this end all efforts and methods must be adopted for reformation of the criminal. Whitey knew he had made a complete reformation before he was discharged from Alcatraz. He was no threat to Brenda or anyone else as his only crime was taking food that he had already bought and paid for.

"To hell with Whitey!" was the attitude of Brenda, the D.A. and the judge who sentenced him to fifteen years in prison? "Give a dog a bad name and hang him!" Sums up the treatment of the man with an Alcatraz record. All the D.A.s and judges, and the average citizens who simply do not believe that it's in the nature of the leopard to change his spots, or that the time-honored remedy of imprisonment is really adequate; but they will always release the leopards and dogs to be hung, and the coyote remains a rebel.

CHAPTER 7.

It was the summer of '68 and Whitey had made more acquaintances at Folsom Prison than he had expected. Even a few guards liked him because he was a quiet man who did his own number, and even with his violent temper he was no longer a troublemaker. He didn't make any close friends other than McCulley for it was not in his nature to think of an acquaintance as a friend. McCulley was an exception, he was a close friend. When he had cigarettes, Whitey had cigarettes, and when Whitey had candy, McCulley had candy. They shared what they had with each other, they were true friends.

Occasionally Whitey would go to the yard, but not too often for he did not want to get involved with the many different gangs out there. Most of his spare time was spent in his cell painting.

One day while working on a picture he heard reports of rifle shots coming from the yard. Quite frequently the tower guards would fire shots down into the yard to break up a fight in progress, and occasionally they would fire shots to discourage a fight before it started. On many occasions' prisoners had been hit and injured by flying fragments from bullets ricocheting from the asphalt. The tower guards could also be angels of mercy for an inmate who wanted to end it all, he merely had to make a run at the wall, and if he were lucky, he wouldn't even hear the shot.

The next afternoon for a change of routine Whitey decided to go to the yard. It was an extra warm day, and to get out of the sun he selected a shaded bench next to the wall of Number One Building. He was about to light a cigarette when someone called his name.

"Well I'll be goddamned, Whitey, Whitey Thompson you fucking termite!"

Before he saw him, Whitey recognized the voice of Lou Peters as Lou dashed across the walkway. He started to get up and immediately he was sent flying against the building from the collision impact of Lou! With arms around each other in a bear hug it was all they could do to maintain their balance. Both men were excited, shouting and pounding each other on the back.

"Goddamn Lou, I can't believe it!"

"Neither can I, damn I'm happy to see you."

The two friends were so overcome with emotion that they didn't

33

notice the guard in the high tower taking aim at them.

"Hit the ground, hit the ground!" someone yelled.

Within a split second both men fell to the asphalt as did the rest of the convicts in the vicinity. Whenever someone yelled "Hit the ground!" It meant bullets were going to fly. The guards would not fire shots near a man if he were lying perfectly still on the ground. To the eyes of the officer it looked as though the two friends were fighting the way they were stumbling about, and if it were not for an alert convict they might have been shot. The guard now realizing that there was no fight, lowered his rifle.

"Damn Lou we almost got our asses shot off!" Laughing, the two men sat on the bench.

"I'm happy to see you Whitey, really happy."

"Me too. You know Lou, when I left the Rock I never thought I'd see you again. What brings you here?"

Laughingly Lou replied, "I heard you were here, what else?"

"You crazy bastard! When did you leave the Rock?"

"A few months after you left Whitey. I got reinstated and all my good time returned. I got out in January '63."

"But what the hell are you doing here Lou? When did you get here?"

"Ah you know me, how I like to gamble, the state got me for making book, nothing serious, just a nickel. I got here three weeks ago. How about you Whitey? How long you been here?"

"Two and a half years, no three, it will be three years this September."

"Damn I'm happy to see you Whitey. Where do you work? What's your job?"

"I'm Lead Cook on the morning cook crew."

"No kidding!" Lou laughed. "No wonder the food is fucked up!"

"Fuck you Lou! Where're you working?"

"R and R, Receiving and Release."

"How did you get a bonarue job like that?"

"Juice Whitey, juice! Hey you remember the Green Lizard don't you? Remember how he snatched up the Christmas tree in the Dining Hall and got himself thrown in the hole? Well after you left Alcatraz they let him out for Christmas. They felt sorry for him it being Christmas and all that shit, and he'd been in the hole for a whole year. Well they let him out of the hole a couple of days before Christmas, and he did it again! The fucker grabbed the tree and ran all over the chow hall with it. He tore that thing up and was sent straight to the hole. So tell me Whitey, what the hell are you doing here?"

For a moment Whitey sat staring at the ground, and then in a slow angry voice he recounted the whole story to Lou.

"What a dirty fucking deal Whitey. They railroaded you back to prison for nothing, the sons of bitches! And that broad, what the

34

fuck's her name? Brenda? You should waste that slut when you get out!"

"I can't Lou, I told you about the kids."

"Yes that's right, I forgot about the kids, but you should at least punch her lights out."

Whitey was feeling a little angered, "I don't want to talk about it anymore. Let's forget the bitch, okay?"

"Yeah okay Whitey. Well looking on the bright side, you got your old buddy back with you!" Laughing, Lou gave Whitey a playful punch on the shoulder.

"Yeah that's right Lou, everywhere I go you come chasing after me! From the county jail to McNeil, to Alcatraz, and now Folsom. Where will it be next time?"

"I hope it will be on the bricks," Lou replied with a laugh, "but who knows."

Both men were still laughing and did not see McCulley walk up.

"Hey Okie, you're just in time, I want to introduce you to an old friend of mine. Lou this is my cell partner McCulley, McCulley this is Lou Peters, we done Federal time together."

"If you're a friend of Whitey," Lou said, "then you're a friend of mine."

"Thank you," McCulley returned, "that goes both ways." Addressing Whitey he added, "I got to run, I'll catch you later."

"Well now," Lou said to Whitey, "when do you go up for parole?"

"I'm scheduled to go back next year, but there's a rumor that I may be going up sometime in September, it don't make any difference, I don't expect a date anyway."

"You never know Whitey, you might get a parole this time, hell you don't belong here. By the way I live in Three Building, how about you, where do you live?"

"I'm over in Five Building in cell. . . ." At that moment yard recall sounded. "Well that's it Lou, I'll see you in the yard tomorrow afternoon."

Every day for the following two weeks the two friends met out in the yard. They laughed and joked as they relived the past and talked about long remembered escapades spanning over a period of nineteen years. From their chance meeting in the county jail, to McNeil Island Federal Penitentiary, Alcatraz, and now Folsom Prison.

Monday afternoon of the third week of their meeting Lou was disappointed because Whitey had not come to the yard. He was concerned, but the disappointment faded after talking to McCulley who was standing on the sidelines watching a handball game. "Hey have you seen Whitey? He was supposed to meet me out here."

"Yeah I know. He told me to tell you he was called back up for a parole hearing."

35

The rumor was true, unexpectedly the previous evening Whitey had received a ducet to appear before the Adult Board at 1:00 P.M. the next day.

Upon entering the Board room Whitey immediately realized nothing had changed since his previous appearance six months ago. The same cold stares greeted him as he crossed the room and sat down. Don't these people ever smile? He thought.

Larkin was the first to speak, "Well let's see," Larkin mumbled as he leafed through some papers. "It has been six months since your last appearance Thompson. What have you accomplished since then?"

"Showing no disrespect sir, I've been keeping my nose clean, you have my progress report in front of you."

"Is that what got you transferred to Alcatraz Thompson? By keeping your nose clean?" Morson asked sarcastically.

Whitey refrained from answering as he knew the panel was deliberately trying to provoke a hostile reaction out of him. He displayed no anger as he sat there in silence with his hands on the armrest of the chair. It was hard at times to endure all their insults, but he didn't respond to any of them.

It is a long time to wait between each parole hearing, months, sometimes years, and when the day finally arrives, you go before the Board only to be insulted and condemned. Each member of the Adult Authority was being paid a substantial amount of money just to play cat and mouse. They set themselves up as gods, and meted out relief to a select few.

"Answer me Thompson," the member shouted, "is that why you were sent to Alcatraz? For keeping your nose clean?"

Again Whitey said nothing, he just sat there, very still, very quiet. The Board members could not get a rise out of him, and one could see they were frustrated and angered.

Striking the table with his open hand, Larkin verbally lashed out at Whitey, "You are nothing but a worthless drunkard and deserve no consideration. Now speak up damn it when you are spoken to. Do you deserve any consideration?"

In a straightforward voice Whitey replied, "Yes sir I do. Every time I have appeared before this Board I've been accused of being an alcoholic. I'm no alcoholic, I never was nor will I ever be one. But to try to please the Board, for the last two years every Sunday afternoon I have been going to A.A. meetings. It is a good program and even though I'm not an alcoholic, I've gotten a lot of good out of the meetings. The fact is I'm trying to better myself. I have a good attitude, I'm a dependable worker as the record shows. I get along with people, and yes, I deserve consideration, I deserve a lot of consideration."

When Whitey stopped talking the room became absolutely quiet, the Board members seemed to be aghast, looking from one to the other, then back at Whitey.

Larkin's vibrant voice broke the silence, "I think that about sums it up. There is no need for any further discussion with this man; this hearing is ended. We'll let you know Thompson."

Whitey quietly left the room, and as the door closed behind him he knew perfectly well that he was turned down again. Two days later, it came as no surprise when he received his results—parole denied, placed on the R.R. Panel March 1968. It was only a six-month denial, and Whitey's spirits were high, for he knew he would receive a parole next time. He was happy as he felt he had beaten them at their own game. *They* were the ones who had lost control and showed anger. They failed to hold their composure, and they knew it.

Whitey had a magnetic personality, powerful and strong. All eyes seemed to be watching him as he attacked his art work and kitchen duties with a new vigorous intensity. Immediately after his Board appearance he wrote a letter to Cliff Strange of Strange Truck Parts. Cliff had been a good friend, and had helped him out when he was first released from Alcatraz. The man had a passion for antiques along with arts and crafts. He had purchased fifteen of Whitey's paintings, and notified him that upon his release to come to his office, where with no down payment he would get him started with another diesel rig. Whitey was overjoyed with the prospect of once more owning his own truck, but the enjoyment came to an abrupt end when he received the news that Cliff had suffered a fatal stroke.

CHAPTER 8.

The first week of October Whitey was offered the position of Diet Cook in the hospital. The workload was nil in comparison to the Lead Cook's work in the main kitchen, so he readily accepted the job. The working conditions were pleasant. With the exception of Sergeant Parker, the hospital crew worked under no supervision as each man was extremely proficient and knew exactly what to do.

As a prison guard, Sergeant Parker was of the old school. He was a strong muscular man of six feet, blond hair, blue eyes and a solid chin. He was rough and tough, but above all fair and immediately took a liking to Whitey. With their magnetic personalities, both men seemed to come from the same mold, the only difference, Parker was a prison guard and Whitey, a convict. The Sergeant was well liked by everyone. Whitey had great respect for him, but being a true convict he would never engage in conversation with him unless it pertained to his work. Small talk with Parker never went beyond "good morning," or "how ya doing Sarge?" or "goodnight Sarge see ya tomorrow."

The only drawback to working in the hospital Kitchen were the hours, 5:00 A.M. every morning until 6:30 P.M. each evening. It didn't leave Whitey with much time to oil paint. However, the job had its fringe benefits. When day was done, he would return to his cell, but never without food. Each evening as he left the kitchen he would take such items as hamburgers, ham sandwiches, containers of milk, ice cream, or whatever he wanted from the huge walk-in refrigerator. Sergeant Parker would be stationed at the main hospital door where each inmate must return through on his way to the Cell Blocks. Every evening when Whitey approached the door Sergeant Parker would smile and say, "Hello Thompson, done for the day? What's in the paper bag, your laundry?"

Holding tightly to the brown paper bag Whitey would reply, "Yeah Sarge, it's my laundry."

Sergeant Parker would pass him by and never shook him down; as for the food, Whitey always shared it with his cellmate.

Guards were not allowed to eat institutional food, they either carried their own lunch or paid for their meals served to them in the outside cafeteria. In the case of Sergeant Parker, without fail every day at precisely 1:00 P.M. Whitey would have a full course dinner

38

setting on the kitchen table. Parker would come in, sit down and eat; then with a wave of hand as thanks, he was out the door. At various times throughout the day, Parker would drop in for coffee and a sandwich, or some little snack. For these favors' Whitey was allowed to carry food to his cell.

Autumn passed by quickly, Christmas and New Year had come and gone. Before Whitey realized it March was upon him, and so was his appearance before the Adult Board. It was a repetition of previous appearances. Once more he was reminded of Alcatraz, and again he was a bastard and not fit for society. Sitting upright in the chair Whitey held his composure with arms folded across his chest. He held his chin high as he looked down his nose into the eyes of the Board members. They were shouting at him, but he did not hear the onslaught of insults for he had blanked out the sound.

"Thompson, did you hear me?" Larkin was addressing him. "I said this hearing is terminated. We will let you know."

"Thank you sir, thank you very much for your time and consideration."

Once more in a military fashion, Whitey stood erect, about faced and marched out. As he walked down the corridor, he had the urge to jump in the air and click his heels!

The following day, he was alone in the Diet kitchen drinking a cup of coffee when Sergeant Parker walked in.

"Morning Sarge, knock any heads in lately?"

"Oh one or two! How's the coffee?"

"Help yourself."

After filling his cup Parker sat at the table, and looked over the rim of his coffee mug at Whitey, "You think you may of made a parole date?" he asked.

"I have a feeling I did Sarge, but I'm not sure."

"Will it upset you if you were denied again?"

"Hell no, if I don't get a date this time, I'm sure to get it next year, or the year after."

Parker leaned toward Whitey, "Look Thompson," he whispered, "I'm not supposed to tell you this, so keep it quiet, you got a RUAPP." (Release Upon Approved Parole Plan)

Whitey stared wide-eyed across the table at Parker, "Is that for real? You seen my results?"

"Yes I talked to your counselor Mr. Clark last night on my way home. He's a friend of mine, he said you have a RUAPP. You'll be gone in about thirty days or less, depending on how fast they set up a program and process your papers."

"Thanks Sarge, thanks for letting me know."

Two days later Whitey received his official results Parole granted and to be Released Upon Approved Plans.

The following afternoon he went to the yard and met Lou, "I got my results yesterday Lou, I got a RUAPP."

"Wowwwww man that's great!" Lou was delighted, and jumped to his feet to pump Whitey's hand. "Hell man you'll be gone before you know it, how do you feel?"

"Pretty good Lou, but not like I felt when I was released from Alcatraz though."

"Well at least you know what to expect out there this time. It should be easier for you Whitey. When do you go out to the Ranch?"

The Ranch, about the size of a forestry camp, was located just outside the prison walls. The living conditions there were entirely different from those inside the main prison. The buildings, including the dormitories, Mess Hall, and Control Center, were constructed of wood. The inmates were allowed to move about at will, there were no fences to keep them in, but they had to stay within the boundary-lines of the Ranch. On rare occasions an inmate would walk away, but this was the act of a foolish man.

"When do you go out to the Ranch?" Lou asked again.

"In a few days," Whitey replied.

"I'll see you before you get out Whitey. As you know I work in R and R, I'm the guy that takes your pre-release mugshot."

"Attention on the yard—attention," the PA system announced. "Thompson A-92856, report to your Cell House officer, on the double!"

"I gotta go Lou, I think that's for the Ranch."

Within the hour Whitey was transferred to the Ranch.

On Monday two weeks later, Whitey returned inside the walls for dress-out, and stood outside the door to Receiving and Release. He was waiting for the guard in the tower to press the button that controlled the door. He called down to Whitey, "Identify yourself."

"Leon W. Thompson A-92856."

The guard checked over his list, and found Whitey's name and number on it. Then he pressed an electric switch releasing the catch which opened the door. Passing through the door, Whitey walked toward the R and R officer who was standing directly behind a counter. A few feet short of the counter Whitey sensed someone coming up from behind him, and without warning a pair of hands made a grab for his neck. With the reflex of a cat Whitey spun on his heels. In the same motion he dropped his body-weight giving him the opportunity to drive a fist into the attacker's mid-section.

"It's me damn it!"

Recognizing Lou's voice Whitey pulled up short, but not before his fist made contact to the stomach partially knocking the wind out of him. Half-bent over holding his mid-section, Lou shouted, "You bastard, didn't you know it was me?"

Whitey's first impulse was to follow through with another punch, but refrained as he recognized Lou.

"You son of a bitch," Whitey was angry, "you know better than to come up behind me like that."

"Hey man," Lou chuckled, "you're still quick on the rebound."

"I'll rebound you, you fucker!" Whitey retorted.

Lou turned to the guard who was laughing, "What the hell you laughing at?"

"I'm laughing at a man who made a fool of himself."

"Yeah I sure did." Turning to Whitey he continued, "Whitey this is my boss Officer Smiley."

There was no response from Whitey, he was still angry.

"Ah come on Whitey goddamn it, laugh; hey I saw your name on the list, I knew you were coming in for your mugshot this morning. I told Smiley I was going to jump you when you came through the door. Come on man, smile. Besides I owe you one anyway."

"What'd you mean you owe me one? What for?"

"I haven't forgotten how you flooded me out at McNeil Island—we were in the hole, remember? You flooded my cell."

"Aw for Christ sakes, that was many years ago." He held his hand out to Lou. "Okay fucker, so now we're even, right?" Again he attempted to introduce Whitey to the officer. "Boss, this is my pal Whitey, Whitey this is my boss Officer Smiley."

Whitey nodded his head, "How you doing? You must be pretty hard up for help if you got a guy like Lou working for ya."

"Yeah I'll admit he was no pick of the litter!" Smiley returned with a laugh.

"Hey you're lucky to get me," Lou retorted, "no one else will work for you ya prick!"

"Go on and do your job," Smiley said, "take the man's picture and quit goofing off."

Stepping into the photo room, Lou handed Whitey a white shirt and gray suit coat.

When an inmate makes parole from a California prison, a photo is taken of him in civilian clothes. A copy is then distributed to the local police of his residential town.

Whitey stood on an indicated spot on the floor with a white wall for a background. Lou pressed a switch and several bright lights came on. "Okay Whitey look at the birdie! Hey don't smile you fucker!"

"Well don't make me laugh fool!"

"I'm not trying to make you laugh, be serious now, hold it, hold it."

A picture of Whitey's profile, left and right was taken, and one exposure of him facing the camera with his prison number in view.

"Well that's it. You're all set Whitey, you're ready for the big time!"

"Thanks Lou, I got a 9:30 ducet for the Clothing Room, for my dress-out, I'll see you later. Nice meeting you Smiley."

At the Clothing Room Whitey was dressed out with the usual wear, black shoes, white socks, underclothes, brown pants, brown jacket, and white shirt. This was his going home outfit. The clothes would be waiting for him in R and R on the day of his release.

Before returning to the Ranch Whitey persuaded a guard to let him enter Number 2 Dining Hall. There he found McCulley getting coffee ready for the noon meal.

"Hey McCulley," Whitey greeted him, "I just dropped by in case I don't see you the day I leave."

"I'm glad you did Whitey. I'm going to miss you."

"I'll miss you too McCulley," Whitey said as he started for the door, "Take care ."

"You too pal," McCulley called after him, "Take care Whitey."

CHAPTER 9.

On the evening of April 8, 1969 Whitey's parole papers were in order and signed by the Department head. The next morning April 9, he was released from Folsom prison. Shortly after the 6:30 A.M. count Whitey, under escort, was taken inside the walls to R and R for his dress-out clothes. After his last goodbye to Lou he was on his way.

The bus ride to Sacramento was a short one, and after coffee and donuts in the station cafeteria. Whitey made his way to the parole office.

The time was 9:45 A.M. when he reported to his parole officer Mr. Rosemar. Whitey did not know what to expect as he walked into his office. Sitting behind his desk was a well-dressed man in his late forties. He was a rather handsome man, black hair with shades of silver, smooth olive skin, white teeth, and dark brown eyes. At first glance Whitey knew the eyes were deceiving, for they were not the eyes of a happy man. They reminded him of a person who had performed the same duties for a long period of time. He had gone as far as he could up the corporate ladder with little time left for advancement. All he could do now was to hang on and wait for retirement.

At the sound of Whitey entering the room, Rosemar looked up from his desk. He had been looking at a prison record, and when he closed it, the cover revealed Whitey Thompson's name, prison number, and photo.

"Well you finally showed up Thompson. What time did you leave Folsom?"

"It was just eight o'clock, why?"

"Why? Do you know what time it is now?"

"Sure, the clock in the waiting room says 9:45 A.M."

"Your bus pulled into the depot at nine sharp, where have you been for the past forty-five minutes?"

Whitey did not reply, instead, from his jacket pocket he retrieved a manila envelope that contained his parole papers.

"Look, my parole paper says I have until one o'clock to report in," he said in a surly voice pointing to the document.

"I know what time you were to report in, that's not the issue here. I asked you where you have been for the past forty-five minutes."

"I was at the bus station having coffee and donuts in the cafeteria, why?"

"Thompson, I will often ask you to account for your time, you better be able to. Now, as you know, you have been placed on five years close custody parole, close custody is just what it says, understand?" Not waiting for a reply Rosemar continued, "Each and every week I want you to report to my office for an eyeball to eyeball contact, do you understand? Eyeball to eyeball, I have to see you personally right here in my office each week, and twice a week you are to phone in. Also you are not to have any alcoholic beverages, none at all. You must keep decent hours unless your place of employment calls for night work. You will send in a monthly report and I want it on my desk no later than the fifth of each month, do you understand?"

"Yeah, yeah I understand."

"You better Thompson, step out of line once, no matter how small the infraction I will send you straight back to Folsom. Do you understand?"

"Yeah I understand. What you're telling me is I'm not free."

"That's exactly it Thompson. You are far from being free. You are still doing time, and don't you forget it. Let's see now," Rosemar continued, "you'll be staying at a halfway house on T Street until you find an apartment, is that right?"

"Yeah that's right."

"It so happens there's an apartment building directly across the street with a vacancy. If you like you can inquire about it."

Nodding his head, Whitey replied, "I'll go right over there."

"All right Thompson, if you rent an apartment over there let me know immediately. Also my report says you have a savings account with adequate funds, fourteen hundred dollars to be exact. How do you happen to come by this Thompson?"

"It's from my earnings before I went to Folsom."

"Oh yes, here it is in your record. Let's see now, you were leased out to Senator Truck Service and you were driving your own truck, okay Thompson that's all I wanted to know."

Whitey rented the apartment across the street for ninety dollars a month, this included utilities. The dwelling was a large one bedroom apartment including a living room with a wall fold-down bed, kitchen and dining area. Most importantly to Whitey was the private bathroom with tub and shower. With the parole office directly across the street, he would have no problem making his weekly reports, he was thankful for that.

It required two days to straighten out his personal affairs, including obtaining his driver's license. Once this was accomplished, he immediately set about looking for work, and quite luckily hit upon employment driving a diesel rig for Universal Transport System. The job was approved by Whitey's parole officer, and his first trip for

44

Universal was hauling a cargo of bulk cement to Crescent City. The rig he drove was a three thirty-five Peterbilt with a set of double tank trailers behind it.

Toward the end of the second month with the firm, Rosemar gave him permission to purchase a car. His selection was a 1959 Ford Thunderbird. For a ten year old vehicle it was in excellent condition.

Being conscious of his parole conditions, Whitey was regularly on time making his weekly appearances. During the last seven days of July he was driving out of state and failed to report in person or phone in. When he returned to Sacramento he immediately drove down to the parole office. He was sitting in the waiting-room when the receptionist called out.

"Mr. Thompson Mr. Rosemar will see you now."

Rosemar was busy behind his desk when Whitey entered the room.

"Be seated Thompson, I'll be with you in a moment," he said sharply.

Sitting, Whitey watched the parole officer as he studied a document. After leafing through several pages, Rosemar fixed his attention on Whitey.

"All right Thompson, what's your excuse?"

"Excuse, excuse for what?"

"You know perfectly well Thompson. Why didn't you report in last week?"

"Look, last week I pulled a load out of Calaveras to. . . ."

Rosemar interrupted. "You know the conditions of your parole. So why didn't you report in last week?"

"Last week I. . . ."

"Never mind," Rosemar cut in again, "I have a caseload of twenty parolees under my jurisdiction, so what happens when one doesn't report in? I can't go chasing all over the county after him. So I wait a number of days for him to report in, but on the seventh day, if I haven't heard from him, I put out a warrant for his arrest, and you can be sure he will be violated and sent back to prison. I was just about to put out a warrant on you when you appeared. Now I want to know why you did not report in last week."

"Damn it I've tried to tell you I'm a long-line truck driver, and last Sunday. . . ."

"I don't want a long line of crap Thompson," Rosemar scowled, "I just want to know why you did not call in."

Whitey was angry and shouted back, "If you don't give me a fucking chance to answer your question I'm gonna walk right out of here."

"And if you do," Rosemar hissed, "I'll have you picked up within ten minutes, and send you straight back, so you want to walk out there's the door!"

Without moving Whitey sat staring at the parole officer, and after a few tense moments had elapsed Rosemar spoke, "I guess you don't feel like walking out. Now explain last week to me."

"All last week I was driving back and forth between Sparks Nevada, and Calaveras County. I didn't get back until this morning, and when I did I came right down here."

"Before you left for Nevada why didn't you tell me you would be gone for the week?"

"Because I didn't know it myself until after I got to Nevada. My orders were changed, I had to run a load a day for the next six days out of Calaveras County to Sparks, and that's why I didn't report in."

"Then why didn't you telephone?"

"All right now listen to me, I'm not trying to be a fucking wise-guy but listen, when I applied for the job as long-line truck driver with Universal, I could not accept the job until you approved of it. And you did approve of it knowing I would be on the road for days, even weeks on end. I don't think it's fair for me to have to pay for long distance phone calls to let you know where I am, when all you have to do is make a local call right here in Sacramento to Universal. The dispatcher will be more than happy to tell you my location at any given time."

"All right Thompson your situation as a long-line driver is not the customary type of work my parolees do, so under the circumstances I'm going to give you a pass, and from now on whenever possible you call in. If I want to see you and you are out of town, I will notify your dispatcher. Do you understand?"

"Yeah okay, sure I understand."

In the middle of September, Whitey, along with another parolee was seated in the waiting room of the parole office. Whitey was casually leafing through a magazine when the silence was broken.

"Hey bud, can you spare a cigarette?"

Looking up from his magazine Whitey said, "Yeah, I guess so." Fumbling with his shirt pocket, he pulled out a pack of Winstons, extracting a cigarette from the package he tossed it into eager hands.

"Thanks a lot buddy." The parolee lit the cigarette, took a deep drag, and held the smoke in his lungs a moment before he exhaled.

"The name's Jay Holt," he said as he walked across the room and sat next to Whitey.

Whitey was in no mood for conversation but replied, "The name's Whitey, Whitey Thompson."

"Glad to know you. Who's your parole officer?"

"Rosemar," Whitey replied.

"Rosemar? They tell me he's a prick. Martin's my P.O., he's okay though. How long have you had Rosemar for a P.O.?"

"Since I got out of Folsom five months ago."

"Folsom huh, myself, I paroled from Quentin ten months ago."

Whitey wasn't in the mood for informal talk, and he was tired of

Jay's jailhouse questions, and was getting ready to explode and tell him so. Turning his head slightly, Whitey took a closer look at Jay. He was sightly on the slim side, a well-dressed six-footer, his good looks were aided by his pencil-thin mustache, hazel eyes, and receding brown hair; he obviously considered himself somewhat of a ladies man.

"So what kind of work do you do Whitey? I'm a carpenter myself."

"I drive truck."

"Not a bad job. Do you live close by?"

"I live across the street."

"I live out in the boondocks myself. I don't have a car, it's a pain in the ass getting to work. I'm looking for a rent closer in. You wouldn't want a roommate to share expenses would you?"

Suddenly the pull-down bed came to Whitey's mind. The rent was $90 a month, it would only be $45 if he shared the apartment.

"Come on, what do you say?" Jay asked, "Is it a deal?"

"I don't know much about you only that you are on parole."

"Same here," Jay returned, "I don't know much about you either."

"Yeah, but I'm the one with the apartment not you."

"You got a point there! Okay anything you want to know about me just ask my P.O."

"Fuck your P.O. I won't ask him nothing, if he approves of it, you can move in."

Rosemar and Martin both agreed on permitting the two paroles to share an apartment. Jay was waiting in front of the parole office building when Whitey came out.

"It's all set with my P.O. Whitey, how about your's?"

"Yeah he said it was okay, but before you move in I'm setting some ground rules. The rent is $90 the first of each month, your half is $45."

"What about the rest of this month? What do I owe for that?" Jay asked.

"There's only a week and a half left before the first, I won't charge you for that. Okay, now here are the ground rules. Number One, we pay for our own food, we split on the phone bill except for long distance calls, you pay for your own. I'm on the road most of the time, so when I'm gone I expect you to keep the house clean. When I do come home I'm tired, I don't want to hear a lot of noise. Them are my rules and remember one thing, the apartment is rented to me. You live by my rules, if you don't, then out you go. Agreed?"

Reaching for Whitey's hand, Jay replied, "That's a good deal. Hell yes I agree!"

He moved in and everything worked out satisfactorily until the second week of December. This was when the carpenter work slowed down and Jay was laid off. Jay assured Whitey that there was nothing to worry about as he would be eligible for unemployment, $60 a week.

"I'm sorry you got laid off Jay. I'll tell you what I'll do. Instead of forty-five dollars a month, just give me forty dollars and I'll pay the telephone bill too, but not your long distance calls, okay?"

"Hey that's fine Whitey. I sure appreciate it."

There was no work for Whitey over the holidays, so he took advantage of the time off by getting plenty of rest. The apartment was quiet without Jay, for he had left on Christmas Eve and did not return until after the holidays. Whitey was pleased having the place to himself, and celebrated the in coming year, 1970, with two cans of beer before retiring to bed.

CHAPTER 10.

On January 2 Whitey was behind the wheel of a big diesel rig heading for Florence, Arizona. After a one day layover in Florence, he was back on the road, arriving in Sacramento on the sixth. When a long trip was over it always felt good to return to the comforts of his home, but on this particular run his return was a disappointment. As soon as he opened the door he was greeted with an odor of stale wine and beer. He made a quick inspection of the rooms only to find the floors littered with empty beer cans, wine bottles, and cigarette butts. In the kitchen he found the refrigerator empty with the door partially open. He was furious, Jay was nowhere about. It was 2:00 P.M. when Whitey commenced to clean up the apartment; he did not finish until late afternoon.

Once the job was accomplished, he took his dirty clothes to the Laundromat to have them ready for his next trip. His laundry completed, he went to the supermarket for groceries and a six-pack of beer. He returned home, and after putting the groceries away he fixed himself some ham and eggs, and had a beer. Then he took a hot shower and retired to bed. His long road trip, plus the cleaning of the apartment had worn him out.

The following morning he woke up bright and early and discovered that Jay had not returned home. Whitey was disappointed as he was hoping to see him before returning to work. He took a quick shower, had a breakfast of hotcakes and eggs, then went to see his parole officer. After a brief session with him he went back to the apartment, and as he unlocked the door he heard the phone ringing. Thinking it might be Jay calling he hurried to answer it; it was the dispatcher from Universal who was calling to give him his trip orders.

Before leaving for work he wrote a note to Jay, and carefully stuck it on the refrigerator door where he would be sure to see it. The note read:

> "Jay,
> I don't appreciate coming home to find the
> Refrigerator empty and the apartment a disaster.
> I'll be returning on the 11th. You better be here.
> Whitey."

Twenty minutes later he arrived at the terminal where he fueled up the truck, and checked the oil and tires. Once the big rig was ready he climbed up behind the wheel, switching on the ignition, the huge engine fired up. Slowly the eighteen-wheeler pulled out of the terminal yard heading for the open highway.

Whitey returned on the evening of the eleventh. Jay was just leaving the apartment and almost collided with him in the doorway.

In a nervous voice Jay said, "Hi Whitey I was just on my way out."

Showing no emotion Whitey stood there blocking Jay's way, and in a cold voice said, "Stick around a minute I got a few words to say to you."

"Can't it wait until tomorrow? I'm late for a date."

Looking him straight in the eye Whitey placed his hand against Jay's chest and gently pushed him backwards. " No it can't wait until tomorrow. You're going to hear me now."

Taking a step back Jay said meekly, "If it's about the mess I left, I don't blame you for getting mad, but I promise it won't happen again. I mean look around, you see this last time I kept it clean while you were gone."

The apartment was reasonably clean, but not enough to satisfy Whitey, he was still mad.

"Sure it's clean now, but what was it like last night or the night before? The only reason it's clean now is because you knew I was coming home today. I want this place clean all the time, understand? All the fuckin' time!"

"You got it Whitey, I'll do my share and keep it clean, I promise."

"You better do your fucking share or you can get the hell out, and while I'm on it man, I don't appreciate you eating up all my food and drinking up all my goddamn beer."

"Hey I'm sorry Whitey, I really am, and it won't happen again, no kidding I mean it, it won't happen again."

"If you're in a tight spot Jay, I don't mind helping you out, but you get sixty fuckin' dollars a week, and all you do is piss it away on booze. Also I told you about the fucking phone, you already ran up a twenty-eight-dollar long distance bill. I want my freaking money."

Not giving Whitey a chance to finish talking Jay cut in, "Look man, my next unemployment check I'll pay you for the phone, okay? And I'll give you ten dollars each week toward the rent. Is that okay?"

"Okay Jay, just get your act together, but don't try fucking over me, you'll get yourself hurt."

"Don't worry Whitey, I won't try to pull anything on you. When I return to work, I'm really going to make it all up to you, you'll see."

The way Jay was pleading, Whitey had no idea what would follow during the next three months. Each time he returned home from a road trip Jay would be gone, and he would stay away from the apartment until Whitey was on another trip. Jay would wait until

Whitey's car was gone from in front of the apartment. He then assumed Whitey was off on another trip, but he had to be sure, so he would phone the dispatcher at Universal Transport System.

"Hello, is this the dispatcher?" he asked. " This is Whitey Thompson's roommate, can you tell me if he's on a trip, and if he is, when will he be back?"

"Yes" the dispatcher replied, "he's on his way to Arizona, he'll be back on the eighteenth."

"Thank you very much. Oh do me a favor, don't tell Whitey I called. I don't want him to know I worry about him when he is on the road!"

In this manner Jay evaded Whitey for three months.

Tired, Whitey turned off the truck ignition, and using his arms for a head-rest, he leaned across the steering wheel.

"Hey Thompson, turn in your manifest and driver's log before you fall asleep!"

Raising his head Whitey looked across the parking area toward the terminal. From the window of his office, Harry, the dispatcher, was calling out to him."

"Come on Thompson, I'm going home in a few minutes, turn in your papers."

"Yeah Harry, I'll be right in," Whitey shouted back. He climbed down out of the cab and walked to the dispatcher's office.

"Hello Whitey," Harry greeted. "You're back early, I didn't expect you until tomorrow."

"Yeah, I made good time. How's it going Harry?"

"Things are okay Whitey, but you sure look tired. Are you too tired to have a beer?"

Harry was a tall heavy-set man in his early forties. He had been Universal's dispatcher for the past twelve years, and was well liked by all the drivers.

"I'm in a hurry Harry, I wanna get home and catch up to my fuckin' roommate."

"Your roommate? What do you mean catch up with him?"

"The son of a bitch has been ducking me for three months. He owes me money."

Harry looked bewildered, "You mean you haven't seen him for three months?"

"No, when I show up, the fucker is never home."

"Whitey I'm sorry, but it's my fault. Your roommate has been calling me to find out when you were coming home, I didn't see anything wrong, so I would tell him."

"You mean every time I went on a trip he called you?"

"That's the size of it Whitey."

"Well didn't you think it funny, him always calling?"

"I would have thought so, but he asked me not to tell you he'd

51

called, he said he didn't want you to know he worried about you when you were on the road."

"That son of a bitch, him worried about me! The only thing he was worried about was me catching up to him, the bastard!"

"Gee I'm sorry Whitey, damn if I had only known."

"Well you didn't, so forget about it Harry, it's not your fault. He doesn't expect me until tomorrow night, right?"

"That's right."

"By the way have you got me scheduled to go out soon?"

"Yes Whitey, you take off Monday night at eight for Arizona. If there's a change in dispatch I'll call you at home."

Whitey walked out to the parking lot, got in his car and drove home. He found the apartment halfway clean, but Jay, as he expected, was nowhere in sight. The rest of the evening was uneventful; after dinner and a shower, Whitey called it a night and went to bed.

The next morning, Saturday, he made his regular trip to the Laundromat and the grocery store. He spent the remainder of the day puttering around the house. He was happy to see evening come, and like the previous one, after dinner and a shower, he retired to bed, but before falling asleep he set the alarm clock for 4:30 A.M.

He felt as though he had just fallen asleep when the alarm went off. Immediately he got out of bed, dressed, left the apartment, and went out to his parked car. At this early hour nothing was moving on the streets as Whitey slowly pulled away from the curb. He drove approximately two miles; then parked and locked the car, and walked back home.

He was still tired from his Arizona trip, and went straight to bed. It was shortly after 2:00 P.M. when he woke up. He showered, ate a late breakfast, and then relaxed leisurely sipping on a can of beer. He seldom drank more than two cans, but on this afternoon his thoughts were on Jay Holt, and he drank one beer after another. As he sat there, he patiently watched the front door waiting for Jay to enter. Suddenly the phone rang startling him and causing him to spill his beer. He was angry at the sound, and started to throw the beer can when the phone rang again. He reached for the receiver, but hesitated to pick it up. The caller might be Jay ringing to find out if he was there, but then again it could be Harry calling to change his trip schedule. The phone rang a number of times before Whitey decided to answer it.

"Hello Whitey, this is Harry. Hey I'm sorry but I have to change your trip plans. I need to have your truck in Davenport by 2:00 A.M.. You're to load up for Santa Rosa, you got that?"

"Yeah Harry I got it, I'll be there."

Harry did not respond right away, all Whitey could hear on the phone was the hum of the wire.

"Hey Harry goddamn it, did you hear what I said? I said I'll be

52

there."

"Yes I heard you, you sound like you're drunk Whitey, are you?"

"Hell no Harry, I'll be truthful with you though, I had a few but I'm not drunk."

"Okay Whitey, if you're okay then you're scheduled to be at Davenport at 2:00 A.M."

Whitey hung up the phone, he wished he had told Harry he was intoxicated, but was afraid it might get back to his parole officer. He looked at his watch, the time showed 6:00 P.M. He didn't have to leave until 11:00., there was plenty of time he thought as he opened up another can of beer.

Darkness had overshadowed the room, it was ten minutes to ten. With a can of beer in his hand, Whitey sat in the gloom facing the front door. Suddenly it opened, and for a second Jay was silhouetted in the doorway before he closed it behind him.

Jay's eyes had not had a chance to adjust to the darkness, and he didn't know Whitey was sitting in the chair until he switched on the wall lamp.

"Whitey, I didn't expect you to be home," he exclaimed in a shocked voice.

"Where did you expect me to be? After all this is my home," he replied sarcastically.

"I thought you were on a trip, I didn't see your car out front."

"Is that why you came home? You thought I was gone?"

"No, no what makes you think that?"

Whitey was getting hot under the collar and shouted back, "That's exactly what I think, I haven't seen you in three months. You're never here when I come home."

"That's just an accidental occurrence Whitey, just a coincidence."

Whitey jumped out of the chair, he was furious, "Coincidence, you lying bastard, is it a coincidence when you phone my dispatcher to find out when I'm returning off a trip?"

Jay was taken aback, his face was pale as he stood there with his mouth wide open.

"Tell me fucker, was it a coincidence?" Whitey shouted again.

Stalling to regain his composure Jay removed a handkerchief from his rear trouser pocket, and proceeded to wipe a few beads of perspiration from his forehead.

"All right, all right it's true, I did call, but not for the reason you think. I wasn't trying to dodge you, honest. I would call just to find out when you would be home, the reason was, I wanted to be away so the apartment would be nice and quiet for you."

"The reason was, you lying bastard, you was dodging me. How long did you think you could get away with it?"

"Honest Whitey, believe me, I wasn't dodging you. Why would I do that?"

"Money you son of a bitch! It's almost May, you haven't given me a dime since the first of the year, and I'm fed up paying your phone bills."

"Listen a minute Whitey, listen."

"Listen shit! You listen to me mother fucker before I punch your lights out!" Whitey was in a rage. "The last four months you collected nine hundred and sixty dollars from unemployment, you pissed it all away, you never even tried to help out, and you want me to listen to you."

"Look Whitey, please listen to me a minute," Jay pleaded in an apologetic voice. "I'm sorry, and you are right in everything you said, but listen, I have good news, my union told me I'll be going back to work in two weeks. When I do I'll pay you back double, okay? How much do I owe you now?"

Whitey ignored the question and walked out of the room and returned with a can of beer.

Jay looked longingly at the can, "Can I have a beer Whitey?" he asked innocently.

That did it! Whitey was furious, he hadn't been this mad since his last day with Brenda. "You got a fuckin' nerve, you owe me over four hundred dollars and ask me for a beer! What do I look like?"

"I'm gonna pay you back double," Jay shouted. "I'm gonna. . . ." He didn't finish, Whitey jammed his hand against his chest and shoved him up against the wall holding him there, he shouted in his face, "You want a beer fucker? Here's your beer." He poured the beverage over his head. Jay started to struggle; Whitey released him, and with a shrug of the shoulders he left the room, only to return in a few moments with another can of beer.

"You freeloading bastard, I'll tell you how you're gonna pay me back. I'm going on the road shortly, when I get back I want you packed and gone—moved out. If you're still here when I return, I'll knock you right through the fucking wall!"

Jay stood there, his mouth agape, afraid to speak.

"Do you understand me? I want you gone. I don't want nothing more to do with you."

"Okay Whitey if that's what you want, I'll be gone."

"You better, I'm going on a short run, you don't have to call the dispatcher to fine out when I'll be back. I'll be home tomorrow afternoon, your ass better be out of here."

Without another word Whitey went into the bedroom to change clothes in preparation for his trip. Shortly after, he left the apartment, and drove to work. It did not take him long to get his rig fueled up and ready for the road. Fifteen minutes later the heavy vehicle was rolling south on 99 Freeway. The cool night breeze coming through the window was refreshing. The big Peterbilt was purring right along. Whitey glanced out the window to his left side rear view mirror. In the distance he could see a flashing red light coming up from behind. Automatically he checked his speed, the indicator needle was pointing to fifty-five miles per hour. Maintaining his speed Whitey skillfully eased the big rig to the right side of the road allowing the Highway Patrol adequate room for passing. To his surprise the patrol car made no attempt to pass; instead it stayed just to the left of his tailgate with its siren wailing and lights flashing. Whitey wasn't speeding or swaying all over the road; he couldn't understand why a patrolman was pulling him over. He began applying the brakes, and as the rig slowed, he pulled well off to the curbside of the Freeway. After stopping the truck, he set the brakes and shut down the engine.

With his eye on the rear view mirror Whitey watched the patrol car pull up behind his rear trailer. He could see the officer as he stepped out of the car, walked the length of the rig, and stopped just to the left side of the cab looking up at Whitey.

"Climb down out of that truck," he ordered politely.

In disbelief Whitey sat there not moving, "What's wrong officer? Why did you stop me?"

"Never mind why, just come down out of that truck."

Whitey reluctantly opened the door and climbed down out of the cab.

"Is your name Leon Whitey Thompson?" the officer asked.

Whitey wondered how he knew his name. "Yeah officer that's my name," he answered.

"Then I got the right truck. We received a call that a Universal truck would be coming this way, and that the driver had been drinking. By the smell of you I'd say you were drinking. You want to show me your driver's license?"

After verification the officer ordered Whitey to turn around and face the truck with his hands behind him.

Whitey's first impulse was to take a swing and make a run for it. Instinctively he glanced toward the patrol car; he saw a shadow of movement within the vehicle. He was sure it was a backup patrolman who had him under his sights.

Facing the truck, Whitey held his hands so that the officer could handcuff him from behind. Then kicking his legs apart the patrolman shook him down.

"Why're doing this to me?" Whitey asked.

"I'm taking you in for driving under the influence of alcohol."

"Hey come on," Whitey pleaded, "sure I had a few beers, but I'm not drunk. Come on give me a break, I won't move the truck for a couple of hours, I'll sleep, okay?"

"The only place you'll sleep is in a cell at the county jail. You're drunk and you know it."

Twenty minutes later he was booked on a 502 (drunk driving) at the Sacramento county jail. Whitey was absolutely positive Jay Holt had notified the Highway Patrol.

CHAPTER 11.

The morning following his arrest Whitey was taken to Elk Grove where he appeared before Traffic Court. He was found guilty and received a sentence of ninety days, and was returned to the Sacramento County jail. Early the next morning he was transferred to the Branch County jail located in Elk Grove. He was placed in a ten-man cell, and as he entered he felt weak and dejected. He was not prepared for the greetings that were bestowed on him.

Voices in succession called out to him, "Hi Old-timer, welcome to the club!"

"How you doing Bro? What brings you here?" The welcoming committee was a group of nine young inmates between the ages of eighteen and twenty-four. Recognition was in their eyes—recognition of a man who had done time—big time. They looked up to him with respect, and in doing so they restored his strength, and Whitey felt he was back in a position of rank.

The chorus continued, "How much time you bring? What you in for?"

A resonant voice dominated over the eager questions of the group. "Shut up, all of you shut the fuck up. Be quiet you bastards!"

Everyone including Whitey, turned to face the speaker who was standing on a steel table towering over the group. He was impressive-looking with long black hair, dark piercing eyes. A muscular specimen of a man wearing motorcycle boots, oily Levi's, and a leather vest over his bare torso. At a glance he gave the impression of a rugged early-day mountain man.

"Shut up you bastards!" he shouted again. "What the fuck's wrong with you guys asking such juvenile questions? How much time you bring? What you in for? You don't ask a man questions like that. Show some fucking class you ass-holes!"

Jumping down off the table, the young scooter-tramp turned to face Whitey with an outstretched hand, "The name is Ben Vakno."

Accepting his hand in a brotherhood grip, Whitey returned, "Glad to know you Ben. I'm Whitey Thompson."

"Right on man! It's my pleasure to meet you."

"Why's that?"

"Because I know you've done time," Ben replied with a knowing look. "I overheard a pig this morning talking about you."

"Hell these cops don't know me."

"Maybe not, but they have your name and record, they knew you were coming out here this morning from downtown. Anyway I heard a pig say to another one, 'We got a parolee out of Folsom coming in on the chain this morning and guess what? He's an ex-con from Alcatraz!' "

"Word sure gets around!" Whitey growled.

"Welcome to the Branch!" a chorus rang out. "Your seniority counts with us man!"

Whitey became popular with the inmates of the Branch county jail. Also, a lasting friendship was building between the forty-seven-year-old ex-con, and the twenty-year-old scooter-tramp.

"You know Whitey if you ever need a place to stay, you're always welcome at my pad."

"Thanks Ben, I'll keep that in mind."

During the second week of incarceration Whitey was unexpectedly visited by his parole officer. Rosemar was seated and waiting when Whitey entered the room.

"Well well Thompson, I would of been down to see you sooner, but there was no rush because I knew where you were, and that you would be here when I arrived."

Whitey was expressionless as he sat in his chair staring at the parole officer.

"Why did you get drunk Thompson? Is there a reason behind it?"

"I just had a few drinks, that's all there is to it."

"A few drinks Thompson, I've heard otherwise. The police report says you had a considerable amount. Also I bumped into your roommate Jay Holt, he told me you had quite a bit to drink that Sunday."

"Hey, I got drunk. I got drunk and that's all there is to it."

"Yes I know you got drunk, but I want to know why. Were you having any sort of trouble with your roommate?"

"No, I wasn't having trouble with anyone."

"I just don't understand it, you had a good job, you were doing well on parole, but you just had to screw up. Well maybe we can salvage something out of this yet. You keep your nose clean and we'll see what happens. I'll check in on you from time to time."

"Look before you go, tell me right off the top if you're gonna reinstate or violate me."

"I'm undecided Thompson, just keep out of trouble and we'll see what happens."

After Rosemar had departed, Whitey was returned to the cell.

"Who came to see you?" Ben asked.

"No one really," Whitey replied, "just my P.O."

"Did he mention your parole? Is he gonna to violate you?"

"I don't know. All he said was, keep my nose clean and stay out of trouble."

"Hey that's sounds good, I bet when your ninety days are up you'll walk."

"Yeah, right back to Folsom!" Whitey returned with a sneer.

Three weeks elapsed before Rosemar returned, and he was in a cheerful mood. "I see you kept your nose clean, and with thirty days good-time that will put you out the twenty-ninth of June. You have twenty-six days to go."

"And then what happens on the twenty-ninth of June?" Whitey asked. "Are you sending me back to the joint, or are you gonna cut me loose?"

"I've taken everything into consideration Thompson, you have done well on parole except for the one mishap. On the twenty-ninth I will be out to pick you up."

"I guess that means you're gonna violate my parole, right?"

"Not necessarily Thompson, the only way you can be released is to my custody. So you see, I have to be out here on your release day. You keep out of trouble, don't mess up, and I'll see you on the twenty-ninth."

A guard returned Whitey to the cell.

"How did it go?" Ben asked. "Are you gonna be reinstated?"

"It looks that way from what my P.O. says, but I don't count on it."

"Ah you'll make it Whitey," Ben was excited. "Don't forget, I get out a few weeks after you leave. You got the address to my pad, you can stay there as long as you want."

"I may take you up on that Ben—we'll see."

On the morning of June 29 at 9:30 A.M., a guard called out to Whitey, "Thompson, Leon W. Thompson. Roll 'em up—roll 'em up!"

A chorus of voices rang out, "Good luck Whitey. Go get 'em pal!"

A guard unlocked the cell door, and before Whitey departed he reached out for Ben's hand, "I'll catch you later Ben. Good luck, and I'll see you at your pad."

After shouts of farewell, Whitey was escorted under guard to the Control room where he signed a release form for his personal property. Once the paper was signed the officer behind the counter handed him his clothing and wallet. No one had to tell him to change clothes. He quickly slipped into his civilian dress and was just slipping on his boots when Rosemar entered the room.

Whitey's happy expression turned to bewilderment when he saw the articles the parole officer held in his hands. Rosemar caught his stare and glanced at the handcuffs and chain he was holding.

58

Quickly looking back at Whitey, he smiled; then with a laugh he said, "Don't let these chains and cuffs disturb you Thompson. This is just a formality, once we get to my office the chains will be removed, but I have to cuff and chain you now, it's just the rules."

Whitey's expression turned to anger, "Come off it Rosemar, don't bullshit me, you're gonna violate my parole. That's why you got the irons."

"No no Thompson, I'm taking you downtown to my office, but I have to cuff you up, those are the rules. After we get there you will be reinstated on parole. Then you can go home free. So come on now, the quicker I get these on you the quicker we can get this over with."

Reluctantly Whitey held his hands behind him while Rosemar placed the handcuffs on his wrists. For double security, a chain was strapped around his waist and attached to it was another length of chain that ran down to a set of leg-irons.

"That's an awful lot of iron for a trip to your office."

Taking a step back, Rosemar said, "You're not going to my office Thompson, your parole has been violated, and I'm taking you back to Folsom!"

"You son of a bitch! You conned me, you lowlife bastard!" Whitey made a lunge at the parole officer, only to succeed in tripping and falling to the floor. "You're lucky I'm chained up you bastard!"

With the aid of a deputy, Rosemar helped Whitey to his feet.

"Thompson, you can make it hard on yourself, or you can make it easy, either way you are going back." Turning to the deputy sheriff he continued, "Is he all set to go?"

"Just as soon as you sign these papers you can have him," the deputy answered.

Rosemar signed the papers, and with the aid of the deputy Whitey was ushered to a waiting car. There was no further communication between Whitey and the parole officer.

The movement of the car was bearable until the shackles began to chafe his ankles. It reminded him of another time when he was a prisoner in shackles and irons on a train bound for Alcatraz. At this time he had been incarcerated for ten years in the Federal Penitentiary at McNeil Island, Washington. He was doing fifteen years for bank robberies. During his stay at McNeil he was a constant troublemaker. He was considered incorrigible, and was transferred to Alcatraz, better known as "The Rock."

Once inside the double gates of Folsom Prison, the loneliness, anger and despair were with Whitey once again.

Rosemar turned over Whitey's wallet and personal belongings to the gate officer along with his commitment papers. Then he removed the leg-irons, and handcuffs. Whitey immediately began to rub circulation into his wrists and legs, and while doing so he stared coldly at Rosemar who had turned to leave.

"Good luck Thompson," he said.

"Shove it up your ass!" Whitey retorted.

A few moments after Rosemar left, a guard appeared at the main gate to escort Whitey to Sergeant Parker's office at the hospital.

"Thompson, well-well-well, I've been expecting you," the Sergeant greeted Whitey.

"Hi Sarge, how's it going," Whitey said with a faint smile.

"Just fine, but what are you doing back here?"

"I'm sure you know Sarge, there's no need me telling you."

"You're right. I received a notice about you over a month ago, stating you would be returning today. What the hell's wrong with you Thompson? Why did you fuck up?"

"It's just one of those things Sarge, I felt like a drink, and here I am! At least I'm not back on a new beef."

Holding out his hand to Whitey, Sergeant Parker smiled, "I'm sorry you're back. I guess you're wondering why you were delivered here to the hospital instead of Receiving and Release."

Shaking his hand Whitey replied, "Yeah, what is the deal? Why did they bring me here?"

"They've started a new program, it's called the STRU program, STRU is short for Short Term Release Unit. You will be free in six months or less."

"Are you pulling my leg Sarge, are you serious?"

"I'm serious Thompson, it's a new program for inmates with a drinking problem. You were sent back for getting drunk. They want you back for a dry-out period of six months or less, and then you return to the streets. That's all there is to it. You see technically you are still on parole, it has not been violated as yet. In a few weeks you'll go before the Adult Board for a hearing, and when you do, you tell them the truth about being drunk. A new parole date will be set for you, it won't exceed six months, and then you will be going home."

"But suppose I wasn't drunk Sarge, suppose I was just feeling good?"

"Don't tell them that," Parker replied in a stern voice, "if you tell the Board you were not guilty of being drunk, your parole will be revoked, and you will wind up doing another year or two instead of just six months. Do you understand?"

"Yeah I get the picture Sarge. I understand, thanks for the tip."

"That's okay Thompson. You just do as I said and you'll be out of here by January. Now then, you will stay up here in the hospital in a cell until tomorrow, at that time you will receive a physical examination. . . ."

"What do you mean a physical? For what?"

"We don't want you bringing back the clap or any other social disease with you," Parker replied with a laugh.

"Shit Sarge I didn't even get a piece of ass while I was out!"

A grin appeared on Parker's face, "Sorry Thompson, you are still required to have a checkup, and right after the exam you'll be moved to 2 Block. You'll only be there a week, then you'll be transferred outside to the Ranch. You know Mr. O'Leary, the Ranch Food Supervisor don't you?"

"Yeah I know him, what about it?"

"I hear he's in need of a lead cook. I'm sure he'll want you for the job. You will be in charge of the Ranch kitchen under no supervision. Well that's about it Thompson, right now I want you to get out of your street clothes, and put on these blues." Parker pointed to a set of prison blues setting on his desk. "You can change right here Thompson, I have to take your street clothes before I put you in a cell."

After the change of clothes Whitey was escorted to a single cell where he was locked up. A few minutes later the Sergeant returned carrying a large paper bag; he opened the cell door and handed it to Whitey.

"What's this Sarge?" Whitey asked.

"It's from your former cell partner McCulley. You remember him don't you?"

"Hell yes, how's he doing?"

"He's doing good, he saw your name on the movement sheet, that's how he knew you were here, and he sent this stuff up to you."

"Hey thanks Sarge, if you see him tell him I'm obliged."

"You'll get a chance to see him tomorrow, you can thank him yourself."

After Sergeant Parker left, Whitey opened the bag, inside he found five packs of cigarettes, five books of matches, a jar of M.J.B. instant coffee, and three paperback books.

CHAPTER 12.

The following morning, immediately after his medical examination Whitey was moved to the third tier of 2 Block. Shortly after the
move was completed and he was settled in, his cell door slid open for
the 10:00 A.M. unlock. He decided to walk over to Number 2 Dining
Hall to see if McCulley was there. The officer in charge of the dining
area was Mr. Lasher who opened the gate to admit Whitey. Lasher
was a middle-aged easygoing veteran of fifteen years with the prison
system. He was well-liked by most of the inmates, especially the crew
who worked for him. He was very fond of arts and crafts, particularly
oil paintings. He held out his hand to Whitey as he came through the
gateway.

"Whitey Thompson, what in the world brings you back here?"

Ignoring the officer's hand Whitey replied, "It's a long story Lasher,
How ya doing?"

"Just fine Thompson, what can I do for you?"

"I dropped by to see if Okie is around."

Lasher pointed to the dining tables, "He's right over there rolling
cigarettes."

Whitey looked in the indicated direction and saw McCulley seated
at a table with his rolling machine. Beside the machine stacked like
cord-wood, was a small pile of cigarettes. At that moment McCulley
happened to look up and saw Whitey walking toward him. In his
excitement of joy at seeing his old friend he almost fell off the stool!

"Hi Whitey, goddamn man how are ya?" he yelled so loudly his
voice echoed throughout the Dining Hall.

"Hi pal, I see you're still rolling them cancer sticks!"

Both men embraced for a second, then stood apart and shook
hands.

"Sure glad to see you Whitey, but I'm sorry you're back."

"Me too Okie, I guess you heard what happened."

"Yeah I heard all about it. It's a bummer sending a guy back to the
joint for getting drunk."

"Well it was more than that Okie, they busted me for drunk
driving."

"Well even so they didn't have to send you back," McCulley

62

"Well it was more than that Okie, they busted me for drunk driving."

"Well even so they didn't have to send you back," McCulley sympathized. "By the way did you get the smokes and coffee okay?"

"Sure did pal, thanks a lot. How come you gave me tailor-made smokes and you're rolling your own? You should have kept the Camels and gave me the Bugler."

Shrugging his shoulders McCulley replied, "I like Bugler tobacco better than tailor-made."

"You fucking Oakie liar! But thanks anyway McCulley, I sure appreciate the smokes."

"Forget it Whitey. Hey Sergeant Parker told me you're on the STRU program. Shit you'll only be here about six months, I can hold my breath that long!" McCulley chuckled then continued, "You'll be going out to the Ranch then, right?"

"Yeah, I'll be going out there in a few days. The Sarge told me O'Leary needs a lead cook out there. I guess that's what I'll be doing."

"I bet them sons of bitches violated your parole Whitey, just because they needed a cook at the Ranch!"

"You may be right Okie, I wouldn't put it past them!"

"You know Whitey, if I had taken bets on you I would of lost. I would of bet my life that you would never come back to prison."

"Let me tell you something Okie, when you are on parole it's easy as hell to come back. An ordinary citizen can get drunk, and if he's stopped by the law, he may have to go to jail or pay a fine, whatever, then he continues with his life like nothing had happened. But when you are on parole like I was, it's different. They busted me for drunk driving and I was sent to jail for ninety days. When I finished my jail time, my ass was snatched right back here to prison. I feel like I'm being punished twice for the same offense."

"Well in a way you are. I guess that's all part of the parole system, but you'll make it the next time Whitey, I'm sure you will."

"I don't know about the next time," Whitey spoke in a whisper, "I'm getting to where I don't give a fuck, you know what I mean? I'm getting tired of the game."

"I don't like to hear you talk like that."

"I'm not bullshitting. The next time I get out I might just hang it up, hold court in the fucking streets, and get it over with."

"Ah come on Whitey, don't talk like that. You're too good a guy to hang it up."

"Thanks Oakie, but I'm getting fed up with trying. You know when I left Alcatraz I made up my mind to go straight, and what happens, I get fucked over and get hit with one to fifteen years, for what man? And now for the past year on parole I've worked my ass off, that's all I did was keep clean, stay out of trouble and work. I didn't even go out with a chick, I didn't even get laid man because I didn't want to take a chance of getting into a jam, and what happens? I tried to be decent to a guy on parole and the son of a bitch calls the cops, and I get busted for drunk driving, and here I am, back in prison."

"I understand how you feel Whitey, and I don't blame you, but don't give up now, you'll be getting out in a few months, give it another try, what do ya say?"

"I don't know yet, I'll just play it by ear for now. Say have you seen Lou lately? Is he still over in R and R?"

"Lou? Yeah he's still working in R and R, I see him once in a while in the chow line."

"Listen I might not get a chance to see him before they send me to the Ranch, so say hello for me will ya?"

"I sure will Whitey, you can count on it."

"All right pal, and thanks once again for the smokes, coffee, and books."

Whitey turned and walked toward the Dining room gate.

"My pleasure," McCulley called after him.

Whitey did not get the opportunity to see Lou, for on the following Monday morning he was transferred to the Ranch. Shortly after his arrival, Mr.O'Leary, the Supervisor, made him the Lead Cook. There were seven inmates in the Ranch kitchen crew counting Whitey. Whitey's sole job was supervising and cooking. The other inmates performed dining room duties, such as waiting on tables, serving food, washing pots and pans, cleaning, and of course performing other chores required by the Lead Cook. Cooking for two hundred men was a breeze for Whitey compared to the twenty-eight hundred inmates he prepared food for inside the walls. He fell into the routine and before he realized it, July had passed, and it was the middle of August.

On the evening of the eighteenth Whitey was notified to appear before the Adult board, and the following morning at 10 o'clock he was seated in the hot-seat waiting his turn to make his appearance. When his name was called, he walked in. Nothing had changed, there in front of him was the long table, and seated behind it were familiar faces, a member and representative of the Adult Parole Board, Larkin and Morson.

Without any introductions Whitey sat facing the panel. It was a warm summer day, but as he sat there he could feel a slight chill in the room. There were no greetings, no smiles, and above all, no warmth from the faces staring at him.

Larkin was the first to speak, "Thompson A-92856, you love that number don't you?" Not waiting for a reply he continued, "You must love it, if not, why did you come back?"

Whitey was quiet and without moving he sat there listening to Larkin rant and rave.

"Why did you come back? I'll tell you why. It seems you like to tip

64

the sauce a bit, as a matter of fact, you like to tip it quite a bit, to the point of getting arrested for drunk driving. What is your excuse Thompson? Do you have an excuse?"

"I have no excuse," Whitey answered promptly.

"Well now, isn't that strange?" Larkin said in a supercilious voice. "Here is a man with no excuse! He has no excuse for being sent back to prison."

"That's not what I meant," Whitey shot back.

"Now we are getting somewhere, you admit getting drunk, and are you guilty of the drunk driving charge?"

Whitey sat there quietly staring at Larkin, he knew full well Larkin was trying to get a rise out of him, but as yet he had not succeeded.

"How do you plead to this charge? Guilty or not guilty? Answer me Thompson," he shouted.

Whitey did not answer, in a defiant manner he quietly sat there glaring at the man.

"Answer me Thompson, are you guilty or not guilty? Speak up!"

For God's sake an inner voice in Whitey seemed to say, answer the man, why don't you answer him? If you are trying to get a rise out of him, you have succeeded, he is angry now, so for God's sake answer him before it's too late.

"Guilty," Whitey sneered, "I'm guilty as hell."

Larkin turned to Morson, "Do you have any questions for Thompson?"

"No, I think you about covered it."

"Fine, then this hearing is terminated. We'll let you know Mr. Thompson."

Whitey stood up, and with a nod of the head, left the room.

Three days later, August 21. Whitey received his results, Parole granted. Effective date, January 4, 1971. Conditions, placed on Close Custody Parole, totally abstain from any alcoholic beverages. Must attend Alcoholic Anonymous meetings weekly.

A.A. meetings were held each Sunday right after breakfast in the Ranch Dining Hall. Whitey decided to attend. Occasionally members from outside groups would come to Folsom to attend the weekly sessions, and it was during one of these meetings that Whitey met Lonnie and Bernie Kirkland. Lonnie was an attractive woman of 48, trim figure, with radiant red hair, and flashing brown eyes. To the opposite sex she was outgoing, and at times too friendly to the point of being a flirt. Her husband was a quiet unassuming man of 65, six foot two, black hair with traces of gray, deep brown mystic eyes, and like his wife, he too could be outgoing.

After being introduced to Whitey the Kirklands became quite friendly with him. Both Lonnie and Bernie had been with the A.A. program for over ten years. At first their conversations with Whitey pertained strictly to the subject of A.A., but it did not take them long before they became fond of him. When they learned he was soon to be released, they invited him to live in their home, subject to approval by his parole officer.

Whitey knew his P.O. would never approve of him staying with Ben Vakno, so he accepted the Kirkland's offer.

"Of course I have to get permission first, but right now I don't know who my P.O. is going to be. I sure hope it isn't Rosemar."

"I can find out for you if you want," Lonnie said.

"You?" Whitey was surprised. "How the hell can you find out?"

"Easy, you see once a week on Tuesday evenings, we attend the A.A. meeting held at the Sacramento Parole Office. My husband and I know all of them. When we find out which one is your P.O. we'll ask him if you can live with us. That's all there is to it."

"You know all the parole officers?" Whitey was amazed.

"Yes all of them." Lonnie and Bernie began laughing at the expression on Whitey's face.

"Tomorrow morning," Lonnie continued, "I'll call their office, then I'll write a letter to you and let you know, okay?"

On the following Tuesday Whitey received a letter from Lonnie, but the news it contained was a disappointment, the letter read:

"Dear Whitey,

This letter will be short and sweet. I called the Parole Office and your P.O. is going to be Rosemar. I know you don't like him, but believe me he is okay, and he told me he will give his approval for you to live with us. Isn't that nice?
I have to close now, but I will see you next Sunday at the meeting, we will have a nice long talk.

Love Lonnie."

Whitey was not too excited about Rosemar being his parole officer, as a matter of fact, he was disappointed, but there was nothing he could do about it.

One afternoon toward the end of September, Whitey was called out of the kitchen for a visit. He had no idea who had come to see him, and was delighted to see Ben Vakno walk into the visiting room. After a brotherhood handshake, the two men sat down at a table.

"This is a surprise Ben, a hell of a surprise. I didn't think you would show up here. When did you get out of jail?"

"Last Monday."

"How did ya know I was back in the joint?"

"I heard about it the same day you left jail. We thought you went free, until a trusty who worked out front told me he seen your P.O. with two deputies dragging you in irons to his car. It didn't take much brains to figure out where he was taking you, anyway here I am!"

"Yeah the son of a bitch lied to me, I thought I was getting out that day, instead I wind up here. But to hell with that! What's happening with you Ben? How's it going?"

"Never mind me, I want to know what's happening with you. How long you gonna be here?"

"I'm getting out January 4."

"Far out man, far out!" Ben exclaimed. "I'll be up on your release day to pick you up."

"Thanks Ben for the offer, I appreciate it, I really do, but I know my P.O. won't approve of me staying with your motorcycle gang. You know that as well as I do, right?"

"Yeah, I guess so," Ben agreed reluctantly. "But where the hell will you be staying then?"

"I know a couple of squares, Lonnie and Bernie Kirkland, I'm gonna be staying with them, but don't worry, I'll keep in touch with you."

"You better you fucker! You give me a call right after you get out."

"Sure Ben, just as soon as I get settled in I'll give you a ring."

"Okay, I'll have a little coming-home party set up for you. How does that sound? I'll fix you up with a little fox, you can get your dick wet!" Ben said with a laugh.

When the visit expired Ben promised Whitey that he would visit him at least one more time before his release date. He kept his word.

On the first of December Whitey was taken back inside the walls for dress-out. After this was accomplished, he reported to Receiving and Release to be photographed. Since his return to prison this was Whitey's first opportunity to see Lou Peters who greeted him with a crushing bear-hug.

"Damn, I was about to give up on seeing you Whitey, you've been back over five months."

"Yeah I know, I wanted to see you, but they shot me right out to the Ranch. What's happening with you Lou? When are you gonna get out?"

"Oh I won't get a date for at least three more years. In the meantime I put in a transfer for Quentin."

Whitey was surprised. "What the hell ya wanna go to San Quentin for?"

"All my visitors live in the Bay Area, they can't make it up here to Folsom, it's too far for them."

"Well wherever you go I wish you luck Lou. You know I'm leaving on the fourth don't you?"

"Yes I know, I saw your name on the list yesterday. Sure wish I were going with you Whitey. You and I would make a good team out there."

"Yeah I think we would Lou, but who knows, maybe we will meet out there one day, you never know."

After Whitey's picture was taken, the two friends said their goodbyes.

On the evening prior to his release Whitey signed his parole papers. The following morning, January 4. at 7:00 A.M. he took a final shower before getting dressed in his street clothes. He was ready to leave, and under an escort, he was led to the main gate. Once he was beyond the gate outside the walls, the escorting guard gave him a gentle pat on the shoulder, "Good luck Thompson, you're on your own now."

Ignoring the warm gesture from the guard, Whitey picked up his duffle bag, slung it over his right shoulder and turned toward the parking lot. If he was excited about his release, it did not show. Twice before the gates of freedom had opened for him, Alcatraz and Folsom, and each time he was locked up again. Will it happen once more? These thoughts were running through his mind when a voice interrupted him.

"Yoo-hoo Whitey! Over here." Lonnie Kirkland was standing alongside a Ford pickup truck, beckoning to him.

"Hi Lonnie," he called as he walked the short distance to the truck.

"Congratulations Whitey, you're free, congratulations."

Whitey was surprised, totally surprised when Lonnie threw her arms around his neck, pulling him close, embracing him with a lingering kiss.

PART TWO.

RUN FAR—RUN FAST

1971—1972

CHAPTER 13.

The drive to the Kirkland residence located in North Sacramento, was a pleasant one. The house was a comfortable two bedroom home, and after Lonnie showed Whitey his room, she prepared a light breakfast of coffee and donuts. Then she drove Whitey to their business establishment. She and her husband were the owner-operators of a Payless Cleaners pickup station.

While Lonnie was at Folsom Prison picking up Whitey, Bernie was in the shop with work piling up on him; he was happy to see both of them walk through the door.

"It's good to see you on parole Whitey," Bernie greeted. "How does it feel to be out?"

"It's too soon to tell," Whitey returned.

"Have you reported in to the parole office yet?"

"No, Lonnie and I just had breakfast, then we came right over here."

"Well you better report in. How did you figure on getting down there? Do you still have your driver's license?"

"Yeah sure, I got a class one, it's good until nineteen-seventy-three, why?"

"Long as you got a license, then use the pickup."

"Hey that's swell Bernie, thanks." Whitey started toward the door, before he reached it Bernie called after him, "Hey Whitey, do me a favor will you? Come right back we sure can use a hand here. We're away behind on bagging and ticketing the clean and dirty clothes."

I'll get back as soon as I can," Whitey replied.

It was 10:00 A.M. when Whitey reported to the parole office receptionist; after a ten minute wait he was summoned into his office. Rosemar looked in an unpleasant mood, but this was nothing new for Whitey, as he had never known him to smile.

Whitey greeted Rosemar in a surly voice, "Good morning Rosemar."

"Never mind the formalities," he retorted. "You've been on parole before so you know the rules as well as I do. You are on Close Custody Parole, so don't step out of line or I'll send you back. Do you understand? And another thing, I know the Kirklands well, very well, so don't do anything out of the way. Now do you have anything to say?"

Without uttering a word, and with a look of contempt, Whitey turned on his heel to leave the room.

"Thompson!" Rosemar shouted. "I asked you if you had anything to say."

"No. Like you said, I know the rules, so I don't have nothing to say, okay?"

"That's fine Thompson . As long as you know the rules."

Rosemar breathed a sigh of relief after Whitey left the room. He knew about his violent temper and felt uneasy in his presence.

After leaving the parole office he hurried back to the Cleaners to help the Kirklands catch up on their work. With Whitey's aid the backlog was caught up by 3:00 P.M. The first half hour after Whitey's return was spent learning how to sort, bag and ticket the clean clothes. He also learned how to sort, bag, and ticket the incoming dirty clothes. Once the cleaned clothes were ticketed and bagged, then they were hung on racks in alphabetical order. As for the dirty clothes, it was quite a chore getting them ready for the evening pickup man who hauled them off to the plant for dry-cleaning.

It did not take Whitey long to master the cash register, and handling money was natural to him! As the week wore on he became more proficient than either Lonnie or Bernie, and before he realized it, he was carrying the brunt of the workload.

It was Tuesday afternoon of the second week; shortly after 2:00 P.M. Bernie complained that he wasn't feeling well.

"What's wrong honey?" Lonnie asked.

"I don't know, I just don't feel well."

"Well come on, I'll drive you home." Then turning to Whitey, "Can you handle things until I get back?"

"Yeah, go ahead take him home."

After they had left, Whitey began sorting out dirty shirts, but was interrupted when a customer came in for her dry-cleaning. While waiting on her, an elderly man came after his shirts. No sooner would one customer leave the establishment when another would enter. For the next three hours Whitey was very busy, and did not realize the time until business slacked off and he noticed the clock. Damn it's five o'clock, she should of been back long ago. It's only a half mile to the house. I wonder if I should call her up; maybe I'd better.

The phone was next to the cash register, and at the precise moment he reached for the receiver, the phone rang. He let it ring four times before answering it to give the caller the impression that he was busy.

"Payless Cleaners, Whitey Thompson speaking."

"Whitey this is Lonnie."

"Hi Lonnie, how's Bernie doing?"

"Not too well, that's why I didn't come right back. How's it going? Have you been swamped?"

"Yeah I've been busy for the past three hours, but it's slow now."

"Okay Whitey, at five thirty start getting ready to close up, I'll be there by ten to six to help you finish. Can you handle it all right?"

"I've been doing it so far."

The shop was open six days a week from 7:00 A.M. to 6:00 P.M.. It did not take the Kirklands long to realize that Whitey could handle the pickup station with ease, so occasionally the two of them would leave the shop early. It soon became an everyday occurrence until finally one day they didn't work at all. Bernie wasn't feeling well and Lonnie decided to stay home with him. She asked Whitey if he would mind opening up the shop alone that morning. He agreed to do so, but he felt it was a little too much to ask of him for just a place to stay. Lonnie turned over the shop keys to Whitey, and after that day, each morning he would drive to work, and in the evening after he had closed up, he would return with the day's receipts.

The Kirklands were taking advantage of his situation, and slowly burdening him with all the work. Running the shop was no longer easy for him. In addition to the regular work, every morning before he left the house he would prepare breakfast for Lonnie and Bernie, do the dishes, and clean up the kitchen. Without fail, every evening after returning from work, he would cook dinner for the three of them. When the meal was over, he would wash the dishes, tidy up the rooms, and see to their needs right up to his bedtime.

Toward the middle of February Bernie was admitted to the hospital for a severe case of arthritis of the right knee joint. For three previous years he had been suffering minor symptoms of the disease. Now the knee was so inflamed and painful that he was unable to stand. His only alternative to walk again was through surgery, and the day after his admittance to the hospital, he was operated on. It was successful and the doctor assured him he would be up and about within a few months.

Three days after Bernie's surgery, Lonnie went to the hospital for a hysterectomy, and like her husband, she too was bedridden after returning home. Whitey was run ragged, he had absolutely no time to himself. Every single minute of every single day found him working either in the shop or running errands for the Kirklands or waiting on them.

On May 30 Lonnie and Bernie returned to work.

CHAPTER 14.

Five months had passed since Whitey's release from prison, and he felt he had more than paid his obligation to the Kirklands. Lonnie and Bernie had been back to work for more than a week, and Whitey decided it was time to get his own life together.

Lonnie had just finished with a customer when Whitey said, "Lonnie, because of the circumstances I stayed here longer than I had planned to. You and Bernie are in good shape now health-wise, and it's about time I went out and looked for a job."

"You don't have to do that Whitey, you can stay with us as long as you want."

"Thanks Lonnie, but that's not getting on my feet. I've got to find a paying job if I expect to have anything. I'm gonna start job-hunting today, I'd like to know if I can use the pickup."

"I'm sorry Whitey I can't let you use it."

He was positive she would let him use the truck and was taken aback by her refusal.

"Why not?" he asked.

For a moment Lonnie seemed at a loss for words, "My insurance, my insurance company won't allow it," She blurted.

"Ah come off it Lonnie, that's a crock of shit and you know it."

"Honest, no one is allowed to drive it except Bernie or myself. That's the way our insurance is set up."

Whitey knew she was lying about the insurance and he could not comprehend why she refused him the use of the vehicle. It just did not make sense, he had been driving the pickup an average of twice a day for the past five months. Suddenly it hit him; she didn't want him looking for work. The simple fact was if he found employment she would have to pay someone else to take his place or do the work herself. Up to this point, Whitey had thought highly of the Kirklands and was willing to help them out any way he could. But now he felt he had been used by them, and it saddened him to think that they disregarded his welfare and only thought of their own.

"What did you say?" Whitey was beginning to anger. "Only you and Bernie can drive the truck? What the hell have I been driving for the last five months? I'll tell you what I've been driving, I've been driving your goddamn Ford. I drove it all over hell for you and Bernie, to the fuckin' grocery store for your groceries, the goddamn pharmacy for your medicine, to your stinking slave-shop so I could do your work; everywhere I drove it was for you. I broke my ass for you people and never asked for a dime, I never asked for nothing. Now I ask if I could use the truck to look for work, and you refuse me; well I'll tell. . ."

"Wait a minute," Lonnie shouted, "just you wait a minute buster and listen. . . ."

That was as far as she got, Whitey was furious now; his old violent temper had returned. He took a step toward her. His sudden move frightened her, and she quickly backed up.

"Fuck you bitch," he shouted, "you listen to me, take that truck and shove it up your ass!"

Whitey had forgotten all about Bernie who came running around the counter shouting at him. "Just where do you get off talking to my wife like that? I'm going to knock your. . . ."

Whitey spun on his heel holding his hands high to block the onslaught, and in doing so he knocked Bernie up against the counter.

"Get out of my way old man before I hurt you." Whitey stormed out of the shop and hurried down the street to the Kirkland's home.

A few minutes after he arrived at the house Bernie came home. Whitey was in his room when he knocked on the door.

Bernie entered the room and approached Whitey who was lying across the bed. Acting somewhat humble he said, "Whitey look, I don't blame you for being mad."

"Don't blame me for being mad did you say? Hey I'm not mad man I'm fuckin' pissed off, pissed off do you hear me?" Whitey jumped up off the bed, Bernie thought he was going to attack him and started for the door.

"Wait a minute," Whitey shouted. "I'm not pissed off at you."

He was not mad at Bernie, for in reality he felt sorry for the old man, and did not blame him for Lonnie's actions. Bernie stopped short, and turned to face Whitey who was lighting a cigarette.

"Whitey will you listen to me for just one minute please."

Whitey took a deep drag on the cigarette, "Sure go ahead, but no matter what you say, your old lady is still a bitch!"

"Like—like I said, I don't blame you for how you feel, you have helped us out a great deal. I don't know what we could of done if it weren't for you. We couldn't of hired someone to run the shop or take care of us like you did Whitey, so for myself I want to thank you, and you can take it for what it's worth, and I hope you believe me."

Whitey took a step forward and looked directly into the old man's eyes. "I believe you Bernie, but that's as far as it goes."

"Thanks for believing me Whitey and it's hard for me to say this, but Lonnie wants you to go, she says she's afraid of you. I'm sorry Whitey, I really am."

"No, I'm the one that's sorry, I'm sorry I ever came here in the first place."

"You didn't have much choice Whitey; you had to have a home to parole to."

"But not to your house. I only came here because I thought you and Lonnie were nice people, real nice people to offer me a home. Maybe that was your intention Bernie, but it sure as hell wasn't your wife's intention, she didn't care about helping out a parolee, all she wanted was some fool to do all the fuckin' work. But let me tell you something, I didn't have to come here."

"Then why did you?"

"I thought it was wonderful of you people to offer me a home. I thought it nice to get out of prison and live in a home atmosphere. But you can tell Lonnie I didn't come here out of desperation, I have over two thousand dollars in savings, I can go where I want, I don't need her or her fuckin' house."

Bernie was astounded when Whitey mentioned two thousand dollars.

"Wherever did you get that amount of money?"

"The last time I was out on parole, it's money I saved from Universal Transport. I worked for them. Did you think I had stolen it?"

"No, nothing like that, I was just surprised you had so much money."

"Well I have. I'll get out of here just as soon as I make a call. I'm going to use your phone."

Not waiting for a reply Whitey walked into the living room, picked up the phone and dialed a number. Bernie remained by the bedroom door watching him, as Whitey stood there waiting for someone to answer his call. He could hear the phone ringing at the other end of the line.

The ringing ceased and a soft voice said, "Hello."

"Hello, who am I talking to?" Whitey asked.

"This is Sharon, who did you wish to speak to?"

"Hi Sharon, this is Whitey Thompson, you don't know me, but I'm a friend of Ben's."

"Oh I know who you are, you were at Folsom, Ben went to see you, right?"

"Yeah I'm the one. Is Ben around?"

"Yes he's outside, I'll call him. Are you going to come see us?"

"Yeah, I may even be staying, it's up to Ben."

"Far out, he told us about you, I'll go get him now."

While waiting for Ben, Whitey lit a cigarette, and a moment later a sonorous voice sounded over the phone, "Whitey you cad, is that really you? Is it true you want to stay with us?"

"Yeah, if the offer still stands."

"You bet it does," Ben answered with elation. "Where you at? I'll come pick you up."

Whitey gave him the address, and Ben said he would be there in fifteen minutes. After hanging up the phone Whitey turned toward the bedroom. Bernie was still standing by the door.

"I'm gonna get my things together," Whitey said as he walked by. "Then I'll be out of here. I'm sure your bitch will be glad to hear I'm gone!"

"Whitey I wish you wouldn't call her names like that, after all she's my wife."

Whitey did not reply, instead he packed his few belongings in his duffle bag. Minutes later the task was accomplished; he tossed the duffle bag over his shoulder and walked to the front door. Before opening it he turned to face Bernie.

"I know she's your wife," he said in a surly voice, "and I don't mean to hurt you, but she's still a bitch, a sorry bitch!"

Bernie's face turned red with anger, but he was afraid to move or say a word.

"You tell her what I said," Whitey continued, "she's a sorry bitch, and I know she'll call my P.O. the moment I'm gone."

"She's not that kind Whitey, she won't do that," Bernie tried to defend his wife.

Whitey shouted angrily, "I don't give a fuck if she does call, I know she'll fill my P.O. with a lot of bullshit. That stupid low class parole officer will believe everything the lying bitch says."

"Look Lonnie's not. . . ."

Bernie's speech was interrupted as Ben's convertible pulled up in front of the house. Almost immediately Ben started blowing the car horn. With a firm hold on the duffle bag, Whitey swung the front door open and charged down the steps to the waiting car.

Bernie was watching from a window. Whitey dashed to the vehicle, and toss his bag into the back seat. Then he jumped into the vehicle while Ben skillfully put the car in motion, and with an earsplitting squeal of burning rubber, the car sped away.

CHAPTER 15.

After picking up Whitey Ben drove north out of Sacramento.

"What happened Whitey? You was supposed to give me a call when you got out."

"Yeah I know Ben, but the reason I didn't I was trying to play it cool. I was trying to do my parole without any problems, you understand?"

"Yeah I can dig it, but what came down to make you leave now? What happened?"

Whitey recounted the events of the last five months.

"The bitch was using you Whitey, she was taking advantage of a man on parole. Boy she's something else! Can't you explain all that to your P.O.? Won't he understand?"

"Shit no! He won't believe me after the Kirklands finish talking to him. The fuckin' Kirklands are like mini parole officers, I'm not kidding, they know every goddamn Sacramento P.O. including mine."

"So what do you want to do?"

"I'm gonna hang it up, fuck it, live for today, and to hell with tomorrow!"

Ben was surprised at Whitey's remark. "Are you sure that's the way to go?"

"Hell I'm forty-eight years old, I spent most of my life in prison, I'm tired of trying to do good when the cards are stacked against me. It's not in the deck man, time is running out, so what have I got to loose? Fuck it!"

"I guess there's no need in trying to persuade you to change your mind, is there?"

"No my mind's made up."

Over the roar of the engine, Ben shouted in Whitey's ear, "If your mind's made up, so be it! It's party-time tonight and the gang is waiting!"

The car, at a very fast clip was heading toward Carmichael, or at least it seemed that way until suddenly without warning Ben applied the brakes. As he did so he pulled on the steering wheel making a sharp turn. Without hesitating he jammed the accelerator to the floorboard, sending the Ford screaming across the intersection. This caused a southbound car to apply its brakes, as the convertible crossed in front of it.

Ben held his fist in the air and shouted at the unfortunate driver, "You fucking red-neck get off the road!"

With a blast of bellowing exhaust pipes, the Ford convertible shot down Eagle Road where Ben lived. As the car rolled to a stop in front of his house, Whitey could see a half dozen motorcycles parked in the backyard. Both men barely had enough time to get out of the car before a handful of rough-looking scooter-tramps came out to greet them. Most of them carried cans of beer, while the rest of them were drinking from wine and whiskey bottles.

"Hey you guys, this is by buddy Whitey Thompson. You bums can introduce yourselves."

As each man gave Whitey a brotherhood handshake, he was beginning to feel more at home with them. Their ages ranged from twenty-one to thirty-five, Ben himself, had just turned twenty-one, but he appeared much older than his years.

Before the introductions were over, Whitey had received six drinks of Wild Turkey whiskey from six different bottles, four swigs of wine, and a can of beer!

"Come on in the house," Ben invited Whitey. "I want you to meet my mother, Jo."

Whitey was surprised at the name. "Your mother what?" he asked.

With a chuckle Ben replied, "My mother Jo, it's short for Josephine."

Upon entering the house both Ben and Whitey were immediately greeted by four fierce growling dogs.

"Get back dogs, get back goddamn it, this is a friend, get back you sons of bitches!" Ben yelled at them.

Still growling, the dogs moved back a few paces and held their ground.

"Don't worry Whitey, they won't bite you."

"Do the dogs know that?"

Ben laughed, and with a kicking gesture, he again shouted at the dogs, "Get back dogs, get back you mother fuckers!"

The dogs ceased their growling, and Whitey was relieved that they obeyed Ben's command, but he still didn't trust them. As he walked past eight pairs of eyes were fixed on him. The owner of one set of eyes was a huge 115-pound German Shepherd who was backed by a large Blue Tick Coonhound. Standing next to him was a black fierce-looking Belgium Shepherd, and bringing up the rear was a half-breed Coyote.

"Whitey I want you to meet my family," Ben said, and as he made the introductions Whitey nodded his head to each one of them.

Jo was a short rotund woman of five foot two, with shoulder-length brown hair, and hazel eyes. She was a pleasant person with a ready smile that would reveal two missing front teeth. She had a heart as big as the whole outdoors, and was loved by all. She greeted Whitey with open arms.

Ben had two sisters, Jackie, nineteen and Tammy eight years old. Jackie was an attractive girl, and like her mother, she too had hazel eyes and long brown hair. She embraced Whitey with a hug and kiss. Tammy was a pretty little thing, shy and bashful, and only after some extensive coaxing was Whitey able to shake her hand.

The last person to be introduced was Sharon, Ben's girl friend. She was a lovely looking young woman of twenty-one, very attractive, full of life, and a picture of health. Like Jackie and Jo, she too greeted Whitey with a warm embrace.

"Ben told me a lot about you Whitey, I've been looking forward to meeting you," Sharon said with a warm smile.

"Thank you Sharon, it's nice meeting you. Ben told me you were a pretty girl, man he fell short of the mark. You're no girl, you're a woman, a very lovely looking woman!"

Blushing slightly Sharon returned, "Thank you Whitey, thank you , no one has ever paid me a compliment like that."

"Did you hear that?" Ben said with a laugh. Then imitating Sharon he said in a falsetto voice, " 'No one had ever paid me a compliment like that!' Bullshit woman! I paid you one like that the day I met you."

"You liar!" Sharon laughed and gave Ben a friendly slap on the shoulder.

Turning to Whitey Ben said, "Come on Romeo, let's go out back, we're going to party!"

Both men went out to the backyard. Whitey was surprised to see a large swimming pool, and behind the pool off in a corner of the yard stood a spacious single room building. It was fifteen by twenty feet that was converted into a motorcycle clubhouse. The inside of the building contained a long table lined with chairs all around it. Meetings were held here one night a week. Posters were hanging in all available places including the ceiling, and on the far side of the room were three shelves, one over the other, running the length of the wall. Lined up on the shelves were rows of empty wine and whiskey bottles, at least three or four hundred of them. On the opposite wall was a large electric sign and when the switch was turned on, a display of letters flashed in brilliant red and gold, K K K. At either end of the room was a set of built-in bunk beds, one of which was in use.

While Whitey inspected the clubhouse, the atmosphere was filled with the sound of hard acid rock music. He turned to go outside and join the party, and at that precise moment someone turned up the stereo amplifier to full capacity. Mounted at various angles in the yard, were six four by five foot speakers, and discharging from each one of them was a violent outburst of rumbling thunderous sound. The time was 4:00 P.M., and the party was well under way.

80

Walking up to Whitey, Ben gave him an affectionate slap on the back, and at the same time yelled in his ear, "Where's your drink?"

Before Whitey could answer, Ben disappeared into the house, and returned a moment later with a fifth of Wild Turkey. He offered the bottle to Whitey who took a long stiff pull, and as he handed it back to Ben, his eyes drifted in the direction of the pool. There were a number of people kicking and splashing around in the water, while off to one side, three lovely young girls were seated completely nude at the pool's edge watching the activity.

An amused smile appeared on Ben's face when he noticed the direction of Whitey's eyes. Using his elbow, he nudged him and said, "This is your party, you want to get fixed up?"

"Does a bear shit in the woods?" Whitey replied with a laugh.

"How about one of those chicks sitting over there?" Ben was referring to the three girls sitting by the pool. "Do you see one you like?"

"How about that dark-haired one that just dove into the pool?"

"Hey you got taste man, she's a fox."

The moment she stepped out of the water Ben called to the girl, "Hey Debbie, come here."

As she walked toward them Whitey was amazed by her beauty, and with each step she took, drops of crystal clear water ran down her olive-hued skin. She had a striking figure that most females would envy. Her peach-size breasts were firm and beautiful. Over one of them she had a tattoo of a small green leaf and a cherry, with the words, "Property of Ben Vakno."

Whitey looked at the tattoo and smiled at Ben, "They ought to get you for violating the Pure Food Act!"

Ben laughed and returned, "Hey man, she's still pure pussy!"

Debbie was within hearing distance, and looking directly at Ben she said, "Whose pussy is pure?"

"Yours babe, who else?" Ben replied with a laugh. Turning to Whitey he continued, "This is a brother of mine, Whitey Thompson."

Before Ben could finish his introduction Debbie took Whitey's hand and said, "Hi Whitey, I've been hoping to meet you."

He was surprised at her remark. He wondered how she had heard of him. "You been hoping to meet me? I don't understand, how'd you know about me?"

"When you called this morning for Ben, Sharon told me about you."

"Okay then," Ben interrupted, "I don't have to tell you he just got out of the joint five months ago."

"Yes Sharon told me he was in prison, I know all about it!"

"Good, then you know he needs to get his pecker wet!" Ben blurted out.

Debbie quickly glanced at Whitey, then at Ben, and started to blush.

"Like what?"

"You could have used a little finesse! You could of said I have not been with a woman in about a year now, or something like that!"

"Sorry about that Whitey, finesse or no finesse, you've got to get fucked! So take him in to clubhouse Deb, and fix him up!"

"Are you serious Ben?" she asked.

"Hell yes, he hasn't been balled in a long time!"

Ben started into the clubhouse, halfway there he turned and called to them, "Come on you two, what're waiting for?"

Whitey shrugged his shoulders and looked at Debbie. "Do you want to?" he asked.

"Sure why not?"

Inside the clubhouse there were two couples sitting at the table drinking and talking.

"All right everyone out of here! Come on move it you bastards—now!" Ben bellowed.

After they all cleared out Ben said, "Okay Whitey, the place is yours. There's some beer in that cooler on the table, help yourself."

The door closed leaving Whitey and Debbie alone; he took two cans of beer out of the cooler and sat down on the bed next to her. Debbie reached for the two cans, opened one and handed it to Whitey. Then she popped the other one open and began to sip from it.

Whitey offered her a cigarette.

"No thanks, I don't smoke."

After lighting one for himself he leaned back on the bunk bed, and in between puffs on the cigarette he sipped his beer. Except for the noise of the party outside it was very quiet inside.

"What was you in prison for?" Debbie finally broke the silence.

"It's a long story," Whitey replied, "I don't care to go into it, okay?"

"Sure that's fine, if you don't like to talk about it, that's fine with me. Ben said you used to be a scooter-tramp, when did you ride a motorcycle?"

Whitey didn't hear the question, his mind was on her nudity and sex! She was very attractive sitting there in the semi-darkness, and her body was extremely inviting.

Debbie gave Whitey a nudge on the shoulder as she raised her voice, "Whitey I'm talking to you."

"What—what did you say?"

"I asked you, when did you ride a motorcycle?"

"Oh that. It was a long time ago, just after World War II."

"Gee Whitey, just how old are you?" Debbie asked with a look of astonishment.

"I'm forty-eight, does it make any difference?"

"No, what makes you think that?"

"You seemed to be amazed at my age."

"Well yes and no. What I mean is, you had me fooled."

"Fooled? What do you mean? I didn't try to fool you. How old did

82

you think I was?"

"You look like you are in your thirties, your early thirties."

Whitey began to beam, "That's a real compliment, I can take that."

"You know what, I love your blond hair, and you're sort of handsome in a rugged way. You sure don't look no forty-eight, but it don't matter anyways."

"Why not?" Whitey asked.

Smiling Debbie replied, "Because I like older men, I like you Whitey."

He beamed all the more. "How old are you Deb?"

"I just turned eighteen May first, but never mind that, you were telling me about when you first rode motorcycles."

"Yeah, it was just after World War II, I was in my hometown then, I bought a. . . ."

"Where is your hometown?" she interrupted.

"New Haven Connecticut. Anyway I bought this new hog . . ."

"What the hell is a hog?" She interrupted again.

"A hog? Hell everyone knows what a hog is! It's a Harley Davison motorcycle, okay?"

"Then what happened after you bought the hog—I mean motorcycle?"

"Well I left the east coast, bound for California, and ended up in Seattle Washington."

"Boy that must of been nice to ride a motorcycle all the way across the U.S.A.. What did you do after you got to Seattle?"

Whitey recounted the story to her of how he shipped out of Seattle with M.S.T.S., and then meeting Rose, and how she rode with him to Los Angles where they later parted company.

"Why did you part? She seemed like a nice girl," Debbie asked.

"That's exactly why I parted, she was a nice girl, and I knew if she stood with me I would only cause her hardships, so I let her go."

"Did that have anything to do with you going to prison?"

"You know for a pretty girl you're sure a nosey one!"

"Tell me, did it? Did it have anything to do with you going to prison?"

"More or less, I got busted behind armed robberies and got hit with fifteen years."

"Fifteen years! God, where did they send you?"

"To the Federal pen at McNeil Island."

"Sharon told me you were on Alcatraz, were you?"

"Sharon's got a big mouth! Yes I was on Alcatraz. Anything else you want to know?" he asked in a rather sarcastic voice.

"Yes about Rose, did you love her?"

"Yeah I loved her. I guess I always will."

"Did she ever come to see you while you were in prison?"

Whitey closed his eyes, and for the moment Debbie didn't think he was going to answer, when suddenly in an angry voice he said, "No

83

she got killed. She was killed on a motorcycle."

"Oh no, I'm sorry Whitey, so sorry."

"No need of being sorry, it's just one of those things. Hey wait a minute, what the hell am I telling you all this for? I came in here to screw, not to tell my life story!"

"Well come on then!" Debbie said with a laugh. "Take your clothes off, let's ball!"

Anticipating what was to follow, he hurriedly undressed and turned his attention to Debbie who was waiting to receive him. For a moment he stood at the side of the bed looking down at her. God what a delicious sight! He was excited by her beauty the moment he laid eyes on her sitting by the pool. He couldn't believe how horny he was until his body made contact with her's. His heart was pounding, a thunderous pounding so loud that not only could he feel it's vibration, but he could hear the sound of it hammering in his ears—faster and faster, pounding and pounding, louder and louder. Her lovely body had the feel of satin, so soft, but yet so firm, and as he kissed her ripe red lips, he felt her fiery silken tongue penetrate his hungry mouth. The movement of her torso beneath him was an uncontrollable pleasure, it was too much for him.

"No!" he cried aloud. "Damn it, damn it, damn it!"

Debbie held him closer trying to comfort him. "It's okay, you were just a little excited."

"Bullshit I fucked up!"

"Don't be silly Whitey, you didn't fuck up, you were just too hot to hold it!"

Whitey gently rolled over and rose from the bed. He stood there for a moment, then walked over to the ice cooler where he retrieved two cans of beer. After offering Debbie one, he sat next to her. The cold can felt good in his hand, he pressed it against his forehead for a moment, then took a long drink: he didn't stop until the can was empty.

Debbie was calmly watching him, "How do you feel now Whitey? Any better?"

"I'm embarrassed, that's how I feel."

"Please don't feel that way Whitey," Debbie whispered, "I understand how it's been for you, not having any in a long time. It could happen to any man."

"It's nice of you to understand Deb, do me a favor will you? Don't tell Ben what happened, he'll laugh like hell if he knew I had a hair-trigger!"

Debbie began to laugh, and before he realized it, he was laughing with her. It took a minute or so before they could stop laughing and get themselves under control.

"Don't say nothing to Ben," he repeated.

"Don't worry about it Whitey, I won't say a word to him. I like you, and listen, anytime you want to try again, just let me know, okay?"

84

"The day ain't over yet," Whitey returned.

"You're right, it's not over yet." With a mischievous smile she quickly kissed him on the lips, then pulling away from him she shouted, "Let's take a dip, last one in sucks!"

Outside, the party was in full-swing. Sharon and Ben were sitting under a huge umbrella at a patio table when the clubhouse door burst open. The couple screamed with laughter when they saw the two nudes streaking toward the swimming pool!

"The last one in sucks!" Debbie shouted again.

After diving in, Whitey swam across the pool to the far end and back. Then he went into the clubhouse to get dressed. Debbie was still in the water when he walked up to the table and sat down with Sharon and Ben. Ben handed him a fifth of Wild Turkey, Whitey took a long pull on it before handing it back. He lit a cigarette and relaxed in the chair.

"Well come on," Ben said with excitement in his eyes.

Whitey turned with a blank expression on his face, "Well come on? Come on what? What the hell are you talking about?"

Smiling, Ben answered, "Ah come on bro, you know what I'm talking about." Still smiling, he nodded his head toward Debbie who was just diving into the pool.

"Oh you mean Debbie!"

"You know damn well what I meant. How did it go?"

"She was okay, she's a little fox."

"Is that all she was? Just okay?"

"No, she's a fine chick, I like the broad, what more do you want me to say?"

"I mean how well do you like the bitch? Do you like her well enough to want her for your old lady? You know what I mean, if you like her, she's yours."

"What about that little cherry tattooed over her left tit with the words, 'Property of Ben Vakno?'"

"Ah hell Whitey, I busted it months ago! It don't mean nothing. Debbie thought it would be kicks to put that tattoo on. Besides you know Sharon is my old lady." Turning to Sharon he said, "Isn't that right babe?"

"It better be right!" Sharon returned.

"See, there you are Whitey, it's all settled, Debbie is your old lady from now on."

The music was still blaring, the booze was flowing, there were drugs of all kinds to be had, and sex galore as the party progressed on through the night until the wee hours of morning.   It was like a dream world with everyone having a ball, most of them were loaded and flying, while others were just plain drunk. Everyone was enjoying themselves except for the ones who had passed out, and even they had had a good time!

It was a wonderful evening for Whitey, but the affects of the party were catching up to him. The music had been turned off an hour ago, and the only sound that could be heard were the soft whispering voices of Sharon, Ben, Debbie and Whitey. They were the sole survivors of the party, and they too were ready to call it a night.

Whitey yawned and held his arms over his head to stretch; turning to Ben he asked, "Where am I gonna sleep bro?"

"Just crash wherever you want!"

Debbie, who had gotten dressed hours ago, was sitting next to Whitey.

"What do you say fox?" he asked her, "You want to crash?"

"You know I do, but wait a minute, I'll be right back." She ran into the house and a moment later she reappeared carrying a sleeping-bag.

Debbie and Whitey walked to the side of the clubhouse. Whitey called back to Ben, "I'll see ya tomorrow bro."

Ben laughed, "It's already tomorrow!"

"Well whatever, I'll see ya. You too Sharon."

On the far side of the building, away from everyone, Debbie unrolled the sleeping-bag, and spread it out behind some rose bushes next to a huge Australian tree fern. Without the slightest hesitation Whitey immediately got undressed and crawled into the sleeping-bag. He laid there watching Debbie undress, and as he viewed her graceful movements it was like watching a scene from the South Sea islands where a native girl was undressing in the tropical moonlight. It was a lasting scene, a scene to remember, and when Debbie eased her way into the sleeping-bag, it was more than he could hope for. The early morning air was crisp and cool as they wrapped their warm bodies around each other. Only this time nothing happened prematurely, and it was beautiful.

CHAPTER 16.

It was daylight, Debbie and Whitey were awakened with a start, the morning silence was broken with a thunderous roar of motorcycles and the sound of straight pipes. They took off down the driveway, one after another. With a squeal of tires and smoke they blasted down Eagle Road and out of sight.

With the motorcycles gone silence reigned again, the couple closed their eyes and dozed off in the warmth of the morning sun.

It was midmorning when they awoke, together they hopped out of the sleeping-bag, and in the nude they dashed around the clubhouse and dove into the pool. The water had a cool refreshing sting to it as they swam from one end to the other.

After a refreshing swim they returned to the sleeping-bag to get dressed. While doing so they heard the opening and closing of the back door to the house. The sound alerted Whitey, he wondered who it might be, and was relieved when he saw Sharon and Ben appear around the corner of the clubhouse.

"Hey good morning Ben, hi Sharon, I didn't know you guys were still home. I thought everyone had left this morning."

"Shit no!" Ben returned. "There's no way I'd get up that early in the morning!"

"Where the hell were they going anyways?" Whitey asked.

"Who knows. They'll be back later on you can count on it."

"What time is it getting to be?"

"Hell I don't know," Ben answered as he looked to Sharon. "What time ya got babe?"

Glancing at her wristwatch Sharon replied, "It's just ten A.M."

Whitey acted surprised, "Damn is it that late already?"

"Late? Hell man that's early unless you have a nine o'clock appointment, and I'm sure you don't have one," Ben said with a laugh.

With mock sarcasm Whitey informed him, "It so happens I do have an appointment."

The laughter ceased, Ben was surprised, "What? You mean you *really* have an appointment?"

"That's what I said."

"Where Whitey? What time?" questioned Sharon.

Hesitating to answer he just stood there smiling.

"Come on," Debbie persuaded. "You never said anything about an appointment to me."

"Well I have one, but first we're going to a restaurant for some breakfast. How does that sound?"

"Food sounds great to me," Ben volunteered, "but you still didn't say where your appointment was, or the precise time."

"It's within the hour if you must know, but first we're gonna eat some breakfast. Then I want you to drive me to the B of A downtown."

"The B of A!" Ben exclaimed. "You mean the Bank of America? What the hell you gonna do? Hold it up?"

With a slow sly grin Whitey answered, "Yeah, I might just do that!"

After breakfast at Sambo's restaurant, Whitey had Ben drive him to the Broadway branch of the Bank of America. Ben eased the Ford along slowly hoping to find a parking place in front of the bank.

"There's no place to park. Where the hell we gonna park?" he asked anxiously.

"Don't worry about it," Whitey said in a gruff voice, "double-park right in front and keep the motor running!"

The girls had been kidding and laughing with each other until they heard Whitey say, "Keep the motor running!" They were not laughing anymore.

Ben double-parked the car directly in front of the bank, with the convertible top already down, Whitey jumped over the door, landing on the curb. He turned back to face Ben, and in a low voice he whispered, "Don't let that motor stall, keep it running whatever you do. I may be coming out of that bank on the run, so be ready to move out!"

If the girls were not frightened before, they were now.

Sharon started to stutter, "You—you're really going to hold up that bank?"

Whitey's expression was cold, and in a serious voice he said, "You chicks keep your mouth shut." Then looking at Ben he repeated, "Keep that motor running, be ready to drive!"

With that he disappeared through the front door of the bank.

"I don't believe this," Ben cried, "I'm sitting out here behind the wheel of a getaway car!"

"God Ben!" Sharon exclaimed. "What are we going to do? We can't just drive away."

"We're gonna wait," Ben replied. "We're sticking here until he comes out that bank, so shut up, and don't you chicks stare at that bank door, it's a dead giveaway."

Whitey had been inside the bank approximately ten minutes, but it seemed more like an hour to the girls who sat nervously waiting in the car.

"Damn I wish he would hurry up." Ben complained, "we're gonna run out of gas setting here!"

"I put in two dollars yesterday Ben."

"Goddamn it Sharon, that was yesterday, we're sitting on empty now!"

"What are we going to. . . ."

Suddenly their attention was drawn to the sound of sirens off in the distance.

"Whitey better get out that bank!" Ben exclaimed. "The fuckin' pigs are on their way!"

Both girls were praying out loud, "Oh God please make Whitey come out that bank door! Hurry up please!"

The trio had cause to be worried for the blaring sirens were drawing dangerously close. Any second now the police would burst into view.

"Oh come on Whitey, come on!" Debbie cried.

The girls were anxious for him to appear, while Ben sat nervously behind the wheel gunning the engine. Suddenly both girls screeched with joy as Whitey appeared in the bank doorway. Without hesitation he ran to the car, at full speed he sprang for the vehicle, and using the trunk as a stepping-stone, he landed in the rear seat.

The car was already in gear when Whitey yelled, "Hit it man! Let's get out of here!"

With a screech of burning tires and a cloud of smoke, the old convertible shot down Broadway. At the first intersection, Ben subsequently spun the steering wheel and jammed the brakes, causing the Ford to spin around. Then with motor roaring, tires squealing, the car went careening off in the opposite direction back toward the bank. As the convertible whizzed past the building, there was no sign of activity, there was no one in hot pursuit.

From the rear seat Whitey shouted, "Slow down man, slow down! I can't see anyone chasing us. Slow down damn it, you're gonna get us busted!"

Ben glanced at the rear-view mirror, saw no one giving chase, then he quickly looked over his shoulder for clear vision. This time he was convinced that no one was pursuing them, and slowed the vehicle to a normal speed, making a left turn on to 16th Street.

With no threat of an immediate police chase, the girls relaxed while Ben leisurely guided the convertible toward the north area, and home.

A few minutes later found the group safely in the confines of the clubhouse. Whitey went directly to the ice cooler, but found it empty.

"Damn no more beer!" he said as he turned to Ben. "Do you have any in the house?"

"Fuck the beer! What happened back there at the bank!" Ben was excited. "Did you do any good!"

Shrugging his shoulders Whitey replied, "I can't remember a thing until I have a beer."

"Ah man, what's all this bullshit?" Ben complained as he turned to Sharon. "You heard him, get your ass in the house and bring out some beer—hurry."

Whitey lit a cigarette while they waited for Sharon to return. A minute or two later she came in with a half dozen cold beers. Quickly Ben ordered her to open one for Whitey.

"I'm not his old lady," Sharon protested, "let Debbie open his beer."

"But you're *my* old lady," Ben shouted, "and I told you to open him a beer, so open the fuckin' thing or I'll open your nose!"

Without any more sass Sharon opened a can of beer and handed it to Whitey.

Ben waited impatiently for him to have a drink, then with a trace of anger he said, "Okay bro, what it is? Did you score or not?"

Reaching into an inner pocket of his Levi jacket Whitey pulled out a wad of money and plopped it on the table. There were shouts of jubilation with Ben shouting the loudest.

"You did it man! You did it! How much is there? Count the fucking money Babe, hurry count it!"

Sharon reached for the money, and as she did so Whitey knocked her hand away. Picking up the bundle, he returned it to his pocket.

"No need to count the money," he said. "I know exactly how much there is; two thousand, one hundred and thirty-four dollars." Reaching in his pants pocket he produced two dimes. "Two thousand, one hundred and thirty-four dollars and twenty cents!"

Ben was astonished, he was filled with wonder as to how Whitey knew the exact amount of money.

"How did you know how much you had?" he asked. "You didn't have time to count it."

"Sure I did, when the teller handed it to me I counted it."

"Bullshit! I don't believe that crap, here you are robbing a bank, and you take time to count the loot, bullshit!"

"Well then how did I know how much money there was?"

"I don't know yet, but I'll figure it out unless—hey wait a minute, if you held up that bank, what did you use for a weapon? You don't have a gun."

"I faked it!" Whitey told him with a prankish grin.

Ben was becoming suspicious, "You mother fucker, I don't think you robbed that bank!"

"Well if I didn't, then tell me how I got the money."

"Easy, you must of had a savings or checking account. All you had to do was go in the bank and draw the money out, right?"

Whitey's mischievous smile turned into a chuckle, "That's it Ben! You smart fucker, you hit it on the head!"

"Then you *did* have an account. You didn't rob the bank, you fucker! You son of a bitch! We could of got busted for speeding. I thought we were making a getaway from the bank!"

Ben raved on and on, and as he did so he could see the humorous side of the episode and began to laugh. It was too much, Ben's actions were extremely comical to the group, and they all ended up in hysterical laughter.

After the laughter subsided , Debbie asked Whitey, "How in the world did you ever manage to have that kind of money in the bank?"

"It's from my earnings the last time I was on parole," Whitey replied. Then he went on to tell them how he had previously worked for Universal Transport System.

"Well you sure fooled me," Debbie commented. "I was convinced you had robbed that bank, but I'm happy now that you didn't."

"Me too," Sharon added.

Whitey did not hear the girls' comment for his attention was focussed on a distant sound. It became louder and louder, a moment later he was able to separate and classify the sound, it was not one, but two motorcycles coming down the street.

The group stepped outside the clubhouse door and greeted the riders as they turned into the driveway. Whitey immediately recognized Chris and Fuzzface. They had both been at the party the previous night. Except for their height they were almost identical. Chris, the tallest of the two by three inches, stood six foot two and was in his early thirties. While Fuzzface was in his mid twenties. Both sported long blond hair and a heavy growth of beard. They were clad in greasy Levis', leather vests and black boots. Each one was adorned with a chain around the waist. Chris wore a swastika earring in his left ear, while Fuzzface wore a skull and crossbones in his.

The two scooter-tramps parked their motorcycles and walked toward the clubhouse, a distance of twenty feet. Both men hobbled along as though their legs were made of sponge. Suddenly Chris tripped over an unseen object, or more than likely his own feet, causing him to stumble. In his fall he made a desperate grab for Fuzzface who was himself having difficulty standing up. Both men became entangled with each other and fell to the ground in a fit of laughter. A moment passed while they attempted to regain their feet, and in doing so, their voices of merriment echoed throughout the yard. At last, still laughing, they were up and navigating again. Both men were loaded, and unaware of having a fall!

Chris was the first to notice the foursome standing in front of the clubhouse and blurted out, "Aaaaah, so here you are! Where you been?"

Fuzzface, with his eyelids closed, complained to Chris, "Who you talking to? I don't see anyone."

Chris halfheartedly raised his arm pointing in the direction of the clubhouse, "They're standing right there, you can't see them fool unless you open your eyes!"

Fuzzface doubled over with laughter, "So that's it! No wonder I couldn't see them." But even then the people who stood in front of him were nothing more than blurred figures. It took a moment or two before he could distinguish who they were, and when he did he blurted out, "Hey Ben—Whitey, I knew I'd find you fuckers. You should of been with us. Where the hell were you guys?"

"Nowhere, we've been here all day," Ben answered.

"No we were gone about an hour. We went to town about ten A.M." Whitey said.

"It doesn't matter," Chris informed them. "Fuzzy and I made a good score this morning.".

"Yeah," Fuzzface cut in, "we ripped a fucking redneck off for three bags of reds."

Chris pulled a quart-size plastic bag out of his inside vest pocket and flipped it to Ben, and said, "There you go man, have a party!"

Catching the bag Ben responded with, "Far out man! What did you do with the other two bags?"

"Don't worry bro I've got them," Chris replied as he pointed to his inner jacket pocket.

Along with Chris and Fuzzface, the small party moved back into the clubhouse where Ben opened the bag and handed Whitey a half dozen reds. Immediately he swallowed two and chased them down with beer. Ben was busy doing the same and when the beer ran out both men continued dropping reds, and instead of beer, they washed them down with Wild Turkey.

"How about Deb and me?" Sharon asked Ben. "Don't we get to take some reds?"

"No," Ben replied harshly, "if I wanted you to have a red I would of gave it to you. You know better than to ask. Go into the house and get some more beer."

"We don't have any more in the house."

"Goddamn it go to the fucking store and get some more. What's wrong with you?"

Whitey pulled out a twenty-dollar bill and handed it to Sharon, "Here Sharon get it with this and buy me a couple packs of Camels."

"I'm going with Sharon, will it be all right Whitey if I go?" Debbie asked.

"Yeah sure, but hurry back."

A few minutes after the girls left eight more motorcycles riders came to a screeching halt in front of Ben's house. Each rider was accompanied by a girl friend.

Whitey, Chris, and Fuzzface staggered out of the clubhouse, while Ben walked out the driveway toward the front of the house to greet the incoming riders.

"Hey you fuckers, don't park them scooters out front here. Push them out of sight in back. Come on move them fucking things!"

After this was accomplished, the party continued in the backyard. Fuzzface, and Chris, with their arms around each other, were

92

attempting to sing a duet. Both men were trying to sway to the rhythm of their song, and in doing so they lost their equilibrium, falling backwards into the swimming pool. In a burst of laughter, both men dragged themselves from the water.

Suddenly Ben stopped laughing and yelled at Chris, "The reds, the fucking reds—you got them all wet, you dumb fucker!"

Without a word Chris made his way back into the clubhouse. A moment later he reappeared laughing as he held the two bags of reds high over his head.

Shortly after this episode Sharon and Debbie returned from the store. Whitey was so loaded by now that he did not realize the girls had been gone until Sharon handed him the cigarettes. It was touch and go from then on, for he began to stagger all over the backyard. He would have fallen over or fallen into the swimming pool a dozen times or more if it were not for Debbie staying close by him. She would light his cigarettes, wait on him, and take care of his needs, all the while trying to keep him in sight. At one time he stripped off his clothes and dove into the swimming pool. The water was crystal clear enabling Debbie to see his every move. When he dove into the water he went straight to the bottom and immediately started toward the surface. Halfway up his body turned and he headed toward the bottom again, only this time striking it with force. Disoriented, he quickly swam to his right, then sharply spun to his left. Debbie, who had been watching his every move, suddenly realized that Whitey had lost his sense of direction. He was so loaded on drugs he did not know up from down. Without hesitation she dove in. Putting one arm around his torso, she guided him to the edge of the pool, and up the ladder.

Sharon, seeing Debbie struggling with Whitey rushed over to help her, and between the two of them they managed to carry him around to the side of the clubhouse.

"Sharon, would you run in the house and get me a towel so I can dry him off?"

Debbie went back to the edge of the pool and retrieved Whitey's clothes and made sure his wallet and money were intact.

After Sharon returned with the towel, Debbie dried him off, but before she could get him settled in the sleeping-bag he was sound asleep. To the west the beautiful California sun was starting to set, the evening was young, but the party was over for Whitey Thompson.

For the subsequent weeks each day was a repeat of the previous one. It was party after party, drugs, and more drugs, beer, wine, and whiskey, and of course the continuous blaring music of hard acid rock.

"Let it all hang out!" Whitey would yell, and that's exactly what he did—let it all hang out!

Sure, he knew he was doing wrong, there was no denying it, but for the first time in many years he was actually enjoying himself. Ben and his scooter-tramps were his type of people, and when no one else would accept him, they did; they accepted him with great respect for the man he was. To them he was a symbol, someone they admired, like the famous baseball star was to the young ball player, so was Whitey Thompson to these young scooter-tramps.

CHAPTER 17.

It was the last Monday in June, Whitey had been with Ben Vakno for a month now. As always, there had been a party the night before that had carried on over to the wee hours of the morning. The time was 10:00 A.M.., and Debbie and Whitey were still asleep in the clubhouse bunk-beds when Ben came bursting through the door. In three strides he was across the room shaking Whitey awake.

"Whitey—Whitey wake up, come on man move it!"

With eyes half-open Whitey made a grab at Ben's intruding hands, and hissed at him, "What the fuck's wrong with you? Get the hell out of here!"

"Come on Whitey," Ben continued to shout in his ear, "I haven't time for any bullshit, get up!"

Whitey became angry, and opening his eyes wide, he blared at Ben, "What the fuck is it man? Can't it wait?"

"No goddamn it, it can't wait! My mom is at the front door Whitey, she's talking to some dude. I think he's your P.O."

"My P.O.?" Whitey quickly jumped out of bed, he hurriedly began to dress, and as he did so he shook Debbie awake.

"What is it Whitey? What's wrong?" her voice was excited.

"I don't know yet, just get dressed and get the hell out of here." Then turning to Ben he said, "Go back to the house, make sure it's my P.O., if it is, and if he starts to come out here, signal me by turning the stereo on, and turn it loud. I'll be ready for him."

"You got it Whitey." Ben turned and rushed for the door.

While Debbie was still getting dressed, Whitey slid his hand under the pillow and extracted a twenty-two semiautomatic handgun which he had purchased a few days earlier from one of the members. The gun clip held nineteen shots. Debbie had just finished dressing when she looked up in time to see Whitey slip the weapon behind his belt, concealing it with his jacket.

"Whitey, what is the gun for?"

Her voice was unexpected and it startled Whitey. Angrily he turned to face her, "Never mind, just get your ass in the house, stay with

95

Sharon and don't come out. Now get!"

Debbie knew better than to question him further, and hurried through the doorway with him right behind her. She made a run for the house while Whitey scurried around to the back of the clubhouse, and disappeared into the bushes. Lying down on the ground behind some foliage, he positioned himself so as to have a clear view of the house and the backyard. Okay Mister Parole Officer, come out and find me! With gun in hand, nineteen shots in the handle clip, he was ready, but why? Why not just run? Unless—unless you just want to kill him, is that it? Has it come to that? It doesn't have to be that way, you can jump the fence and run. Behind Whitey was a high wooden fence, all he had to do was climb over it, run to the next street, and he could be gone. For a moment it looked as though he had decided to run, but just as he started to get to his feet he heard voices; he immediately realized it was neighbors beyond the fence. He laid there scarcely breathing, his only exit was blocked leaving him with one alternative, the stereo's signal.

He was beginning to get impatient, when suddenly the back door shot open, and Ben came out of the house with Sharon and Debbie walking a few feet behind him.

"Come on out Whitey, he's gone, it's all clear," Ben called.

Placing the gun in his belt, he emerged from the bushes. "Was it my P.O.?" Whitey asked.

"Yeah, he said his name was Rosemar."

"What did he have to say, how the hell did he know I was here?"

"My mother did all the talking, let's go in the house, she can tell you all about it."

Whitey and the small group entered the house and found Ben's mother sitting at the kitchen table having coffee.

Before Whitey sat down he said to Debbie, "Get me a cup of coffee will ya?"

She immediately went to the cabinet and retrieved a cup, filled it with black coffee and set it down in front of Whitey. He took a sip, then looking across the table at Jo he asked, "Well what is it Jo? What did he say?"

Ben, his mother, and Sharon had been sitting at the kitchen table when the front doorbell rang.

"I wonder who that could be," Jo complained. Leaving the table, she walked to the living room with Sharon a few steps behind her. As she reached for the door knob, the bell rang again.

"Wait a minute—wait a minute will you!" She opened the door, standing on the stoop in a dark gray suit was a gray-haired middle-aged man.

"Sorry to disturb you, but is this the Vakno residence?" he asked.

"Yes it is," Jo replied.

"Very good. My name is Mr. Rosemar, I'm with the Department of

Corrections."

Without waiting to hear anymore, Sharon retreated to the kitchen and told Ben to warn Whitey that his P.O. was here.

"The Department of Corrections!" Jo exclaimed. "What is it you want here?"

"I have been informed that one of my parolees, a Leon W. Thompson, had been staying here, and I would like to see him."

"Do you know for sure he is staying here?"

"Oh yes I'm quite sure. You see I happen to know that it was your son Ben Vakno who drove Leon Thompson away from the Kirklands where he had formerly been staying. I have reason to believe he has been staying here."

"Well so what if he had? What's wrong with that?"

"There's nothing wrong with that Mrs. Vakno, I just want to see him. Is he at home now?"

"No, he's not here, and I don't know where he went."

"When was the last time you saw him Mrs. Vakno?"

"I'm not really sure when I last seen him. It was two or three days ago. I don't remember."

"All right Mrs. Vakno I'll be in touch, but in the meantime, if you do see Leon Thompson, and I'm sure you will, please inform him that I only want to see to him. He has absolutely nothing to worry about, I just want to talk to him, but if he does not report in, then I have no alternative but to put out a warrant for his arrest. Is that clear Mrs. Vakno?"

"Very clear." Jo closed the door, not giving him a chance to say more.

"I'm sorry Whitey, real sorry, if I had known who it was at the door I never would of answered it," Jo said.

"Forget it Jo. Hell you got a right to answer your own door, so don't feel bad, okay?"

"Well anyway," Jo continued, "I'm sorry I opened the door, but all he wants is for you to report in. He said not to worry, he won't violate you."

"Bullshit! The lying bastard, and them dirty fucking Kirklands—the low-class-jive-ass snitches, kick me out of their house, then give Ben's license plate number to my P.O. That's how he found out where I was, he checked the plate out with the D.M.V., the bastards!"

"It doesn't really matter how he found out you're here Whitey. The fact is he knows you're here now; all you have to do is go see him, that's all there is to it," Jo persisted.

Whitey lit a cigarette, and after taking a deep drag he exhaled watching the dingy blue smoke drift toward the ceiling.

"Are you going to see him Whitey?" Jo asked. "He said he wouldn't violate you if you reported in."

Whitey looked straight at Jo. "Do you know what will happen if I

97

go see him? I'll tell you what will happen, he'll ship my ass back to prison. He did it to me before, he'll do it again."

"Oh Whitey I don't think so. I think you are exaggerating," Jo said condescendingly.

"Ma, be quiet," Ben spoke sharply. "You don't know a damn thing about his P.O. Whitey don't trust him, and I don't blame him."

"Well it's up to you Whitey. What are you going to do?" Jo asked with a worried look. Ben's mother was a kindhearted woman who worried about her son and all his friends. She knew Ben and his gang were always in trouble with the law, they were all of age, and there was nothing much she could do about it, except try to be a mother to all of them.

"What are you going to do Whitey?" she asked again.

"I don't know yet, I guess take it on the heel and toe. I know I got to get out of here before he comes back." Turning to Debbie he asked her for another cup of coffee, and as she set if down in front of him, she said, "Do you have any place to go Whitey?"

"I don't know yet. Right now I'm a little mixed up, I'm sorry I'm the cause of the heat coming to the door."

"Hey forget it Whitey. If the pigs were not after you, they would be coming for me or someone else!" Ben assured him with a laugh.

"Listen—listen, I hear someone coming!" Debbie cried excitely.

Turning their heads toward the door, everyone listened. From far off in the distance came the sound of a motorcycle.

"Ah it's just someone going down San Juan," Sharon said.

"No no, it's coming this way, it's getting louder," Debbie insisted.

Sure enough, the roar of a motorcycle was becoming louder; then suddenly it was silent. Chris had turned off the ignition half a block away, and a moment later he came coasting into the driveway. After parking his bike he came striding into the house. Ben and the rest of the group watched him as he stormed into the kitchen and plopped in a chair.

"Hey what's happened?" he asked. "Why the gloom? Don't anyone say 'hi' or smile when I walk into the house?"

"The only one who would smile at a lame like yourself is your mother, and you would have to drop dead for her to do that!" Ben told him.

"Very funny Ben—very funny! I can't stop laughing ha-ha-ha! Now tell me what's happened—what's wrong?"

"Whitey's P.O. was just here looking for him," Ben replied.

"How did he find out where you were," Chris asked Whitey.

"Hey who cares?" Ben snapped. "Right now we have to figure out where he can go before his P.O. comes back. He has to get out of here and soon, You got any ideas?"

"Hell yes! Why not come up to my place?"

"Far out! What do you say Whitey? You want to go up there?"

"Where the hell is up there?" Whitey asked.

98

"It's just out of Auburn," Chris told him. "My shack is just west of Auburn in the boondocks. We can hop on my scooter and take off right now. What do you say?"

"Why not?" Whitey replied, "Just give me a minute to get my gear together."

Debbie walked out to the clubhouse with Whitey to give him a hand with his things.

"You are going to need a sleeping-bag. You want to take mine?" she asked.

"Sure, but won't you need it Debbie?"

Before Whitey could say another word she ran around to the side of the building to retrieve the sleeping-bag. Thanking her, he spread it out on the bed and laid his clothes on it. He removed the gun from his belt, and this too was laid on the sleeping-bag. Then he rolled it up tightly and tied it so that it would not unroll. He took the neat bundle out to the driveway and secured it to the handlebars of Chris's motorcycle.

"Well Deb," he said, "I guess this is so long for a while."

"Please be careful Whitey, I'll be up to see you as soon as I can."

"Yeah that would be nice if you could. In the meantime I want you to take this." Whitey handed her a $20 bill. She was astonished at the sight of the money.

"Whitey you don't owe me nothing," she said.

"Yeah I know, but this isn't for what you think, this if for the sleeping-bag, just in case I lose it."

Debbie accepted the money with a smile and a warm kiss, "Okay Whitey, thank you."

The two of them stood by the motorcycle waiting for Chris, and a minute later he and Ben appeared on the back porch along with Jo and Sharon.

"You all set Whitey? You ready to go?" Chris asked.

"Ready as I'll ever be, but first I got to say so long to Jo."

Ben's mother was standing a short distance behind the group. Whitey gave her a warm hug and said, "Thanks Jo, thanks for everything."

"Oh it was nothing, I was glad I could help, so long Whitey."

He reached for Ben's outstretched hand, and after a hearty handshake, they embraced.

"Just lay low Whitey, I'll be up to see you in a few days. I'll keep you posted on your P.O."

Chris fired up the 74 Harley-Davison, and Whitey settled on the seat behind him. He skillfully kicked it into first gear, and in a cloud of dust, they shot out the driveway. In a moment they disappeared from sight, and all that remained was the settling of dust and smoke.

CHAPTER 18.

The small town of Auburn was approximately thirty miles north of Sacramento. It was shortly after 2:00 P.M. when Chris and Whitey arrived at the house on Ophir Road. Ophir Road itself was at one time the main highway to Reno, Nevada, and points east. After the completion of Highway 99 Freeway, Ophir Road became a forgotten highway of the past, a lonely and seldom used country road. The house Chris lived in was situated a quarter mile from the highway at the end of a dirt road. Just beyond the main house, out of sight, was another home. Both these dwellings were abandoned many years ago, until, one day, by chance, Chris discovered them and set up housekeeping in the first one. Rumor had it that before the turn of the century, this location was a stagecoach stop between Auburn, Roseville, and Sacramento. All that remained standing were two houses concealed by the trees and undergrowth. If one were unacquainted with the area, you could travel by on many occasions, unaware of the houses' existence

Halfway down the dirt road Chris turned off the ignition, and coasted the rest of the way. He parked the scooter under an old wooden shelter alongside the house. The two men dismounted, and after removing the sleeping-bag from the handlebars, they both walked to the back door. Suddenly, without warning, a huge Airedale dog came charging around the corner of the house heading straight for Whitey. Quickly he shifted his bundle to his left hand, and stood ready to strike with his right at the oncoming dog. The Airedale realized this man was someone to reckon with, and broke off his charge, skidding to a halt. The dog froze in it's tracks, and stood there snarling at Whitey.

"Goddamn that's no dog! What the hell is it?" Whitey exclaimed.

Laughing, Chris replied, "That's my Airedale, I call him Tail."

"Well call him off damn it!"

"Go on Tail, get the hell out of here," Chris yelled as he waved his hand at the dog who retreated around the house.

Whitey started to laugh, "Christ, that dog looked like it's been lost in the woods for fifty years! That's the biggest and ugliest looking

Airedale I've ever seen!"

"Yeah I admit he's a funny looking thing, but he's a damn good watch dog. He won't bother you any more now he knows you're my friend."

"I hope you're right, because here he comes again!"

True to his word, the Airedale walked up to Whitey, sniffed his hand, then nonchalantly followed the two men into the kitchen. The door was open, and as they walked in a young girl no more than fifteen or sixteen, came running into the kitchen. She quickly grabbed the broom to shoo the dog out of the house.

"Go on you fucking dog, get out of my kitchen!"

She held the broom as if to strike, but the dog did not move, it just stood there growling and snarling at her. Again she raised the broom threatening to strike.

"Get out of my kitchen damn it!" she screamed. "Get out of here before I lose my temper you fuckin' hound!"

Tail stood his ground, snarling fiercely as he looked at the girl. The dog was actually challenging her with his growls, and seeing that she was not going to give in, he gave a final ferocious growl. With his tail high in the air as if he were giving her the finger, he slowly walked out of the kitchen door.

Whitey was astonished, he was amazed at what he had just witnessed.

"I don't believe it," he said as he looked at the girl. "Weren't you afraid of that dog?"

"No, and he knows I'm not afraid of him," the girl answered.

"Well how about the dog? Was he afraid of you?"

"No, and he knows that I know he's not afraid of me! I have to go through this every time I run him out of the house."

"Did you ever hit him with that broom?"

"Oh no, no," the girl answered as if shocked by the question. "I would never hit him, he knows it, and I know it, and he would never bite me. We are quite fond of each other, it's just a game."

Whitey laughed and it took a moment or two before he could stop and get himself under control. "Hey I don't mean to laugh at you but that was the damnedest thing I have ever seen!"

His laughter turned into a curious smile as his roving eyes drank in the beauty of this barefooted girl. She was standing in front of him clad only in a pair of cut off Levis'. Her breasts were small and firm with turgid nipples, and her long brown hair cascaded halfway down her supple back. She was adorable, and as he stood there drinking in her beauty he did not hear Chris speak.

"Hey Whitey, I'm talking to you—hey Whitey!"

Startled, Whitey answered, "Yeah—yeah, what did you say?" He felt as if he had been caught with his hand in the cookie jar!

"I said I wanted you to meet my old lady. This is Libby—Libby this is Whitey."

Whitey thought, an old lady, God how could anyone call this adorable child an old lady?

"Hello Whitey," she said, "glad to know you."

"Likewise, glad to know you too," he responded.

For a split second their eyes locked, and then she smiled and looked toward Chris who was opening the refrigerator. At a glance Whitey could see very little food in there, and just one can of beer. Chris popped it open, and after taking a long pull he handed it to Whitey who finished it off in one swallow.

"Well that's it," Chris stated, "there's nothing left to drink except water!"

"Do you want to get some more?" Whitey asked.

"I only got a couple of bucks, I need it for gas."

"That's not what I asked you. I asked if you wanted to get some more."

"Hell yeah," he said with anticipation.

Whitey pulled out two twenty-dollar bills and handed them to him.

"Woooweee! Two big twenties!" Chris gloated. "Okay, what do you want from the store?"

"Get some food, let Libby write a list of what she needs, get whatever booze you want, and get me a carton of Camel cigarettes. Do you guys smoke Camels?"

"Hell yes, Lib and I smoke anything!"

Libby sat down at the kitchen table, wrote out a list and gave it to Chris, who immediately left for the store.

Whitey wondered where he would sleep as the house was very small with one bedroom, living-room and bath. He was about to ask where he could plop his sleeping-bag when Libby spoke. The suddenness of her voice startled him; it was eerie, uncanny, almost as if she had read his mind.

"Are you wondering where you will sleep?" she asked.

"Yes, the thought had crossed my mind. I only see one bedroom."

"Come, I'll show you," she said with a smile.

At the far end of the kitchen was another door that opened into a small room leading to a side entrance of the house. Running the full length of the room was an old couch. Tossing himself onto it, Whitey was surprised at how comfortable it was.

"How is it?" Libby asked.

"Hey this is perfect, nice and springy."

"Yes it is. You can spread your sleeping-bag out on it and make yourself to home."

"Fine. Say how long you and Chris been together?"

"Oh about ten or eleven months now. I met him at the State Fair last year."

"Do you come from around here?"

"No, I come from Canada, can't you tell?"

102

"No not really, but you look like you have some Indian in you, do you?"

"Yes, I'm French Canadian Indian."

"No wonder you are so pretty."

"Thank you for the compliment. I'll get your sleeping-bag for you."

In a minute she returned, and after handing the bundle to Whitey, she left the room. Once she was gone he untied the bag and laid it out on the couch. He removed his clothes from it, placing them on a chair, and the twenty-two automatic he hid under the head of the sleeping-bag. The room was not much bigger than a prison cell, but at either end was an unlocked door, and he could come and go as he pleased.

He heard the sound of a motorcycle, and looked out of the window in time to see Chris coming down the dirt road with a huge cardboard box resting on the gas tank. He pulled up to the side entrance, and Whitey went out to help him with the supplies. The box contained a gallon of wine, three six-packs of Coors, a carton of Camels, and sundry groceries and kitchen items. While Libby was busy putting the things away, the men cracked open a can of beer.

Before taking a drink, Whitey lit a cigarette, then looking at Chris he said, "Hey bro, haven't you forgot something?"

Showing surprise Chris replied, "No, I didn't forget nothing. I got everything Libby put on the list. So what could I've forgot?"

Whitey took a sip of his beer. "You don't know what you forgot?"

"No, I don't know," Chris looked dumfounded, "I really don't know."

"My change, how about my change?"

"Oh hey man!" Chris exclaimed laughing, "Ha-ha-ha, I forgot all about it, no kidding!"

Both men were sitting on the living room couch, and from the kitchen they heard Libby say, "Yeah, I bet you forgot about it!"

Still trying to laugh it off, Chris took fifteen dollars and twenty-two cents from his pocket and handed it to Whitey.

"Keep it or give it to Libby to buy more food with, or whatever," Whitey told him."

"Yeah, give it to me," Libby called, "all you'll do is buy more booze with it."

"Fuck you woman!" Chris called back as he crammed the money into his shirt pocket.

The men finished their beer, and then started on the wine. After a few swallows on the jug, they were back to the beer. Libby remained in the kitchen preparing a dinner of pork chops, applesauce, potatoes, gravy, peas, and bread. Sitting on the end of the sink was a small glass of wine, and every now and then she would take a sip from it.

After a few more drinks, Chris went into his room and returned with a huge plastic bag of marijuana. Tossing it to Whitey he said, "Here you go bro, try some of this."

Whitey looked up in time to catch the bag and was surprised at the contents.

"It looks like good stuff," he remarked.

"It is, it's damn good weed, home-grown, go on roll yourself a joint."

Whitey rolled one and handed it to Chris, who lit it up, and after taking a drag, handed it back to Whitey. He took a number of hits, and each time he took a draw on the cigarette he would pull the smoke deep into his lungs. He would hold his breath as long as possible before exhaling. First Whitey and then Chris would noisily suck in the smoke and air, hold it, then exhale. They sounded like a steam engine on it's last mile! When the joint became too small to hold, in order to prevent the burning of fingers, a roach-clip was attached to it. When it became too small to smoke then it was eaten. It was top grade marijuana, and eventually both men were flying high!

"Come and get it!" Libby called.

"What you say Chris?"

"Nothing bro, you're hearing things!"

"Yeah maybe I am, but I swore I heard someone yell."

"You heard me damn it!" Libby shouted from the kitchen. "Dinner's ready, come and get it."

"There you are, I told you I heard someone," Whitey began to laugh with Chris joining in.

Libby was getting mad, "Come on you guys, you're so spaced out. Are you going to sit in there all night laughing, or are you going to come and eat? Come on now."

It took a few attempts to get up from the couch before they finally made it, and leaning on each other, they worked their way to the kitchen.

Marijuana makes a person unusually hungry, and in record time the two men demolished their meal.

Returning to the living room, they left Libby to clean the kitchen and wash the dishes before she was allowed to join them.

It was becoming difficult to breathe in the room. The air was thick and heavy with marijuana smoke as they continued lighting one joint after another.

Libby managed to drink a glass or two of wine in between errands for Chris and Whitey.

On and on it went until 10:00 P.M. when Libby disappeared into the bedroom. Both Chris and Whitey were so loaded that they were unaware of her absence, and did not realize she had left the room.

"Hey Chris—Chris where are you?"

"I'm sitting right in front of you—I mean right behind you. Shit I'm sitting right beside you!"

"Well hand me the wine then."

"Fuck you Whitey, get it yourself!"

"Come on sucker, pass the jug wine—I mean wine jug!"

So it continued through the night until the wee hours of morning. Both men fell asleep right on the spot. Whitey was lying on the floor with his feet up on the couch, while Chris was bent over backwards in a chair.

CHAPTER 19.

Hours later, grunting and groaning, Whitey woke up rubbing his eyes. It took a moment or two before he realized he was on the floor. Only with great effort he dragged himself up and sat heavily in a chair. The bright sunlight shining through the window was more than he could endure, and it took a few minutes before his eyes began to function. As his vision adjusted, he realized that Chris was no longer with him. Well, if he were not here, then he must have made it to bed, why worry? With trembling hands he reached for a pack of cigarettes that was lying on the floor. He managed to retrieve it and shake a cigarette out of the pack. He finally lit up, and with a sigh of relief he closed his eyes to relax. He was just about to take another drag when he heard a cheerful voice say, "Would you like some coffee?"

Opening his eyes he looked toward the kitchen doorway, standing there in the morning glow, dressed only in panties, was Libby.

"Yeah, I—I sure could use a cup."

"You don't look too good Whitey! I bet your head is splitting."

"No, I don't feel too bad except for my mouth, it tastes like the Russian army walked through it barefooted!"

Libby gave a slight chuckle as she turned toward the kitchen table with Whitey right behind her. She poured a cup of coffee and sat down next to him placing the cup in front of him.

"This should make you feel better."

He drained the contents before he set the cup down. "That sure hit the spot. Say—ah do you always walk around in the morning with just panties on?"

"I like to walk around like this, it feels refreshing."

"Yeah you sure are refreshing! But I'm a stranger, doesn't that bother you?"

She turned to face Whitey, their eyes met and held for a moment. "Chris has told me a lot about you so you don't seem like a stranger to me, and besides, if I feel like it I'd walk bare-ass in front of you, what do you think of that!"

Whitey grasped his chin giving the impression he was thinking over what she had just said. He gazed into her dancing eyes, then slowly his vision shifted to her lovely young breasts. Then his gaze traveled the length of her elegant body, only to return to the dancing eyes. She appeared to be waiting for him to speak.

"Well what do you think?" she asked.

"Think about what?"

"What I just said, if I feel like it I'll walk bare-ass in front of you."

He replied in a slow determined voice, "If you ever walk around in front of me bare-ass, Chris or no Chris, you're gonna get fucked!"

With a mischievous smile she answered, "Is that a threat or a promise?"

She rose from the table and poured them both a second cup of coffee. Whitey offered her a cigarette, and as she reached for it he whispered softly, "It's a promise you can count on!"

"Do you always keep your promises?"

He was about to answer when his attention was drawn to the sound of movement from the bedroom. Chris was beginning to stir. The door opened and he staggered into the kitchen. He had the appearance of a crackpot clad only in a pair of Levis', with his long blond hair matted and disheveled. As he plopped down in a chair next to Whitey, he gave him a slap on the back and said, "Hey bro, any booze left? I need a drink."

"I don't know what's left," Whitey answered.

"Ah to hell with it! I'll have a cup of coffee. Get us some breakfast Lib. You want some breakfast Whitey?"

"Yeah I could use some grub."

Without saying a word to Chris, Libby poured him a cup of coffee, and then set to work preparing breakfast. When the meal was ready, she set three plates of bacon, eggs, toast, and coffee on the table. The two men ate hungrily, and when the meal was over, Chris went to the refrigerator to retrieve the remainder of the booze—two cans of beer and a glass of wine each. This they consumed while Libby cleared away the dishes.

"Well Whitey," Chris began, "I have to make a run to Sacramento. I'm going to make a score, but it wouldn't be wise for you to come with me."

"Do you think I'm crazy? I wasn't even thinking of it. How long will ya be gone?"

"I won't be back until this evening, maybe tomorrow morning. I don't know yet. Is there anything I can pick up for you?"

"Yeah, wait a minute." He removed a twenty-dollar bill and handed it to Chris.

"I still have that fifteen you gave me."

"That's all right, you keep it. Bring me back a fifth of Wild Turkey, some beer and wine."

Chris went into the bathroom to wash and dress, and without so much as a goodbye to Libby he left the house. A few moments later Whitey heard the roar of a motorcycle starting up. When the engine had warmed up, Chris took off in his usual manner, rear wheel spinning, and tire screeching as he shot down the dirt road.

Whitey watched him from the kitchen window, and occasionally in between clouds of dust, he would catch a glimpse of Chris heading for the highway and Sacramento.

CHAPTER 20.

Long after Chris departed, Whitey stood looking out the window watching the dust as it settled back down on the road.

Libby was seated in a chair watching his every move. "Would you like another cup of coffee?" she asked.

"No, I just wish I had something cold to drink, but there's nothing left."

"Do you like milk? There's cold milk in the fridge."

"I guess it's better than nothing."

Reaching in the refrigerator Whitey discovered a can of beer hidden behind the milk.

"Hey look what I found," he called out, "a can of beer, do you want to share it with me?"

"No thanks, I'm going to have a glass of milk."

Taking the beer into the living room Whitey sat on the couch. Libby drank her milk in the kitchen then retreated to her bedroom.

After finishing the beer, Whitey closed his eyes and relaxed to the point of dozing off. He did not hear the sound of the bedroom door opening, nor did he hear Libby walk into the living room and sit in a chair directly across from him.

She sat there a minute, then went into the kitchen, returning with another glass of milk. Once more she sat across from Whitey sipping her milk and smoking a cigarette. Her eyes were fixed on Whitey; then suddenly, she made up her mind about something. She hurriedly finished her milk, and snuffed out the cigarette. A coy smile appeared on her face as she looked at the dozing man. Then she spoke to him as if he were not asleep, "Did you really mean what you said earlier?" Libby smiled with anticipation. "Did you really mean what you said earlier?" she asked again in a louder voice.

Whitey pulled himself unright on the couch, barely opening his eyes, he caught a glimpse of Libby sitting across from him.

"Were you talking to me?" he mumbled.

Acting surprised and apologetic, she replied, "I'm sorry Whitey, I didn't know you were sleeping. I thought you were awake, that's why I spoke to you. Gee I'm sorry I woke you up!"

"Forget it," Whitey said as he shook his head and stretched his arms. "What did you say?"

Attempting to act shy, and almost in a whisper, she said, "Did—did you really mean what you said earlier?"

"I don't know what I said."

"Come on Whitey, you know what I'm talking about."

"It could be any number of things we discussed this morning. So what was it?"

"You know perfectly well what I'm talking about, but I'll refresh your memory. You said if I ever walk around in front of you bare-ass, Chris or no Chris, that I'll get screwed. You also said you kept your promises. Did you mean it?"

"There's only one way to find out!"

For a moment they both sat there perfectly still as they looked into each other's eyes. Then slowly, very slowly, she moved her hand over her bare breasts, teasingly her fingers played with her protruding nipples. Her breathing became heavy as she watched the movements of Whitey's eyes following her slender fingers as they gracefully glided over her delicate olive skin. Everything about her was smooth and untroubled as her fingers massaged the cavity of her navel.

Whitey sat there entranced watching the manipulation of her fingers, he could feel a trickle of perspiration running down the small of his back. Just below the navel Libby's forefingers were investigating the elastic band of her panties; slowly she began to maneuver the silken fabric down, exposing a few dark pubic hairs. Watching his movements, she could see the anticipation and excitement in his eyes, and the rise and fall of his chest due to heavy breathing.

Whitey was all eyes as he watched her tangent hands, and thought, if she doesn't stop teasing, and pull those damn panties down, I'm gonna tear them off from her!

Libby shifted her full attention to Whitey's hungry stare. She rose out of her chair, and as she did so her expression turned from a smile to a passionate drool. She stood there transfixed at the sight of Whitey's hunger. She hurriedly pulled down her panties, and stepped out of them. She stood there for a moment as if she was using her magnificent body to throw out a feeler to arouse his sexual drive, but there was no further need of her manipulations.

Whitey remained perfectly still on the couch waiting for her. His wait was not more than a second as she floated across the room into his waiting arms. After a quick embrace, she placed her hands on his chest and gently pushed him backward to a horizontal position. Rapidly her fingers fumbled with the buckle of his belt, and unzipped his fly. Aiding her, Whitey lifted his buttocks slightly as she pulled off his Levis'. In a sweeping motion, his undershorts were yanked off following his Levi's to the floor. Moving herself onto the couch she was ready. Whitey accepted her, and almost as soon as the fornication began it ended.

Gasping for breath they lay there, Whitey with his arms wrapped

110

around her upper body, holding her tightly. His perspiration ran freely mixing with Libby's before being absorbed into the cover of the couch.

"Libby, are you all right?" he whispered.

To his relief she opened her eyes, her arms went around him, and using her hands she pressed his head gently forward until their lips met in a warm affectionate kiss.

When their lips parted, she whispered, "Oh it was wonderful—just wonderful." Whitey kissed her a number of times in quick succession, the nose, eyes, lips, cheeks, and then rising up he disengaged himself from her.

After bathing, and feeling refreshed, the two of them were having a cup of coffee at the kitchen table. Whitey lighted a cigarette and offered one to Libby. He held a match to her cigarette, and as she took a deep drag he noticed a coy smile appearing on her face.

"What's the smile for?" he asked.

"I was just thinking, what would happen if I told Chris you screwed me."

With a look of disgust he responded, "Boy you're really something else!"

"What do you mean by that?"

"Just this, less than a half hour ago while my dick was still soaking in you, you whispered, 'It was wonderful, oh God I thought I was going to pass out.' My prick hasn't had a chance to stop tingling, and you come up with such shit as, 'I wonder what would happen if I told Chris you screwed me.' Well for your information, bitch, I don't give a fuck, you can tell J.C. himself, go ahead and tell Chris. I'll tell him what a lousy fuck you were!"

Her coy smile disappeared leaving her with a shocked expression, and in a seemingly sad voice she said, "Was I? Was I lousy? You didn't enjoy me?" She looked as though she was about to cry, her eyes became misty, but it did not stop Whitey from shouting, "No, I didn't enjoy it, you're a lousy piece, and you can tell Chris I said so!"

If he had slapped her face, the effects of it could not have damaged her as much as his remarks. She sat there staring wide-eyed at him. She was horrified, and the tears began rolling down her cheeks. Suddenly she jumped up from the table banging her chair against the refrigerator. Then ran crying to her room slamming the door behind her.

Ah shit, damn it all, what's wrong with that broad? Why did she have to make that remark about telling Chris? Maybe she was just kidding, but I don't like that kind of kidding, damn it. Now she's in there crying because I hurt her feelings. Hell I didn't want to hurt her feelings, that's the last thing I would want to happen. She's a good lay—a real good lay. Damn it all, she's a hell of a good lay! Well I guess all I can do is go in there and tell her so.

111

Whitey knocked softly on her door, "Libby, can I speak to you!"

There was no reply, so he knocked louder, "Hey Libby, can't we at least talk?"

There was still no reply. He decided to open the door and walk in, but he found it was locked.

"Damn it all Libby, unlock the door will ya? I just want to talk to you, and I don't want to do it through a door, so come on and open up."

"Go away, I have nothing to say to you, besides you don't want to talk to a girl who's a poor fuck, so go away!"

"Ah come on Lib, for Christ's sake, I didn't mean that."

"Then why did you say it?" she shouted through the door.

"Because I was angry with you, that's why. Come on, open the door." There was still no reply. "Come on Lib, will you open the door or not?"

In a shy voice she called, "Whitey, if I open the door will you tell me the truth, I mean the real truth?"

"You got my word on it."

A few moments elapsed and he was beginning to wonder if she was going to open the door. Making a fist, he was about to pound on it, when he heard the lock click, and the door slowly opened. A second later Libby walked out of the bedroom and returned to the kitchen table with Whitey right behind her.

"Would you like some coffee?" she asked.

As she stood at the counter pouring the coffee she turned her head to face him, and in a young and girlish voice she said, "Did you mean it Whitey? Am I a lousy screw?"

He could not contain himself, he began to laugh heartily. Libby was startled, surprised at his outburst.

"What's so funny? Why are you laughing?" she demanded.

"It just hit me that's all, you asking me if you are a good screw or not. I couldn't help it, I just had to laugh."

Libby's frown turned into a smile, and then she too began to laugh. When she was under control again, she said, "Yes I guess it was funny, but tell me the truth Whitey, will you? Did you, or did you not, enjoy making love to me?"

"I enjoyed it very much," he answered.

"How much?" she teased.

"Very much. You're a lovely girl with a very pretty face, you have a beautiful ass, a knockout figure, all over you're a beautiful, eatable fox, and a damn good screw!"

Libby was beaming as she came around the table, and gave him a kiss. Gently he pushed her back a step and said, "Like I was saying, you are a lovely fox, and a nice screw, but I still don't give a fuck if you tell Chris or not, as a matter of fact I'll tell him myself!"

"No, no don't you dare say a word to him, don't you dare! Okay?"

Smiling he replied, "All right Lib we'll forget it. How about making me something to eat?"

After lunch Libby did the dishes, then went into her room, closing the door behind her.

Whitey went to his room and stretched out on his sleeping-bag. Well no doubt, he thought, the parole officer has a warrant out on me by now. That means every cop in the state will be on the lookout for me. Damn it all, I didn't want my life to go this way; if only I could go back to the day I was released from the Rock and start all over again. Better still, I wish I could go back before the war and Richie Gene Smith was still alive. R.G. Smith—it's been a long time pal—thirty years now, and I still haven't got my life together. What life? Maybe—just maybe it's not too late. I'd have to turn myself in, that means going back to prison. For how long I don't know. I'm forty-eight years old, if I turn myself in I might not see daylight until I'm fifty-five or sixty. I'd be an old man, a helpless old man.

Whitey was a person who had always attempted to hide his emotions, especially around people. Occasionally, when alone, it was difficult for him to hide his emotions from himself. This was one of those rare moments, and he felt embarrassed when he discovered a tear descending from his cheek. He was grateful for the confines of the room, and quickly brushed the tear away.

It's too late, it's just too late to get it together. To hell with it all! Run fast, run far, live for today, there is no tomorrow—no tomorrow. Whitey had drifted into a troubled sleep.

"Newspaper Mister? Get your newspaper here."

Stepping up to the news stand, Whitey picked up an early morning edition for the headlines caught his attention.

"EX ALCATRAZ FELON KILLED IN POLICE SHOOTOUT.

An extensive statewide manhunt came to an abrupt end shortly after 2:00 A.M. when Leon W. Thompson, known felon, was seen walking along F Street. Patrolman George Moe of the local police department attempted to apprehend the fugitive when bullets started to fly from the lone gunman. Patrolman Moe radioed for assistance, a gun battle resulted leaving one dead and two wounded. The dead man was identified as Leon W. Thompson, alias Whitey Thompson, formerly of Alcatraz prison number AZ 1465. It was said that Leon Thompson once made a statement that before he was ever returned to prison, he would hold court in the streets. Leon W. Thompson, true to his word, held court in the streets, dead at the age of 48."

Perspiring and breathing heavily, Whitey woke up with a start.No,no, no! It's not true! I'm here—I'm alive! Realizing it was just a dream he lay back down to an exhausted sleep.

113

CHAPTER 21.

The roar of motorcycles woke Whitey out of a sound sleep. Glancing out the window, he saw many of them coming down the dirt road. He lit a cigarette just as Libby stuck her head through the doorway.

"Oh you're awake."

"I guess you know Chris and Ben are riding in," she informed him.

"I know, I already seen them coming." As he looked at Libby his expression changed to one of surprise, then a delightful smile formed on his face.

"What's wrong with you? Why the funny smile?"

"I don't believe my eyes! This is the first time I've seen you with all your clothes on, and wearing a dress and shoes—woweee!"

"Well what's wrong with that?"

"Hey nothing's wrong with it. You really are a pretty girl, clothes or no clothes!"

Libby's face lit up, she was all aglow and smiling, "How do you like me best? Dressed or undressed?"

"Hey whatever, either way you are a fox."

"Well thank you. Sometime when we can get. . . ."

The back door to Whitey's room flew open with a sharp bang. Chris, Ben, and his bike riding gang stormed into the room.

"Whitey you fucker!" Ben yelled as he hurled himself landing on top of Whitey on the couch. Whitey was pinned down by Ben's heavy weight, and had no choice but to accept the scooter-tramp hug and kiss. Ben was overjoyed at seeing Whitey, and with his arms around him he shouted in his ear, "I'm glad you're still here, I was afraid you may of spooked and took off."

Returning Ben's hug Whitey shouted above the noise of the group, "The only thing that can spook me is your ugly puss! You got any news for me?"

Jumping off the couch Ben answered, "Yeah, but first let's have some booze!"

"Right on man! Hey Chris where is my bottle of Wild Turkey?"

"Coming right up Whitey," Chris replied, "it's on my scooter, I'll get it."

Still in the nude, Whitey hopped out of the sleeping-bag to get dressed, and in doing so there were a number of cat-callers, "Woo-

114

woo-wooo! Look at them buns! Woo-woooo! He has a prettier ass than my old lady!"

"Damn right, it's prettier than a gorilla's ass!"

Laughter filled the room. A moment later Chris returned with the whiskey, a gallon of wine, and a carton of Camels. Taking the cigarettes, Whitey put them under his sleeping-bag. Then he and Chris went out to the kitchen, put the wine in the refrigerator and opened the Wild Turkey. After taking a big pull, Whitey handed it to Ben who drank from it and passed it on to the next one. As soon as it was empty someone opened another bottle, and it too went the way of the first. Whiskey and wine were flowing, while beer cans were popping all over the place.

Whitey was lighting a cigarette when Ben grabbed a couple of beers out of the refrigerator, throwing one to Whitey he said, "Let's go outside, I have something to show you."

"Is Debbie out there?" Whitey asked eagerly.

"No, she couldn't make it up, but I have something I think you will like better."

"Hey man, she would have to be a real looker to beat Debbie." Taking hold of Ben's arm, Whitey ushered him toward the back door. "Let's see what you have out there for me!"

Except for Libby who lived there, none of the scooter-tramps women were allowed in the house unless they were invited by their old man (boy friend). The party was in full-swing outside as well as inside the house. Ben and Whitey walked out to where the motorcycles were parked. As they approached them, Ben nudged Whitey on the shoulder. "There she is Whitey, all for you!"

"There's chicks all over the place, who are you talking about?"

"Over there the chick sitting on my scooter."

"Wow are you kidding? She's a doll!" Whitey exclaimed in an excited voice.

The young girl in question was watching the two friends as they walked toward her, and when they were within hearing distance, she called out, "It's about time Ben. Is this Whitey?"

"Yeah this is Whitey," Ben answered, "Whitey I want you to meet Val."

"The name is Valerie," the girl quickly corrected.

For a moment Whitey was speechless, he was overwhelmed, bewitched by her youthful beauty, and the sound of her voice was musical, enchanting and fascinating.

"Hey Whitey," Ben shouted as he snapped a finger. "Come out of it man! This is Val, I mean Valerie."

"Hello Valerie, boy this is a surprise."

"Hi Whitey, I've heard a lot about you. I've been looking forward to meeting you."

"You heard a lot about me?" Whitey asked in a surprised voice, "From who?"

115

"My sister."

Whitey was perplexed, "I don't know your sister."

"Sure you do, my sister is Debbie!"

He almost fell over with amazement, "Debbie—Debbie's your sister?"

"She sure is! She's my one and only sister, and she told me all about you."

"Debbie's her sister," Ben confirmed, "and she sent Val up to you."

"What! You're bullshitting me man! I don't believe it. Why would Deb send a sweet young thing like her up to me?"

"Because she's her sister," Ben persisted.

"Okay, so she's Debbie sister. Why would she send her kid sister up to me?"

"I'll tell you," Valerie volunteered, "because my sister thinks the world of you, that's why."

"Shit if she thinks the world of me, then why didn't she come up herself?"

"Because she can't. Let me explain the whole thing to you. First off my sister told me all about you. Deb and I are real close, we share all secrets, and we have never been jealous of each other, and the. . . ."

"Hey that's all fine," Whitey interrupted, "but what the hell has that got to do with her not coming up to see me?"

"I'm getting to that if you'll stop interrupting me! Please be quiet and listen."

In a joking gesture Whitey clamped his hand over his mouth. Valerie smiled and continued. "You see, the very same day you left Sacramento, Debbie received a waitress job in a classy restaurant. She couldn't take off, so she asked if I would come up and take care of you. So here I am!"

"That's it," Ben joined in, "she's come up to watch over you, and take care of you man."

The smile faded from Whitey's face, and in a harsh voice he said, "I don't need anyone to take care of me; you should know that Ben. I don't need a fucking wet-nurse!"

Ben was greatly surprised at Whitey's outburst, and angrily thrusting his face up to Whitey's he shouted, "Wait a minute you ungrateful bastard, you son of a bitch! You're my brother, my compadre, I worry about you. I worry about you doing something crazy and going back to the joint for the rest of your life. No, you don't need a wet-nurse, but it's nice to have a chick who wants to stay with you while her sister works."

"Hell as far as chicks go, I've been making out okay!"

"Yeah, I'm sure you have," Ben returned with a smile.

Whitey looked at Valerie, and in an apologetic voice he said, "Look Valerie, this all came as a surprise to me. I was expecting Debbie and you show up in her place. I mean I didn't know what to think, I was disappointed Deb didn't come and—well I didn't mean that remark

116

about you being a wet-nurse, so can't we just start over again with the introductions?"

Replaced with a smile, disappointment vanished from Valerie's lovely face, and in a cheerful voice she said, "Hi there, my name is Valerie, if you wish you can call me Val."

Whitey scooped her up in his arms, and gave her a tender kiss. She was a treasure, and he knew it. He held her closely and whispered softly in her ear, "Hi Val, I'm happy you're here."

"I'm happy to be here too," she whispered back.

Ben clapped his hands, "Okay let the party begin!" he shouted joyfully.

"Yeah let's party," cried Chris who had just come out of the house accompanied by Libby, and as they approached the group he addressed Whitey and Valerie, "Well I see you two have met. She's a fox ain't she Whitey?"

"She sure is," he replied, then turning to Libby he went on, "Libby do you know Valerie here?"

Smiling, Libby replied, "We never met. I'm glad to know you Valerie."

"Nice meeting you too Libby," Valerie said returning the smile.

"Take her in the house," Chris ordered Libby, "show her around."

Libby seemed delighted to have a girl companion; hand-in-hand like school girls, they ran into the house. Once they were gone Chris said to Ben, "Did you tell Whitey about his P.O.?"

"What about my P.O.?"

"He came to the house this morning," Ben replied. "I was going to tell you about it. He put a warrant out yesterday for your arrest. My mom talked to him, I didn't see him. I'm sure the pigs will be on the lookout for you now."

"Yeah I know, I've been over that road before," Whitey said with disgust. "I guess I'd best be moving on in a day or so."

"Hey Whitey you're welcome here as long as you want, you know that," Chris told him.

"Thanks Chris, but I don't think it wise for me to stay here too long, know what I mean?"

"Yeah, but where the hell you going to go? Hey wait a minute, I have a good friend who is camping out in Blackwood Canyon, you can. . . ."

"Where the hell is Blackwood Canyon?" Whitey interrupted.

"Lake Tahoe," Chris continued. "John Longley, he's a pal of mine, he's camping out alone in the canyon. It's perfect man, it's a perfect place to hide out, and Longley is good people. What do you say Whitey? Is it a go?"

"It sounds like the spot, all I have to do is get up there."

"Hey not to worry man, I'll get you up there," Ben said. "Look tomorrow I'll head for Sacramento, get my pickup ready, you know, I'll load it up with things you'll need. It will take me a while to gather

117

the stuff together, so on Thursday, I'll pick you up around seven A.M.., be ready and I'll drive you to Tahoe."

Whitey put his arm around Ben and said, "You know you're more than a brother, you're a pal—a real pal. Now it's time to party. Fuck the P.O. and his warrant."

The noise outside the house was gathering momentum. It was not much different inside as Ben, Chris and Whitey entered and made their way to the living-room. Whiskey, wine, and beer were flowing freely, and one could smell pot the moment you entered the house. Whitey was promptly handed a fifth of whiskey, and after a long drink he passed the bottle on to Ben. Then he went back into the kitchen for three more cans of beer, and returned to the living room. Looking sharply around, his eyes were searching for Valerie. Not seeing her, he turned to Chris and asked him, "Where's Val? Where did she go? I don't see her."

"Her and Libby are in the bedroom," Chris replied.

Whitey knocked on the door, and from within Libby called, "Who is it?"

"It's me Lib, Whitey, can I come in?"

"Sure the door is unlocked."

Letting himself in, Whitey entered the room. Libby and Valerie were sprawled on the bed looking at a photo album. Valerie looked up, and seeing Whitey, her face brightened with a smile.

"Would you girls like a beer?" Whitey asked.

"Yes we sure would!" both girls replied.

Whitey tossed them each a can, and as he sat down on the bed next to them, Chris entered the room.

"Is this a private party or is anyone welcome?" he asked jokingly. Then slipping up beside Whitey he whispered in his ear, "You want to really get down? I got some Windowpane (acid), some real heavy stuff. Can you dig it?"

"Why not get down. I'm game for anything!"

"Okay Whitey, if you want, you can fix it, swallow it, or if you're game, you can take it directly in the eye. Place it under your eyelid and it will dissolve, it's a direct shot to the brain. You get off right at the peak of the trip."

Windowpane is a minute clear wafer the size of a pinhead, it has to be handled with care. If dropped, it is practically impossible to find.

Whitey carefully pulled down his lower left eyelid. Chris, with the aid of tweezers placed the acid on his lid. Whitey closed his eye tightly shut allowing the windowpane ample time to dissolve. Once dissolved it worked its way into the bloodstream and shot to the brain.

"Come on Whitey," Chris suggested, "Let's get you comfortable on the couch before it hits you."

Whitey eased himself off the bed, and made his way into the living room heading for the couch. Chris and Valerie were leading the way. Quickly the occupants vacated the couch, and none too soon as

118

Whitey fell across it with a mighty yell, "Weee-oooo!" He immediately started to slide off. Valerie reached out to prevent him from falling to the floor.

"Chris give me a hand," she shouted. "He's going to fall."

Whitey never heard Valerie call to Chris, nor could he hear any other noise; he was hallucinating. He was tied spread-eagled to the front end of a runaway Greyhound bus. Down a mountain highway the vehicle careened along at a very high rate of speed.

Whitey had an exceptionally strong and powerful will, and for some inexplicable reason he was aware of his hallucinations and knew that he could not be hurt. There was a voice coming from within himself, "Play it cool Whitey, play it cool, Just kick back and enjoy the trip. It's not really happening, and you can't get hurt." The runaway bus was picking up speed, faster and faster, he could hear the tires screeching as the vehicle hurled into the turns. His clothes were being torn to shreds, the wind was tearing at his hair, his face, his body, and his eyes threatening to rip out of their sockets. In a miraculous way the bus would sway from one side of the highway to the other, and always just in time to miss an oncoming vehicle. He could hear angry horns blowing as the bus sped past, and the grinding crashes of the unfortunate people who swung their vehicles over the embankments to avoid the oncoming bus. He was yelling with joy and fear, similar to the screams one experiences while on a roller-coaster. "Ooooooooweeeeee!" he yelled. He tried to see who was operating the bus, but was unable to turn his head. Somehow he knew there was no driver behind the wheel, and the knowledge of this made the trip more exciting.

He yelled again, "Howeeeeee—Woweee!"

It was 7:00 P.M. when Whitey had taken the acid, it was now 10:00 P.M. and the Greyhound bus was still hurtling its way down the winding mountain road. At times Whitey could hear the sounds of laughter above the squealing tires and honking horns. Suddenly, everything changed. He was no longer spread-eagled on the front end of a bus, he was in a pitch black room, groping around in the darkness on the verge of panic. From a distance he heard spine-chilling laughter that grew louder and louder. It was so loud that he had to clamp his hands over his ears to prevent his eardrums from bursting. The laughter began to fade until it no longer could be heard. Then appearing out of nowhere, he saw hideous phosphorescent faces glowing in the dark. Suddenly, as quickly as they appeared, they vanished, leaving a brilliant light shining directly in his eyes. The light was so penetrating that his head felt as though it would explode. He was about to scream, but in a flash, the light was extinguished, and once again Whitey found himself on the front end of the runaway bus.

He had no way of knowing it, but he was coming down from the acid trip. It was all flashes now, one second he was strapped to the bus, then total darkness, then he would see faces, then he was back on the bus, total darkness, the faces, then the bus. This was repeated many times, but the faces appeared for longer periods until his recognition began to return, and his eyes started to open and close in quick succession. Everything was toning down, even sound was normal again.

He heard a soft voice say, "Whitey, Whitey, are you all right? Are you all right Whitey?"

His eyes ceased their excessive blinking, and he was able to hold them open, he recognized Valerie's lovely face looking down at him. She had him resting comfortably with his head on her lap while she wiped away the cold beads of perspiration from his face. At first he was not quite sure if he was still hallucinating until he heard Valerie speak to him again.

"It's all right Whitey, just relax, it's okay now."

With his head on her lap, Whitey lay there not quite sure of his surroundings. He saw Chris, and then Libby. Soon more faces appeared, and he was able to recognize them. He was positive he was no longer hallucinating. He looked up at Valerie who was smiling down at him.

"You were on quite a trip," she said, "but you're back now, so just relax."

Whitey tried to smile, and in a labored voice he said, "I'm dying of thirst. Get me something to drink—quick!"

"Here give him this," Ben said as he handed Valerie a can of beer.

She helped Whitey to a sitting position, and with one arm supporting him, she held the beer to his parched lips. He drank like a desperate thirsty man. The moment the moisture touched his lips, he grabbed the can with both hands. In his feverish haste to gulp down the cool liquid, half the contents spilled, running down his chin.

After his thirst was quenched, he inhaled a deep breath of air, then exhaled with a sigh of relief. "Woweee what a trip!" he exclaimed.

Sounds of laughter filled the room.

"You were sure on one hell of a long trip," Ben was speaking. "Do you know what time it is? It's past eleven o'clock. I never laughed so much in my life as I did watching you on that goddamn couch. You were a gas men—a gas!"

Whitey lit a cigarette just as Valerie handed him a beer. The can was full when he put it to his lips, and remained there until it was empty. Everyone in the room were kidding and joking, and trying to talk at once.

Whitey turned to Valerie, "I'm gonna crash babe, man I'm tired, I can't stay awake."

Chris, who was sitting next to Whitey agreed, "That's a good idea Whitey, why don't you get a good night's sleep."

"I think I will Chris, I'll see you later." Whitey called across the room, "Hey Ben, I'm going to pack it in, I'm gonna crash. Don't forget Thursday man."

"You got it bro, but I'll see you in the morning before I leave."

With the aid of Valerie, Whitey made it to his room where she undressed and helped him into the sleeping-bag. After undressing herself, she crawled in, cuddling up next to him, but he was already asleep.

That June day of 1971 came to an end, and so did Whitey's first acid trip, with many more to follow.

CHAPTER 22.

It was not until 11:00 A.M.. the next morning when Whitey woke up. It required a few moments before he could figure out where he was, and even longer before he could remember what had happened the previous night. He lit a cigarette, and as he lay there smoking he suddenly remembered Valerie. Where was she? He tried to recollect the last time he had seen her. He couldn't remember, nor could he remember how or when he had gone to sleep. He had no idea that Valerie had put him to bed and comforted him all night. She had woken up an hour earlier to watch Ben, Chris, and their buddies leave for Sacramento.

Hastily grabbing his Levi's, Whitey sprang off the couch, and as he did so he called out, "Valerie, where are you? Are you in the house? Valll-eer-eee!"

The bedroom door burst open with a loud bang as Valerie came running in all excited. The split second he saw her rush through the door, he heaved a sigh of relief.

"Whitey, Whitey what's wrong?" she cried.

"Nothing babe, I—I thought you were gone."

"No I'm still here, or—did you want me to go?" she asked shyly.

"If I wanted you to go I sure as hell wouldn't of yelled for you like I did!"

"I know," she smiled, and quickly disappeared closing the door behind her.'

After getting washed and dressed Whitey went into the kitchen and found Valerie and Libby having coffee together. Valerie was the first to see Whitey come through the door, and with a smile she said, "Good morning Whitey."

Libby looked up from her coffee, smiled and said good morning.

Whitey sat at the table, "Hi Libby what's for breakfast?" he asked.

"Bacon and eggs, but I'm not the cook this morning, Valerie is."

Without waiting to be asked, Valerie went about preparing breakfast for the three of them.

"Would you like some coffee while you're waiting?" she asked.

"Yeah, I could use a cup. Say where the hell is everyone?"

"Chris took off with Ben and the gang over an hour ago," Libby replied.

"Damn it all, shit! I wanted to see Ben before he left. What time is it anyway?"

"It's eleven thirty," Libby answered.

Valerie looked up from her cooking and said, "Ben told me to tell you not to worry about a thing. He'll be here in the morning around seven to pick you up."

"That's good, that's what I wanted to know, thanks Val."

"Yeah okay," she said in a sad voice.

"What's wrong babe? You don't sound too cheerful."

"Well I didn't know you were going to Tahoe until Ben told me this morning."

"Why should that make you feel bad?"

"I came up here to be with you, and now you're leaving."

"Yeah that's right, I'm leaving in the morning, I have to, but no one is stopping you from coming with me if you want to."

"Do you mean it? Do you really mean it?" she cried excitedly. "Yes, I want to go!"

"Okay then, it's all set, you can come. Right now just get my breakfast ready."

Turning from the stove, Valerie gave Whitey an affectionate kiss, and then resumed her cooking.

After the meal, Valerie and Libby gave the house a thorough cleaning as there was a considerable mess after the previous night's party. While the girls worked Whitey spent most of the time sitting outside on an old wooden bench sipping beer and smoking cigarettes. Each time he ran out of brew he would shout for Valerie to bring him another one. She seemed to delight in the opportunity to wait on him.

"Val will you bring me another beer," he would call, and the words were barely out of his mouth when she would appear with a fresh can. After delivering the beer she would walk to the house with Whitey's eyes following her movements. She was lovely, and at the tender age of fifteen, Whitey wasn't quite sure what to do with her. Sure he enjoyed her company, and why not? She was a joy to have around. Most scooter-tramp girls were well-seasoned and experienced before the age of sixteen, but Valerie at fifteen seemed awfully young and immature to Whitey. Yet he had made love to her sister Debbie who was seventeen, and to Libby who was only sixteen, but for some reason or other fifteen was out of the question. She was young enough to be his daughter. What could she see in a man of his age? Yet she seemed to want to be around him all the time.

Valerie and Debbie had been living with an older sister since the death of their parents in a car accident two and a half years ago. Both girls had a very good upbringing, but since the loss of their parents' things had been touch and go for them. Valerie was

123

attracted and clearly infatuated with Whitey, and it troubled him for he didn't want to take advantage of her situation.

After finishing his beer Whitey went to his room to lie down, and soon fell asleep. He didn't know how long he had slept, but he woke up to discover Valerie lying beside him sound asleep.

Poor kid, cleaning the house, and waiting on me hand and foot, no wonder she's tired, he thought as he edged his way off the couch so as not to disturb her. Just before leaving the room he covered her over with a blanket.

He went directly to the refrigerator, retrieved a beer, took it into the living room, and sat down on the couch. He had just lighted a cigarette when Libby entered the room and sat down beside him. Reaching for his beer she took a drink.

"So you're leaving in the morning and taking Valerie with you." It was more of an accusation than a question.

"Yeah that's right, we're taking off just as soon as Ben gets here, why?"

"Oh nothing, I was just wondering, did you screw her last night?"

"You know I figured you'd ask something like that."

"Well did you?"

"No, I didn't touch her."

"Bullshit! You expect me to believe that?"

"Hey believe what you want, it don't matter to me."

"Will you lay her again tonight? Or will you wait until you get to Tahoe?"

"Ah come off it Lib. Why ya asking me such shit, don't you like Val?"

"Oh yes, I like her very much, she seems like a nice person. I know her sister Debbie real well, and Chris told me how you made it with her before coming up here."

Whitey was getting mad at her insinuations and said, "Look, I didn't make it with Valerie, but I did make it with Debbie, and Valerie knows I did. I also made it with you. . . ."

"Yes, but we were. . . ."

"Shut up, don't interrupt me again, and listen. I made it with you, I hope the hell I can make it with a dozen more chicks before I die—at least I hope so. All this questioning is making me mad. I was hoping when I leave it would be on good terms. I enjoyed our time together yesterday, even if it was only for a few hours. Making love to you was a treasure, and it will always be with me. There are two sides of my life, the happy side and the unhappy side. Most of all my living years were unhappy ones, but the happy side of my life I can't count in years. I can only count in days, and not many at that. I haven't experienced much happiness in the forty-eight years of my life, but what little I have experienced I treasure, I keep it right here within me. The few hours of pleasure I had with you yesterday will always be with me, no one can ever take it away. So you see, no

124

matter what, you've been part of my happiness, and I like to think I've been part of yours. Shit Lib, I can't tell what may happen tomorrow, you and I may not ever see each other again, so please don't spoil what little we had by asking all these questions, okay?"

"I'm—I'm sorry Whitey, honest I am."

"Wait a minute Lib, don't cry, I didn't mean for you to cry. I'm sorry I came down on you." Whitey reached in his back pocket, but realizing he had no handkerchief he pulled off his T-shirt. "Here Libby, let me wipe your eyes!"

"With your T-shirt?"

"Hey I just put it on last month!"

As he wiped away the tears her sobbing turned to laughter, and when the giggling subsided, she said in an apologetic voice, "Honest Whitey, I'm sorry for the way I acted, I was just being a bitch, I really. . . ."

"No, no Libby you're not a bitch, don't ever. . . ."

"Yes I was Whitey, I was being a bitch, but I want you to know I really enjoyed making love with you yesterday."

To comfort her Whitey placed his arm around her shoulders as she continued talking, "I guess I was a little jealous of Valerie."

"Hey you have no reason to be. Hell I'm nothing but a fuck-up, I mean what the hell, you have Chris, he's young, shit I'm three times your age, so you don't have to be jealous of girls I make it with. Don't you see?"

"Yes I see, but maybe I see something in you that Chris don't have."

"I'll tell you one thing he don't have, he doesn't have my rap-sheet."

"What's a rap-sheet?"

"My record, he's not screwed up like me."

"Maybe not, but I'll tell you one thing that he doesn't have. You have manners and. . . ."

"Manners! I don't have no manners."

"Wait a minute Whitey, just hear me out first. I said you have something Chris don't have, and I meant it, and that's manners. You do have manners Whitey even though you don't realize it, deep within you, you have some class. Yesterday morning when I served you breakfast you thanked me, when I showed you where you could sleep you thanked me, and just a moment ago you told me you enjoyed my lovemaking and you would treasure it always. Can't you see how happy it made me feel to hear you say that? Chris may be a nice guy in your eyes, but he isn't in mine. I love him, but he never shows me any respect or had ever thanked me for anything. He takes me for granted, even my love, I'm supposed to do everything for him, and I wouldn't mind it if he would show me a little respect and kindness in return. Is that asking for too much?"

Libby's eyes began to moisten, handing her the T-shirt Whitey took her in his arms and held her gently. "I'm sorry Lib," he whispered softly, "I truly am sorry, I never gave it no thought about Chris. I mean, I didn't realize he never showed you any appreciation. Why don't you try to talk it over with him?"

"I can't Whitey, he won't listen to me, and besides he's always gone someplace, and when he's home he's always loaded or drunk. I just can't talk to him."

She raised her head to look up at Whitey, her eyes were filled with tears. His heart went out to her as he held her close, and in a soothing voice he said, "Don't cry Lib, please don't cry. I'm sure things will turn out okay. I'll tell you what, I'll make you a promise if you stop crying."

"What—what will you promise?" she sobbed.

"Before this summer is over, I'll come back to visit you. I mean if you want me to."

"I would love to see you again. Promise me."

"Sure Lib, I promise. I don't know just when, but I'll come back."

"Thank you Whitey, thank you." She threw her arms around him.

"Don't thank me," he insisted, "if anyone deserves the thanks it's you, here I want you to have this," he reached in his rear pocket and handed her a twenty-dollar bill. "Listen, don't take this the wrong way, I want you to have this for food or whatever, okay?"

Accepting the money she replied, "Thank you, thank you very much."

"Now don't give it to Chris for booze, you understand me?"

"Yes Whitey, I understand, and I understand a lot more!" she pulled his head toward her and held it there until their lips met. It was a straight kiss, but a sweet one, and as their lips held, she pressed her body against his. It was electrifying, and like a magnet he responded to her kiss. She could feel the penetrating heat as she pressed against him, and quickly pulled away.

"I really like you Whitey." Then she turned and hurried into her room closing the door behind her.

Whitey returned to his room and found Valerie still asleep. Carefully, trying not to disturb her, he lay down beside her. He took her in his arms, and brushed his lips across her forehead. At the touch of his lips her eyes flashed open, startled, she pulled away with a cry of fear. She immediately recognized Whitey, and throwing both arms around him, she held him tightly. Then turning her head slightly she whispered, "You made me jump," then she giggled.

"I'm sorry Val, I didn't mean to scare you. I was just kissing your forehead." he said innocently.

She smiled and said, "I was wondering if you were ever going to kiss me, but on the forehead?" Before Whitey could reply she quickly pressed her lips against his, and as she did so he could feel her tongue penetrating his lips in search of his.

The sweet fragrance and electricity of her body was overpowering,

126

so overpowering he was afraid he would lose control of himself. Many thoughts were flashing through his mind. Damn, she's so gorgeous, her lips—her tongue taste so sweet, she smells so fresh, so lovely, I can't let her go. But you must Whitey, she is too young. His mind was screaming now—I can't let her go! I *won't* let her go!

As Valerie held her lips to Whitey's she began to sense something was wrong for she felt his body tremble. "Whitey is something wrong? You're shaking all over, what is it?" she asked in a worried voice.

"Nothing, nothing's wrong. I'm just tired I guess. I'll be all right," he assured her.

Valerie brushed her cheek against his as she cuddled up to him. "Sure you'll be all right Whitey. Close your eyes and rest a while."

Once more Whitey thought, damn, she's so sweet, if she stays with me I might end up doing it to her, and if I make her go back to Sacramento, I'll regret that too! Make up your mind Whitey, does she go or does she stay? Man, what am I to do? Hell she may even be a virgin! Be honest with yourself Whitey, can you take her virginity? Yes—no! Yes I can—no!

Opening his eyes he whispered, "Valerie?"

"Yes."

"Look I have something I have to say to you, so just listen until I've finished. I'm trying to make a decision about you going to Tahoe with me or not, and it. . . ."

"But you already said I could go," she cried.

"I know, but just listen to me first, don't say anything. Look, I'm forty-eight years old, and you're a lovely girl of fifteen. Hell I'm only human, if we share a sleeping-bag and all, you know what I might do, so I have decided it's best I give you bus fare for Sacramento."

He had barley stopped talking when Valerie cried out, "No Whitey, that's not fair, you promised I could go and I. . . ."

"I know I promised you Val, but I changed my mind. . . ."

"I listened to you, now you listen to me!" she exclaimed. "I know all about you, I know you're forty-eight and I'm just fifteen, don't you think I haven't thought about it? Of course I have, and I don't care how old you are, the age part doesn't matter to me. My sister Debbie thinks the world of you, she wanted to come up, but as I told you before, she is working now, so I asked her if she wanted me to come instead. She said yes, she'd rather have me with you than some chippie. But what I'm trying to get across to you is, it was my decision to come here, and I think I should have something to say about you sending me away or not."

"Are you telling me you want to stay with me knowing what may happen to you? You know what I mean, what I may do to you?"

"Yes, I want to stay with you," she insisted. "Come on Whitey, I'm old enough to know what I'm doing."

"Tell me something Val, did anyone ever—you know, have you ever—shit, are you still a cherry?"

127

"If you're asking if I'm still a virgin, the answer is yes. Does it make any difference with you? I've been told that all men like to have a girl that way."

"It don't matter to me if you are a virgin, but most young dudes like to have virgins so they can boast to their buddies, 'You know man, last night I got me a cherry, no kidding, a real virgin!' "

"Did you ever brag Whitey?

"No, I never brag about a thing like that, and I don't care to."

Valerie gave him a short kiss, and remarked, "I'm really fond of you Whitey, and I'm beginning to like you even more."

At that moment there was a knock on the door.

"Hey in there! Aren't you guys ever coming out?" Libby called. "It's almost dinner time, do you people want to eat?"

"Okay Libby," Valerie called back, "we'll be right there."

Hopping off the couch, the two of then went into the bathroom to freshen up. After filling the sink with water, Whitey soaped a washcloth; he grabbed Valerie behind the back of the head and attempted to wash her face. She tried to struggle away from him, and in doing so she got a mouthful of soapy bubbles.

"What are you trying to do?"

"Wash your face, what did you think I was doing?"

"Well you could of waited until my mouth was closed."

After they had finished their clowning, they sat down to a dinner of hamburger steaks, mashed potatoes, carrots, homemade biscuits, and some lovely brown gravy. The meal was delicious, and while Whitey was lighting an after dinner smoke he told Libby so. Her face lit up with pleasure as she said, "Thank you Whitey, I' so happy you enjoyed it."

Libby's cook stove was an antique wood-burning range. The many loaves of bread, cakes, and pies that came out of the over were extremely good considering the primitive equipment she had to work with. Libby was a fantastic cook.

As Whitey got up from the table Valerie announced, "You prepared the meal Libby, so it is only right I do the dishes, and clean the table."

"I'll help you," Libby returned, but Valerie insisted that she go into the living room and sit down with Whitey.

Valerie could be heard washing the dishes, and as she was finishing Whitey called out to her, "Hey Val, will you bring me a beer when you come in."

It wasn't long before she entered the room smiling. As she sat down beside Whitey she open a can of beer for him.

Before he could take a drink Libby remarked, "I see he is getting you trained Val!"

The smile vanished from Valerie's face, and turning to Libby she gave her a stern look and said, "I know you're only joking, but no one trains me. Any time I do something for a man it's because I want to,

128

not because he ordered me to. That is why I never wanted to become a scooter-tamp girl, I won't be a slave to anyone!"

"Val, I was just kidding, don't be mad at me."

"I'm not Lib, I'm not mad, I just wanted you to know how I feel." Turning her attention from Libby she looked at Whitey who nodded his head in approval.

"Well you sweet things, you can sit there and chew the fat the rest of the night, but I'm gonna crash," Whitey stated emphatically. He stood up, stretched his arms, and as he started toward his room Valerie got up to go with him.

"Are you going to bed too? Or are you just walking me to my room?" he asked jokingly.

"I'm going to bed too. Goodnight Libby."

"Goodnight Val, and you too Whitey."

"Goodnight Lib. If Chris comes home tonight, wake me up, okay?"

"Sure," Libby replied, "but I don't think he'll be back tonight. He'll no doubt stay over to Ben's house, and come up with him in the morning."

"Okay Lib, thanks a lot, see ya in the morning."

CHAPTER 23.

Whitey and Valerie went to their bedroom, and after they were both settled in the sleeping-bag, Valerie whispered to Whitey, "You know I may be only fifteen, but I'm old enough to know when a gal is hot for you! I'm sure Libby is. Did you ever make it with her? Tell me!"

Whitey started to laugh.

"What's so funny? What are you laughing at?"

"I'm laughing at you, boy the questions you ask!"

"Well did you?"

"Ah come on sweetheart, it's not nice to ask me a thing like that. I mean what you and your sister tell each other is okay I guess, but look at it this way, let's say I had balled you and someone else asked me if I had ever made it with you, it wouldn't be fair to you to say I did. Do you know where I'm coming from?"

"I think so."

Whitey chuckled, "What do you mean you think so? You know perfectly well what I mean. When you tell one girl you made it with another," he continued, "that's when the feathers start to fly!"

"I don't have any feathers!" she giggled.

They embraced each other, Whitey felt as though he would go wild. Her body was so firm, so refreshing against his own. His chin was brushing the top of her head, while she had her delicate lips pressed into his neck. He could feel the steady rhythm of her breathing, and her breath was warm and sweet. They were both on their sides, with Valerie on her right facing Whitey. He had both arms around her with his hands gripped together at the small of her back. He pulled her closer, she responded with a slight groan; he released his hold, then slowly slid his hand down her back until he touched her panties. It was electrifying. A charge of excitement shot through his body. Under the panties his fingers investigated her firm buttocks.

Valerie was breathing faster now, and as he held her firmly she could feel his hard hot perspiring body tighten. The feeling was a rhythmical quiver, sending electric charges throughout her body. Suddenly he pulled away from her. In the darkness her bewildered face looked up at him.

"What is it Whitey?" she whispered, "Did I do something wrong?"

"No, you did nothing wrong, you're wonderful, but I can't take you now. I know you must be disappointed, and I'm sorry, but I would like to wait until we are at Tahoe."

"If that's what you want Whitey, then I can wait too, but you are going to do it when we get there aren't you?"

"Of course, but only if you want me to."

"I wouldn't be here with you if I didn't want it, don't you know that?"

"Yeah I realize that, but what I can't understand is why you want me to be the first. I mean there are a lot of young dudes who would be happy to accommodate you!"

"But that is just it, I don't want someone like that. I want someone who will be warm and gentle, and has feelings for me. I don't want some dumb boy who is doing it to me just for his own satisfaction, and don't give a shit about me. You know what I mean?"

"I'm really flattered you selected me for the honors. But a lot of people would look down on a man of my age getting it on with you. They would think I misled you."

"Whitey, they are red-necks who think that way. God, you didn't offer me candy to lure me into a car, or offered to buy me nice things, or anything like that. I'm here because it was my idea, I want to be with you, and I want you to love me. So to hell with what those red-necks think!"

"But you know it can't last. I don't want you to be hurt."

"You won't hurt me Whitey, I'm sure of that."

"You don't understand what I mean. I'm on the run, there's no future with me. It could end tomorrow."

"I know," she said sadly, "but I still want to stay with you for as long as you will have me."

"Look Val, I don't like to make promises I can't keep, and right now I'm in a situation where I don't know which way to turn. So for now I guess the best thing is to play it by ear. As for you staying, I would like to keep you for always, but I'm afraid that can't be, I'm sure you understand."

Valerie acknowledged with a nod of the head, "I understand Whitey, I really do, and it made me happy to know you would like to keep me for always."

Whitey did not reply, he merely lay there quietly with his arms around her until finally they both fell asleep.

Because of a horrible dream Whitey did not sleep well that night. He was back behind prison walls, and was standing in front of the California Adult Parole Board. Mr. Morson was speaking in a raucous voice, "Parole is granted Mr. Thompson, effective as of now, so hurry before the big gate closes."

A guard opened the door, Whitey hastened through it down the corridor to the next locked gateway.

131

"Unlock it quick!" he yelled at the guard. "I have to get to the main gate before it closes."

"You have plenty of time," the guard assured him, "it will stay open for you."

Time after time Whitey was delayed at many doors until finally he was at the main entrance. The gigantic one and a half ton solid steel black gate was opened for him. Just as he was about to walk through, like a huge guillotine, the gate came closing down with terrific force, and in a thunderous jolt it slammed shut. He jumped back, not a second too soon to avoid being crushed. The tower guard at the controls smiled then he pressed the button, and the huge gate began to rise once more. Whitey ran for the opening, but the gate quickly began to close, and again he jumped back in the nick of time.

Looking up at the guard and waving his parole papers, he shouted, "I've been granted a parole, open the gate so I can go free."

The tower guard smiled down at him and pressed the button, and the heavy gate began to rise. Whitey started to run for freedom, ten feet to go—five feet to go. He looked up and started to scream at the guard who pressed the button sending the guillotine gate in a downward motion. "Don't close the gate, I have my parole papers—don't close it!"

Whitey was determined to make it under the gate, and ran for his freedom. Three more steps, the gate was hurtling down at a grinding speed. Two more steps—freedom or death? He charged for it.

With a cry of terror, Whitey bolted upright in bed, shouting, "Don't close the gate! I have my papers to freedom."

"It's all right, it's all right babe, you're dreaming. It's all right Whitey—you're dreaming."

It took a moment or two before he realize where he was. Valerie's voice was soothing and reassured him that he was safe. She stroked his forehead, brushed her lips against his shoulder and whispered, "Are you all right? Is there anything I can get you?"

Whitey was extremely dry, and the nightmare had drained him.

"Yeah, would you like to get me a beer?"

She hopped out of the sleeping-bag and disappeared into the kitchen. While she was gone Whitey reached under the couch, fumbled around until his hand found what it was looking for. It was his stash—a bottle of Wild Turkey. He opened the bottle and was taking a drink when Valerie returned.

"You got the beer?" he asked.

After popping the can, she handed it to him. He took a long drink chasing the whiskey down.

Turning to Valerie, he said, "Thanks girl, thanks for being here."

Smiling at him she nodded her head and reached for his beer, after taking a small sip she handed it back.

"You were dreaming about prison weren't you?"

132

"Yes, how did you know?"

"You were talking in your sleep. Then you began to twist and turn; when you started screaming and yelling, I knew you were terrified of something. That's when I tried to calm you down, I was afraid for you."

"I'm sorry to put you through all this but I'm okay now. You go back to sleep."

"Okay Whitey. If you need me, I'll be right here; now you go back to sleep too."

He took another drink—a long pull from the bottle. After replacing the cap he returned it under the couch.

Breathing softly, Valerie drifted off into a deep sleep. Except for the occasional sound of a cricket outside, or some lonely creature of the night, the room became silent. The night silence was deafening, But Whitey took no notice of it as he lay there with his thoughts. He was thinking of the dream, did it have a meaning? What did it signify? Was there still a chance for him, or was it telling him that the end was drawing near? Lighting a cigarette, he inhaled deeply; then finished off the beer. A minute or two later, using the empty can for an ashtray, he snuffed out the cigarette. He was extremely restless, and it was not until the wee hours of morning before he fell into a troubled sleep.

CHAPTER 24.

Valerie and Whitey were awakened when the early morning silence was broken by an approaching pickup truck and a motorcycle. How long he had been asleep he had no idea, it seemed only minutes ago that he had closed his eyes. Reaching under the couch he retrieved the bottle and put it to his lips for a long pull.

The hour was early, the first rays of morning sunlight were beginning to cast their reflections across the sky, while inside the house the darkness of night still had its grip within the room. The gleam of the oncoming vehicles headlights caused eerie shadows to dance on the walls.

"I guess it's Ben and Chris," Whitey said as he took another drink from the bottle.

A moment later their voices could be heard as they walked toward the house. Valerie was just about to hop out of the sleeping-bag, but decided it was too late because the two men were almost at the entrance.

A second later the door burst open, and they came storming in shouting in unison, "Whitey, are you here? Turn on the lights!"

Immediately the overhead lights came on revealing Libby standing by the open kitchen door with her hand still on the light switch. Both Ben and Chris made a beeline for the couch, diving headlong onto Whitey. Valerie, who had seen them coming, barely had enough time to roll to one side.

"Get off me you fucking crumbs! Get off me."

Both men were struggling with Whitey trying to overpower him and take away the bottle of Wild Turkey.

"Go on take the bottle, if that's what you want. Get the fuck off me!" Whitey shouted.

Ben grabbed the bottle as he hopped off the couch with Chris in hot pursuit. In turn they took a drink, and tossed it back to Whitey, who finished it off. Then he threw the bottle at Ben striking him on the shoulder before it fell to the floor. Luckily it did not break.

Jumping off the couch Whitey reached for his jeans. "Well go on, get the hell out of here, go in the kitchen!" he shouted at them. "Do you queens like watching me get dressed?"

"Fuck no man!" Ben replied, "We're waiting to see Val get dressed!"

"Get out of here, what the hell is wrong with you guys? You

134

fucking perverts!"

With one leg in his jeans, he made a dive at them as they scurried into the kitchen closing the door behind them.

"Don't peek through the keyhole, or I'll piss in your eye!" Whitey threatened.

Taking the opportunity to get dressed, Valerie quickly gathered up her jeans, and as she started to put them on Whitey remarked, "Boy, you got the sweetest ass I have ever seen on a woman!"

"I like your compliment," she laughed. "You always use a fine choice of words!"

"What's wrong with my words?"

"Nothing when you're a dirty old man!" Valerie returned as she ran into the bathroom.

Whitey finished dressing, and after washing he went into the kitchen to find Ben and Chris joking and laughing as they drank their beer. Libby was preparing breakfast. Retrieving a beer from the refrigerator, Whitey joined the two men at the table.

"Are you all set to go?" Ben asked.

"Just as soon as I roll up my shit," Whitey replied. Turning to Chris he said, "Just where is this Blackwood Canyon? You better tell us how to get there."

"No sweat Whitey, I'm coming with you guys and show the way. Besides you'd never find Longley's camp without me."

"Are you coming right back?" Libby asked Chris.

"Shit I don't know Lib when I'll be back, why?"

"I was just wondering if I could come for the ride."

"Hell no, we don't have the room."

Valerie walked in the kitchen in time to hear Chris refuse Libby.

"There's plenty of room Chris, let her come so she can get out of the house for a while."

"I said no, and when I say no I mean no! She stays here. You got that Lib?"

Libby did not reply, she turned sadly to the stove and her cooking.

After breakfast they began to gather their belongings, and when Valerie carried her things out to the truck, Whitey concealed the automatic in the sleeping-bag, and this too was loaded up. It only took a few minutes to get ready, and while Valerie was carrying out the last load, Whitey went into the kitchen to tell Ben that they were ready. He felt sorry for Libby, and he could not understand why Chris did not let her come. He would have been out of place to ask Chris, for no one ever interfered with another man's decision pertaining to his woman.

"Okay Ben, we're ready to go. By the way on the truck, what's all that stuff you got under the tarp?"

"It's for you cad, you can't camp without nothing. You have everything you need except a tent."

"I appreciate what you're doing for me Ben, what do I owe you?"

135

"Hey don't worry about it, it's just shit we had laying around the house."

Valerie was waiting in the truck bed for Whitey who climbed in, and they snuggled down together. Ben opened the cab door, getting behind the wheel, and as he started the truck Chris climbed in beside him. Easing the truck into gear, the vehicle started moving slowly toward the highway. Libby was standing by the back door waving goodbye.

"So long Libby," Valerie called out. "Hopefully we'll see you soon."

"So long Val, you too Whitey, take care now."

As the truck picked up speed clouds of dust shot into the air blocking out their vision of Libby and the house. The pickup was a smooth running six cylinder 1948¾ ton Chevrolet. It was painted a deep battleship gray with a decal of a black swastika on each fender. The vehicle was in excellent condition except for the window behind the driver's seat, it was missing. The missing window made it convenient for Whitey to communicate with the driver and passenger in the front seat.

As the truck made its way out onto the highway, Whitey called, "Hey Ben."

Looking through the rear view mirror Ben could see Whitey, "Yeah, what's up?"

"Hey man this display of swastikas ain't going to do it. It'll draw attention from the highway pigs. We've got to cover them up."

"Yeah that's cool Whitey, I'll pull over and scrape them off with my buck knife."

"Shit man it'll take all fucking day to scrape it off. Look, pull into the Auburn shopping center I want to get some booze, and we'll pick up a can of spray paint."

Pulling into the shopping center, Whitey gave Ben $40 to buy some supplies and spray paint. After a short wait Ben returned with the purchases, and once the swastikas were obliterated they were on their way again.

"Hey Whitey, here you go." Chris shouted as he passed a lighted marijuana cigarette back to him. Whitey took a half dozen quick pulls on it and held it deep in his lungs for a moment before exhaling. Going through the same procedure again, he handed it to Valerie who took a drag before handing it back to Chris.

Whitey reached down into the bag of groceries fumbling for the beer, but finding none he yelled, "Hey didn't you get no fuckin' beer? All I see is whiskey and wine, but no beer, pull over man we got to get some."

"I didn't buy any because I got an ice-chest under the tarp, it's full of cold beer. It's for you man, help yourself."

Whitey looked under the tarpaulin, found the chest, and took out four beers, one for each of them.

"Keep your beer out of sight," Whitey cautioned, "we don't want to

136

be pulled over."

Ben eased the truck right along, keeping abreast of the traffic and taking care not to exceed the sixty-five miles an hour speed limit. Whitey was taking no chances either, he was continuously on the alert for patrol cars. The first leg of the journey went by without incident until they were a few miles northeast of Gold Run on Highway 80. It was midmorning, the traffic was light, and with clear visibility Whitey had no difficulty spotting the black and white patrol car coming up from behind. It was a quarter of a mile away, allowing him ample time to conceal himself under the tarpaulin, but before doing so he called out, "Hey Ben, play it cool. It's the heat coming up from the rear. Play it cool."

Looking in the rear view mirror, Ben asked, "Where the hell is he? I don't see. . . .oh yeah, I see him now! Okay everyone hide the beer!"

Crawling under the tarp, Whitey hid himself from view, while Valerie kept her eye on the approaching Highway Patrol.

"Val—Val," Whitey called to her, "can you hear me?"

"Yes I can, your voice is muffled, but I can hear you."

"Okay now, just act cool, act nonchalantly, keep me posted on what that pig is doing."

While waiting for word from Valerie, the subsequent few minutes seemed like a decade to Whitey. The only sound he could hear was the roar of the truck motor blending in with the noise of the highway.

"Oh shit! He just turned on his flashing lights! I think he is going to pull us over. He's coming up fast now!" Valerie cried excitedly.

Fumbling in the darkness under the tarp, Whitey found the sleeping-bag, and slipping his hand in between the folds he extracted the customized semiautomatic. Then pointing it straight up, he flipped the safety-catch. He was now ready for the inevitable, the moment the tarp was pulled back he would open fire.

Valerie called out to Ben, "He's just behind us in the outer lane, you better pull over and stop."

A moment later from under the tarp Whitey heard Ben speak, "Is something wrong officer? What's the problem?"

Ignoring Ben's question, the patrolman asked, "Do you have a California driver's license?"

"Yeah sure," reaching into his rear trouser pocket, he took out his wallet, produced his license and handed it to the officer who carefully scrutinized it. Ben was surprised when he handed it back to him and said, "Where are you headed Mr. Vakno?"

"We're going camping," Ben quickly replied.

"Whereabouts?"

"White Cloud."

"I can't place it offhand, where is it?"

"Not far, we turn onto Highway 20 up here at Emigrant Gap going toward Nevada City."

"Yes, I know where you mean, that's on the other side of Skillman

Campgrounds."

Turning his attention from Ben, the officer looked at Valerie.

"Hello miss, looks like a load under that tarp."

"Yes it's our camping gear, would you like to see it?"

Valerie stood up ready to remove the tarpaulin.

"No that's all right miss," the officer said as he turned back to Ben. "Are you aware of one of your brake lights being out?"

Acting surprised Ben replied, "I didn't know it, they were both working this morning."

"You better stop in the next service station and get it fixed," the officer advised.

"Better still, I'll fix it right here sir. I always carry extra tail and brake light bulbs." Reaching into the glove compartment, Ben retrieved a screwdriver and a brake light bulb. Then he got out of the cab and walked around to the rear of the truck, with the patrolman following behind him. Unscrewing the brake light cover, he removed the bulb and discovered it had blown out. After replacing it with a new one, he called to Chris to step on the brake pedal. He complied, and immediately both brake lights lit up.

"Thanks officer," Ben said, "I sure as hell didn't know that light wasn't working."

"Glad to be of service. I want to compliment you on carrying spare bulbs, I wish more people did."

Beaming, Ben said, "I always carry spare bulbs and fuses too, you never know when one will blow out. Thanks again officer."

"He's gone," Valerie informed Whitey, "he's walking back to his car."

"It's about time!" came the muffled voice from under the tarp.

A moment later the Highway Patrol pulled out onto the Freeway and took off in a burst of speed.

"He's gone Whitey, he's gone!" Valerie cried joyfully.

Getting out of the cab, Ben took hold of a corner of the tarpaulin, and pulled it off Whitey. Ben's face went white. He was staring down the cold barrel of a semiautomatic held in Whitey's hand. It was staring Ben right in the eye."Woooo-eeee!" he cried. "That was one lucky highway pig!"

At the sight of the weapon Valerie's face paled, "Oh my God! I asked that patrolman if he wanted to look under the tarp!"

"If he had it would of been all over for him!" Chris volunteered.

"Wooooo-eeeee!" Ben cried again.

Whitey slipped the automatic back into the sleeping-bag, and turning to Valerie he said, "Open up some beers will ya babe?"

The second leg of the trip was uneventful, occasionally a Highway Patrol would come up from behind and give Ben and company the once-over before passing them. Each time a patrol car was spotted, Whitey would slip under the tarpaulin with his automatic at the

138

ready. It was always a relief when Valerie gave the all clear signal.

At Tahoe City Ben pulled into a Shell service station for gasoline, and added water to the radiator. While this was being accomplished, Whitey, accompanied by Valerie, went to a roadside restaurant where he bought four hamburgers, and french fries to go. The refreshments were enjoyed under the shade of a nearby pine tree.

Out of Tahoe City on Highway 89, they drove a few miles to Sunnyside, a small tourist town located on the west shore of Lake Tahoe. A concise distance south of Sunnyside, Ben made a right turn onto a dusty gravel road not much wider than a logging trail. They were now in the Tahoe National Forest. Shifting the truck into a lower gear, they made slow progress for approximately two miles over the bumpy washboard road. Then veering off to the right, leaving the road, they turned onto what appeared to be a hiking trail. For the next quarter mile they moved at a snail's pace zigzagging around pine trees, rocks, shrubbery, and tree stumps. It was slow progress traveling over this tortuous, treacherous trail. Finally at the edge of a small clearing they came to a halt.

Chris was the first one out of the pickup, and as he slammed the door behind him, he shouted, "Well this is it—Blackwood Canyon!"

It was beautiful, for miles all that could be seen were rolling hills and mountains covered with fir and pine trees. It was breath taking, and at an elevation of six thousand two hundred feet, the air was crisp and clear. Up at the higher levels traces of snow could be seen. Directly across the clearing, camouflaged amongst the pines, stood a small tent. Parked just beyond the tent was an old Ford Ranch wagon.

"Is that Longley's wagon?" Ben asked Chris.

"Yeah, it's his, he must be around here somewhere. Hey Longley!" he shouted.

"Maybe he went someplace," Valerie suggested.

"Na, he's here somewhere. Hey Longley—hey Longley."

"Chris, Ben," a voice called out, "what the hell you guys doing up here?"

Everyone's attention was drawn toward the west end of the clearing, walking out of the woods was a young man in his late twenties.

Chris greeted him, "How's it going John? We were just passing by and dropped in."

"Glad to have some company. How you guys doing?" he said as he shook hands with Chris and Ben. "Who're your friends?"

Chris made the introductions, "John I want you to meet Whitey Thompson, and his old lady Valerie."

"How you doing Whitey—Valerie? I'm glad to meet you."

"Likewise," Whitey returned, while Valerie just nodded her head.

"This is a nice neck of the woods, how long you been camped here?" Whitey asked.

139

"I set up camp about a month ago. Last summer I was over to the other side of the canyon, but I decided to camp here this summer. You know the road you came on? Well instead of turning right to come up here, there's a little trail off to the left that takes you over to the other side of the canyon, It's nice over there, but too many people are getting to know the place. That's why I'm camping here this summer."

"Do you camp every summer?"

"Every year without fail, when winter comes I go back to Squaw Valley. I work on the Ski Rescue Patrol when someone gets lost, but my main job is keeping skiers on the trail. When summer comes I draw unemployment, and to save money I camp out here in Blackwood Canyon. By the way what brings you guys up here? Are you looking for a campsite?"

Before Whitey could answer Chris called John aside.

"Look my buddy's got a little problem, he has to lay low for a while. I thought maybe he could stay here with you."

"Yes sure, but who's after him?"

"He jumped parole, his P.O. put out a warrant on him. He's solid people and you know Ben and me, we look out for our own."

"Hey that's cool, but where do you know this guy from?"

"He's one of Ben's bros', he met him in the county jail. The guy has been fucked over by the state and the Feds, he done a lot of time."

"Is that right? He's done a lot of time? Where at?"

"He just paroled from Folsom a while back, he also served time on Alcatraz for bank robberies."

"Hey we got a real celebrity here! He's more than welcome to camp here with me."

Walking back to the truck Chris called, "Hey let's get that fucking truck unloaded, it's okay with John, Whitey's staying."

When the truck was being unloaded, Chris rolled a marijuana cigarette, while Valerie handed out the beer. Ben had more camping gear in the truck than Whitey realized until they started to unload it. There were four heavy blankets and pillows, Coleman stove, meat, bacon, eggs, and many more useful items besides the ice-chest. Lying next to the chest, still in a paper bag, were two bottles of Wild Turkey, this was not counting the wine and whiskey Whitey had purchased on the way.

He put his arm around Ben, and pressing him tightly in a bear hug, he said, "You're solid Ben, solid people, how can I repay you?"

"Hey when the time comes," Ben laughed, "I'll think of something." He finished off his beer, and yawned loudly. "Well we must be going Whitey, you're all set for now."

"Yeah, thanks again Ben. When do you think you'll be back?"

"I'll be up in a week or so, okay?"

It was shortly after 2:00 P.M. when the formalities of saying goodbye were over, and Ben and Chris departed. Immediately after

140

they had left John announced that he was driving to Tahoe City.

"I have to pick up my mail," he said, "and cash my check. You guys want to come along? Or would you like me to pick up something for you?"

"We'll go with you," Whitey replied. "Come on Val, you want to come?"

"Yes I do," she answered smiling.

While Ben and the group had been busy unloading the truck, Whitey slipped his automatic into his belt behind his back. He felt secure when he had his weapon near at hand.

After their arrival in Tahoe City, John drove to the Post Office where he picked up his mail, and while shopping at Lucky Market, he cashed his check. As John did his shopping, Whitey and Valerie browsed around the store, and after making a few purchases, they returned to the car, but John was not there yet. He arrived a few minutes later pushing a loaded shopping cart.

"Look I have to go to the Laundromat," he said smiling, "and do a few more things. You want to wait in the car, or walk around until I get back?"

"How long will you be gone?"

"About an hour."

"We'll walk around a bit, then meet you at the car, okay?"

Reaching into the back seat for his dirty laundry bag John replied, "That's fine with me. I'll see you here in about an hour."

After he had gone Whitey bought two ice cream cones from a street vendor, handing one to Valerie, they leisurely strolled to the nearby beach. Much to their surprise, there was no crowd. There were a few sunbathers and a number of people swimming, while on the sandy shore, two teenage girls and a boy played with a Frisbee. The warm afternoon sun was offset by the cool breeze drifting in from the lake. The atmosphere was very relaxing, time passed by quickly, and the hour was soon up.

On schedule they met John at the car, and as they were driving back to the camp, Whitey saw a huge dumpster on the roadside.

"Pull over John—pull over!" he shouted.

"What's wrong?" John yelled, as he pulled over and come to a halt.

"I thought I seen a mattress sticking out of that trash bin. Wait a minute while I check it out." Without waiting for a reply, Whitey ran to the dumpster. To his delight he found a surprisingly clean twin size mattress, and lying under it, folded neatly, was a fifteen by twenty foot black plastic tarpaulin.

Putting the vehicle in reverse, John backed up to the dumpster. Whitey tossed the plastic tarp in the back seat, then quickly slung the mattress across the roof, and as he tied it down with a piece of rope he shouted, "We'll sleep like a king now!"

As soon as they arrived at camp, Whitey grabbed the axe and began to clear an area for his makeshift tent. He selected a secluded spot away from the main part of the campsite. After he had a sizeable area cleared, he began to construct a frame out of tree limbs, tying them in place with strips of cloth. Once the framework was completed, he covered it with a section of the plastic tarp. There was enough left over to use as a floor. When this was done, he laid the mattress down, and with his sleeping-bag on top it was quite comfortable—as a matter of fact it was exceptionally comfortable, and Whitey was satisfied with his handiwork

"Okay Valerie," he cheered, "this is your new home!"

"Fantastic," she cried, "you've built me a mansion!"

In a bowing gesture Whitey said, "Thank you my lady! Now if you will, get the blankets and pillows and make up the bed; then help find a home for the rest of this stuff, okay?"

Without a word, she skipped off to take care of the chores while Whitey set up the Coleman stove. Also he hung up the pots and pans on nails he drove into a large pine tree.

The afternoon wore on, and the time was well after five o'clock. He gathered some wood and built a fire in a fireplace of rocks piled in a circle. John joined in with the wood-gathering, and soon they had a huge pile. Then he picked up the axe and proceeded to chop enough wood for the evening fire.

"What's for dinner Val? What're we gonna eat?" Whitey asked.

"I don't know, you guys want something quick, or do you want a proper meal?"

"Something quick is all right with me, how about you John?"

"Sounds good to me, I got an early date over in town."

"How about hot dogs and buns? Is that all right?" Val asked.

"Bring 'em on woman!"

Valerie went to the ice-chest to retrieve the food, while Whitey took his buck knife and cut three selected forked sticks from a nearby tree. Using logs for chairs, the three of them sat down and proceeded to roast their hot dogs and buns over the fire. The franks began to sizzle and swell, and each person cooked his to their own satisfaction, and to Whitey this meant almost black! With toasted buns, ketchup and mustard, it all tasted good when put together. After eating five of them he was ready for a beer. Valerie ate two hot dogs, while John ate three.

As he sipped his beer Whitey remarked, "This six thousand-foot altitude sure gives you an appetite." He laughed to himself as he thought about Alcatraz. And now here he was sixty-two hundred feet up in the mountains. His parole officer, and the police would have one hard time finding him away up here!

John stood up and stretched, "I hate to eat and run, but I'm a little late for my date, so I'm going to take off."

"That's cool man, but before you rush off, where's the best place to wash up? Are there any coves in that stream?"

"Yes there's a nice one about waist-deep. It's about twenty-five—thirty yards upstream, just follow that little path over by the creek. I'll be back late in the morning, if you hear any stumbling around it's only me!"

"Okay John, but I usually shoot first!"

As he walked to his car John laughed and called over his shoulder, "I sure hope you're kidding Whitey!"

A moment later the car started up, and in a cloud of dust disappeared down the trail. Right after John left Whitey stood up, stretched himself, walked to the tent, and returned with a bottle of Wild Turkey. Opening the cap he took a big drink, then offered it to Valerie.

"No thanks Whitey, the beer was enough for me."

"What do you say babe, shall we go upstream and see if we can find this cove and wash up? I feel kind of cruddy."

Valerie jumped up, "Oh let's go," she said eagerly. "I've been thinking of a bath all day."

After getting their towels, toilet articles, and clean underwear, they started upstream. The winding pathway was so heavily overgrown it shut out the late evening sun. It was like walking through a dark tunnel which opened up to a picturesque cove. It was magnificent with the evening sun reflecting off the flowing stream.

With a shout of joy they both ran toward a little sandy beach that ran at the water's edge. With no hesitation whatever Whitey yanked off his boots, followed by his clothes. While Valerie feeling a bit shy, undressed slowly.

"Come on girl, hurry, the creek'll go dry before you get undressed!" Whitey said as he picked up his toilet articles and walked out into the chilly water, and began brushing his teeth. After brushing thoroughly he plunged his head under water, and opened his mouth. Rinsing it out he raised his head, and then plunged it under once more.

Valerie had gotten undressed and was standing at the water's edge modestly holding a washcloth in front of her. When he saw her standing there holding the washcloth, she was a picture of innocent beauty.

"Come on girl, you're not going to get your teeth brushed standing there!" he said as he splashed her with water. With a girlish squeal she jumped back and cried, "Do that again Whitey Thompson and I'll tie your clothes in knots!"

"Come on," he beckoned, "I won't splash you again, honest!"

Holding both her arms out for balance, Valerie carefully lifted her right foot and touched the water with her big toe. Shocked by the chill, she immediately screamed, jerking her foot out of the icy water with such force that she landed on her bottom! It was a comical sight, and Whitey was unable to refrain from laughing.

As she sat there in the sand, Valerie was surprised and embarrassed by the incident until she heard Whitey's laughter, then she too began to laugh.

"It's not all that funny you know, the water is freezing," she said as she regained her feet.

"Only at first, once you're in it's okay. Just make the plunge babe, dive in!"

"Are you nuts?" she cried as she stood there shivering. Once more with caution, she stepped in, first one foot, then the other, until the water was up to her knees. Slowly she edged her way forward until she was close enough to Whitey who handed her the toothpaste. While she was brushing her teeth, he waded to shore for the washcloth and soap; returning to deeper water, he began to bathe.

When Valerie had finished brushing her teeth, she returned the articles to the shore. Then she hurried back to Whitey who had just finished scrubbing his hair. They began to wash one another, and for the next twenty minutes sounds of merriment and laughter could be heard echoing throughout the canyon.

The enjoyment and pleasure of one another was so electrifying that time flew. They were unaware of the sun setting beyond the mountains, and the darkness that was closing in. They were standing in the middle of the stream splashing each other, when Whitey suddenly stood motionless. It took a second or two before Valerie realized that he was no longer splashing.

"What's wrong Whitey?"

"Do you realize it's getting dark? We better get going before we can't find our way."

"Really? Do you think we could get lost?" she asked excitedly.

"Na, not with me! I got eyes of an owl!"

Getting a head start on Whitey, Valerie ran for the shore, calling out, "Come on owl-eyes, I'll race you to the clothes."

He ran after her in hot pursuit, but she reached the clothes first. Excitedly, like a child, she jumped up in the air yelling, "I won—I won!"

She wasn't the same girl of an hour ago as she jumped up and down exposing her nude body. She was a rare treat, and a picture of health. Hastily they dried themselves, donned their clothes, and hurried down the trail.

Back at the campsite it took but a few minutes for Whitey to rekindle the fire. None too soon as a chill drifted through the canyon on the evening breeze.

Moving nearer to the fire Valerie said, "Oooh, it's getting a little nippy, it's going to be cold tonight."

The dancing firelight revealed a smile on Whitey's face. "You won't be cold tonight babe, I'll keep you warm!"

"You better! Did you know there's still snow up in the high country? That's why the stream was so cold this evening."

"But it was clean and refreshing as only virgin water could be out the mountains."

"Why do you call it virgin water?"

144

"Because where we bathed it had never been touched by another human being."

"I never thought of water as a virgin, but I guess you're right."

"Why not? You're a virgin and never been touched," Whitey said with a laugh.

"I may be a virgin, but not as cold as that water!" she retorted.

"Let's see, today is July first. Remember this date Valerie, it's going down in history."

"History?" she exclaimed, "Why is it going down in history?"

With a cunning smile Whitey answered, "Because on the evening of July first at approximately ten P.M. Valerie Vagnault, at the tender age of fifteen, surrendered her maidenhead to Leon W. Thompson who had been after if for twenty years!"

"Twenty years!" she laughed, "I'm only fifteen, how could you have been after it for twenty years?"

"Easy, I knew you were coming!"

"Oh how romantic!" she said in a derisive voice.

Whitey chuckled, "Didn't you know I'm a romantic person?" Not waiting for a reply he continued, "I don't know about you babe, but I'm ready to crash."

Sitting next to Whitey on the log, Valerie did not reply as she watched the glowing glitter of the campfire. The gentle breeze like the tongue of a dragon, lashed hot flames out from the blazing logs. It sent off rays of infernal heat and the embers crackled and exploded shooting brilliantly distinguished sparks skyward like fireflies on a summer's night. She looked beyond the flickering light of the fire in the direction of the tent. She was disheartened, for she couldn't see past the fire's glow, she could only see within the circle of light. It was a ghostly haunting feeling. It was as if nothing existed outside the small circle except total darkness. With a slight shiver she turned to Whitey.

"What's wrong?" he asked with concern for he could see fear in her eyes.

"I don't know," she cried, "it's the darkness. We do exist, don't we Whitey?"

Taking her in his arms, he could feel her trembling. "Of course we do, whatever gave you the idea we didn't?"

"I don't know, I guess it's because we're so alone out here in the forest. It's so dark, I feel nothing exists beyond us. I was afraid, I wasn't even sure of us."

Stroking her head gently he reassured her that everything was all right. "It's only natural for you to feel this way," he whispered softly, "most everyone experiences some kind of fear of the dark."

"Are you afraid Whitey? Are you ever afraid of the dark?"

"Yeah sure, I'm sometimes afraid of it."

"Oh I don't believe you! You are just putting me on."

"No kidding, I'm afraid at times, but I keep it under control. If you

145

let it get out of hand, then you panic. Truthfully it's not the dark I'm afraid of, it's what may be lurking in the dark that I'm concerned with, and I don't mean animals! So you see you have nothing to fear up here in the mountains, there's no one around except you and me, and I don't think you have to fear me."

"Thank you Whitey. Thank you for being so understanding. I've never been in the mountains before, you know, being alone like we are."

"Well there's nothing to fear. By the way do you know where the Coleman lantern is?"

"Yes, I put it in the tent earlier, the fuel is behind the ice-chest."

Whitey retrieved the lantern, filled it with fuel and lighted it. The glow was fantastic lighting up the whole campsite, and at the edge of the clearing they could plainly see the tent.

Before retiring for the night they secured the camp. After making sure the fire was out they picked up the lantern, then arm in arm they walked to the tent. Once inside, using a piece of wire, Whitey hung the Coleman up to one of the tent supports. It threw off a comforting heat as the night air had a definite chill to it. The interior was well lighted, he rolled down the flap covering the tent entrance shutting out the darkness of Blackwood Canyon.

Valerie, who was sitting on the bed, commented, "Whitey this is cozy, it really is. I'm going to love it here."

"I don't think you'll be sleeping for quite a while!" Whitey returned with a laugh.

Pulling off his boots he sat beside her, and as he reached for the fifth of whiskey he said, "Hey this is all right babe. I wonder what the poor people are doing!" Laughing he opened the bottle and took a long drink, then paused long enough to tell Valerie to light a cigarette for him. While she was doing this, he took another long haul on the bottle, then offered her a drink.

"I'd like it mixed with something. I don't like it straight."

Handing her the bottle he told her, "Hold this, I'll be right back." He was out of the tent before she could answer. A moment later she heard him cussing as he stumbled barefooted in the dark. She was just about to untie the lantern to go and rescue him, when suddenly the ice-chest came sliding through the entrance with Whitey right behind it.

After securing the tent flap, he said, "Okay gal, the bar is open. What would you like for your chaser? Beer, wine, Pepsi, or water?"

"Pepsi, Whitey, easy on the whiskey and heavy on the Pepsi," she laughed with delight.

"Coming up miss, one Turkey Pepsi fizzle!" He opened up the cola and after pouring a generous amount into a tin cup, he added some whiskey. Then with a smile, he used his finger to stir the contents.

Removing his finger from the cup, he licked it, "Never fear girl, it's clean!"

"Yes it is now!"

Handing her the drink he said, "If there were any germs on my finger the whiskey would of killed them!"

"What'll we drink to?"

"I don't know Val, why don't we just drink to tonight and us."

"Okay Whitey, here's to you and me, and tonight."

"To you and me babe," Whitey returned.

He took a long drink from the bottle, Valerie put the cup to her lips, took one sip and began choking. Whitey quickly grabbed the cup from her hand, at the same time slapping her back.

"Did it go down the wrong pipe?" he asked.

"No your pound—your." Valerie lost her speech from choking that turned to laughter as she tried to pull back from Whitey's hand. While she was trying to get herself under control, Whitey started to pour more whiskey in her cup. Still laughing she tried to signal him to stop pouring. Whitey shrugged his shoulders and took a big drink himself.

Gaining her composure, Valerie, said, "God, I don't want to go through that again! I thought you would never stop pounding on me!"

"I was just trying to help you catch your breath."

"Yes you did, but when you started to pour more whiskey in my cup, you got me to laughing."

"Why's that? What's so funny about pouring whiskey?"

"It was the damn whiskey that got me choking in the first place, it was too strong."

"I can fix that!" Whitey laughed, and drank all but a third of the contents, replenishing it with Pepsi, and handed it back to her. After she took a sip he asked her if the drink was better.

"Just right, that was perfect. Can I have another one?"

As the evening wore on, they were both feeling high spirited. Especially Whitey, until he finally said, "I think I had enough for one night, how about you babe?"

"Yes I've had plenty, but I would like a cigarette."

"Okay, we'll each have a cigarette, and that's *it*, it's almost ten o'clock."

"So what's with ten o'clock?"

"Have you forgotten already? That's when you go into the history books!"

They laughed together as they smoked their cigarettes. When they finished, Whitey began to unbutton her blouse. After removing the garment he placed his hand gently on her breast, then slowly she stretched out on the bed. He eased his right leg over her mid-section, lying down with half his body weight on her. Still caressing her breast with one hand, he reached for the other. She moaned softly as his fingers made contact with her breast, and an ecstatic feeling magnified a tremble of joy throughout her body. Her breathing increased with the movement of his fingers. Releasing his hold on her

147

he stood up and started to remove his clothes.

"Wait a minute Whitey. Could you, I mean, would you turn off the lantern after you take off your clothes? I would feel better if I took my clothes off in the dark."

"Yeah, okay," Whitey said.

He removed his clothes, and watched Valerie who was laying on her back. She was extremely breathtaking with her black silken hair lying framed around her lovely face. She still maintained her shyness with a somewhat flushed look about her. She was a real gem.

While he was undressing, she lay there watching him; the anticipation of what was to come was overwhelming she could hardly refrain from hurling herself at him. She wanted him—she wanted him right now!

Before removing his undershorts, Whitey had a long drink from the Wild Turkey bottle. Valerie reached for her Pepsi mix and took a small sip, then another one before setting it down. Whitey drank once more from the bottle, then pulled off his shorts, and as he reached to extinguish the lantern, his penis was standing erect. Before the Coleman lantern went completely out it began to flicker, allowing Whitey ample time to lie down beside Valerie before darkness enveloped them.

Valerie sighed. "Whitey it was wonderful. I love you so much."

Whitey did not reply as he was totally exhausted as he laid there enjoying the warmth and comfort of her nude body. She was such a treasure, he realized he was truly in love with this girl, and he wished he could let her know how he felt. He wanted her, he wanted her for always, to share his life, but he knew that this could not be. He mustn't let it happen for nothing could come of it. It was inevitable that one day soon he must answer for his parole violation, and in his attempt to stay free he might have to kill a lawman, or be killed. He had no future to offer, and because of his love for her he must soon send her away. He held her closely as he tried to conceal the tear rolling off his chin.

Lying beneath him, her body suddenly tightened as she shifted her head in the darkness to look at his face. In a soft voice she whispered, "Whitey, Whitey Thompson I do believe you're crying!"

He was angry at himself for showing emotion, and trying to contain his feelings, he said, "I'm not crying, what's wrong with you girl? Don't you know the difference between sweat and tears?"

"Oh I didn't think of that! But you're right, it is warm in here!" With affection, she put her arms around him and held him tightly. She knew they were tears, but said no more about it. She really loved him for making her first act of love, a memorable one.

The next morning Whitey woke to the smell of bacon, eggs, and coffee. Valerie was already up and cooking breakfast. Lighting up a cigarette, he slipped on his undershorts and boots. Then he picked

148

up his toothbrush and towel, and hurried out of the tent down to the stream.

Hearing his footsteps, Valerie turned from her cooking, and saw Whitey walking toward the stream. She called out, "Hey owl-eyes, where you going dressed like that?"

"Good morning Val, make my eggs over easy will ya?"

"As you order sir!"

Later in the day while Whitey and Valerie were walking near the stream, they discovered an old Indian oven built around the turn of the century. It was made out of concrete and red clay bricks, and was constructed in the shape of an igloo. It had a vent hole in the back. The diameter of the oven was about twelve feet. There was no door on the front, just a square opening for tending the fire. Once the coals were hot, you pushed them to either side of the interior, leaving room in the center for cooking and baking. Whitey became quite an expert in using the Indian oven. He made many a dinner in this fashion, such as turkey, roast beef, bread, pizza, cakes, and pies.

Just beyond the oven Whitey carved his name Lee (short for Leon) with the date '71 on a number of trees. He wanted to leave his mark for posterity!

CHAPTER 25.

Celebrating the Fourth of July, Whitey and Valerie spent the day at Tahoe City Beach. It was a day of activities, boat racing, swimming, blanket parties, and picnics. In the evening the holiday was topped off with a brilliant fireworks display.

One week after the Fourth Valerie was preparing breakfast, while Whitey sat next to the fire with a hungry look in his eyes.

"I hope you're hungry," she said as she handed him a stack of hotcakes.

"Does a bear shit in the woods? Just watch me girl!"

Valerie loved preparing food for Whitey, he was not a finicky eater. He was thankful for whatever was placed in front of him, and at the present moment he was doing the hotcakes justice!

While they were eating their breakfast, John Langley approached the fire. "Good morning folks," he greeted them with a smile. "Those hotcakes sure smell good!"

"Would you like some John?" Valerie asked him. "There's plenty of batter."

"I'd love some, thank you." Then turning to Whitey he continued, "What's happening with Ben and Chris? When are they coming up?"

"They'll be up 'most any day now," Whitey replied, "it's hard to tell just when they'll come rolling in. Shit, you know how Ben is."

"Here you are John," Valerie said as she handed him a plateful of hotcakes. Then turning to Whitey she said, "What makes a scooter-tramp the way he is? You, know most of them think they're all bad, they act like they are a little Caesar or something, and God's gift to women!"

"No, that isn't so, they're just looking for recognition. They want to be recognized as someone, that's all."

"But why Whitey? I don't understand."

"Most bike riders who become scooter-tramps felt rejected as a kid. They didn't belong or identify with anyone until they discovered that a motorcycle means recognition. People take notice of a rider wearing dirty Levi's, leathers, a ring in his ear, long hair and beard flapping in the breeze. He feels important, and before long he's a prospect for a motorcycle gang. . . ."

"I think I understand it now," Valerie cut in. "Once he's accepted n the club he feels important because he can identify with them, ight?"

"That's right, he feels he's someone to reckon with for he's a 'ighteous scooter-tramp, he is recognized as such, that's about all here is to it Val."

"Except for one thing," John volunteered. "They are loyal to those vithin the group, and they consider themselves brothers."

"Speaking of brothers, listen," Whitey said cocking his head to one side.

The sound of motorcycles could be heard roaring throughout the canyon. A few moments later Ben and his gang came riding into camp. With a cloud of dust, Ben came to a stop within a few feet of Whitey. As he cut the ignition he shouted, "Hey bro what it is?"

Whitey nodded his head at Ben, "Looks like you have the whole gang with you. What's happening?"

"Nothing much," Ben replied, "just making a little run. Thought ve'd bring you some supplies. Your P.O. has been by three or four imes. As you know, he's put out a statewide warrant on you."

"So what else is new?"

"That's about it bro. We can't stay long, we're on our way to Carson City. There's supposed to be a party in the desert, we're gonna check it out. By the way, how's Val been treating you?"

Whitey placed his arm around her and said to Ben, "She's been vonderful, I don't know what I'll do without her."

"What do you mean, do without me?" She cried, "I'm not going anywhere, I'm staying right here with you."

Looking directly into her eyes Whitey whispered softly, "It's for the best Val. You know it and I know it, so please don't make it hard on me."

"I'm not trying to make it hard on you, I just don't want to leave," she pleaded.

"I'm sorry babe you have to go." Turning to Ben he asked, "Will you ake her to Sacramento?"

"Yeah Whitey, I'll take her, but we're on our way to. . . ."

"Please Whitey don't make me go," Valerie pleaded again.

Ignoring her, Ben continued, "Like I was trying to say, we're on our vay to this gig in Carson, I'll pick her up on my way back tomorrow norning. How's that sound?"

"That's fine," Whitey told him, then turning to Valerie he asked, "Is hat all right with you Val?"

Sadly she replied, "Since I don't have a choice, I guess it has to be."

"That's settled then. By the way, I'll be coming into Sac in a couple of weeks."

"Is that wise?" Ben asked.

Before Whitey could reply Chris interrupted, "Are you crazy man? You'll get your ass busted!"

151

"Shit, no one will recognize me."

This might be true, for Whitey no longer resembled the well-groomed man who left Folsom Prison six short months ago. He was now dressed in oily leather trousers, leather vest, and a pair of grimy black boots. His upper body was tanned to a golden brown. He still maintained the solid square shoulders of a machine-gunner, his body bearing scars of old wounds, a torso that still showed strong muscles under the newly acquired tan. His beard and long streaming blond hair bleached white by the Tahoe sun gave the impression of a beast no longer with the swiftness of youth, but with the cunning of years, and a vigor enough to kill.

"You know I believe you're right." Ben said, "You don't look like Whitey Thompson anymore, you look more like a wild mountain man! You don't happen to know when you'll come down do you Whitey? If you knew the exact day, I'd come pick you up."

"Thanks Ben, but when I do come, I'll hitchhike."

"Hitchhike? Now that *is* taking a chance!" Chris exclaimed.

"No, I don't think so, my P.O. believes I left Sacramento, he won't be expecting me to return, at least not so soon, and they won't be looking for a hitchhiker."

"That makes sense, but why do you want to go to Sacramento in the first place?" Chris asked.

"Change in routine, you know, some excitement, besides I'd like to come see you guys, okay?"

"You're crazy Whitey, but whatever," Chris said with a shrug of the shoulders.

"We'll put out the mat for you Whitey," Ben cut in, "but right now I want to get going to Carson City. We'll see you in the morning."

"Right, but don't get busted in Carson!"

Valerie and Whitey stood watching as the gang started their motorcycles, and a moment later they vanished in a cloud of dust.

"Well that's that," Whitey remarked.""How about a beer John, can you stand one?"

"Yeah, I can do with one," John answered as he glanced at Valerie then he went on, "Are you really going to send Val off tomorrow? It's going to really get lonely for you around this camp."

With a ray of hope Valerie looked at Whitey, but her hopes vanished when he replied, "Yeah, I made up my mind, I think it's for the best. She leaves tomorrow."

"Whitey, I have an idea," Valerie said hopefully, "let me stay until you go to Sacramento, we can hitchhike together."

"I'm sorry Val, I don't care how lonely it gets around this camp, my mind is made up."

"Like I said Whitey, it's going to be lonely when Valerie is gone. You see in a few days I'll probably be gone too. I think I'll be staying at my old lady's place. I'm going to ask her today. She has been hinting for me to move in with her."

"That's great John," Whitey commented, "I hate to see you go."

Shortly after noon John drove into Tahoe City leaving Valerie and Whitey alone in the camp. Whitey began drinking and smoking marijuana, while Valerie put away the new supplies. For the remainder of the day there was very little communication between them, until after they made love that night.

It was very dark in the tent. Whitey had to fumble around for the whiskey bottle, after finding it he took a long drink before lighting a cigarette. Valerie lay still watching the movement of his lighted cigarette, and the glow of his face each time he took a drag.

"Whitey," she whispered. "I want to tell you something. I don't want you to think I'm just a sentimental girl, but no matter what happens, I love you. I always will, and I'm thankful for the moments I had with you. I'll treasure them."

Whitey was touched. He took her in his arms and whispered, "No Val, if anyone should be thankful, it is I who should be thanking you."

Valerie did not reply. Whitey thought she had fallen asleep until he heard her whisper, "Goodnight Whitey, I love you."

The darkness concealed the tears rolling down her face.

Early the following morning while Valerie was preparing breakfast, Ben and his gang rode into camp.

"You guys are just in time to eat," Whitey welcomed.

"Thanks Whitey," Ben said, "But we ate already at South Shore." Turning to Valerie Ben continued, "You about ready to go Val? We want to get going."

"Yes I'm ready just as soon as I finish eating."

While waiting for Valerie to eat, Ben tied her small traveling bag to the handlebars of his motorcycle.

As soon as breakfast was over Valerie cleaned up the dishes and tidied the camp. When she was ready to leave, she faced Whitey and said, "Well I guess this is goodbye for now."

Whitey cupped her face in his hands and kissed her gently on the nose, lips, and then took her in his arms holding her close.

"Take good care of yourself, and I'll see you in a few weeks," he said with a trace of sadness.

"Will you be all right Whitey? You won't feel too lonely will you?" she asked with concern.

"Shit no, ha-ha-ha," Whitey tried to fake a laugh, "I'll be down in a few weeks."

"Are you sure you'll be all right Whitey? I don't want you to be too lonely," she insisted.

"Hell no, I won't be lonely. Go on get the hell out of here, I'll be all right."

Ben fired up his motorcycle, and one by one the rest of the gang

153

also started their engines. Whitey kissed Valerie again; then she climbed up behind Ben.

"Please be careful Whitey," she said, "And take good care of yourself."

"Play it cool bro," Ben shouted over the roar of his motor, "I'll see you in Sac, take care."

Whitey nodded his head in acknowledgment as Ben revved up the engine, dumped the clutch, and took off in a cloud of dust. One after the other the rest of the bikers, including Chris, took off after him.

Whitey stood there transfixed watching them depart. The last rider disappeared down the winding path, and all that remained were clouds of dust. Before the dust settled a feeling of utter loneliness engulfed him. He reached for his cigarettes in his vest pocket, and after lighting one he went to his tent. Seconds later he reappeared with a bottle of whiskey. He held it to his lips, and drank fast and furious. Some of the contents spilled and ran down his chin into his beard. After he had drunk his fill, he held the bottle over his head then suddenly dropped to both knees, and looking skyward he began to scream, "Fuck you—fuck you—fuck you!"

The sound of the hysterical cries could be head echoing throughout Blackwood Canyon. Still looking at the sky he screamed until he could no longer utter a sound. As he knelt there drained, and totally exhausted, he remembered another time, many years ago as a child of thirteen. He had cried out to the heavens for help, and then, like now, no one seemed to have heard.

Slowly he got to his feet, after lighting another cigarette, and with bottle in hand, he went back to the tent. Inside it seemed as though Valerie was still there, for he could smell her scent as he lay down on the sleeping-bag. He felt like screaming again. Instead he had another long drink of Wild Turkey, and finished the cigarette. He rolled himself several marijuana joints and began smoking them one after the other. He was feeling very gloomy, and the weed had no effect. If there had been someone there to take his mind off Valerie it would have helped. He took another long drink from the bottle. With tears streaming down his face, he eventually fell into a troubled sleep.

He dreamed of Alcatraz, and the friends he had made there, long ago buddies of the past. It was a strange world that he had drifted back into. The surroundings were very familiar to him. He recognized the cold steel bars of Broadway, and as he turned the corner into Times Square he thought he heard a familiar voice calling out to him "Hey Killer, Killer Whitey. It's been a long time where have you been?"

Pulling up short in his tracks, he spun around facing the direction the voice came from. Cocking one ear he strained listening for the voice. Nothing could be heard, the Cell Block echoed with loneliness and a shiver went down his spine as the quiet of the prison engulfed him.

154

Once more he cocked his ear, and then shouted at the top of his voice, "Longo, is that you Longo? Lou, Lou. Hey buddies it's me Whitey. Where you guys? Johnny, Johnny House. Come on pal it's me, for Christ's sakes where are you guys?"

The Cell House was cold and damp, but Whitey did not feel it. Perspiration was flowing freely from his pores as he took off running across Times Square. He charged around the corner of Michigan Avenue, and skidded to a halt. He looked up to the second tier, and his eyes focussed on his old cell B-204. He glanced toward the cubicles to the right and left of his cell. They were empty. He started to run along the flats, and each cell he went by was empty. He ran faster and faster, and was at the verge of panic when he realized every cell in the prison was empty. His friends were all gone; nothing was left but the cold steel, and concrete. Yes they were all gone now, nothing was left for Whitey. Nothing but loneliness, and memories of four long years as a prisoner on Alcatraz.

CHAPTER 26.

It was mid afternoon, Whitey was awakened by the sound of a twig snapping. The animal instinct of survival was once more in play. Slowly he slid his hand under his pillow and pulled out the automatic. He made his way quietly to the entrance flap and eased it open. There was no one in sight, but he was not satisfied. He was sure the sound he had heard was made by an intruder. Not knowing what to expect, he held the weapon at the ready and cautiously stepped outside. With the cunning of a cat, he scanned the territory but found nothing amiss. Slowly he edged his way around the tent and in doing so he had a clear view of the campsite. Standing next to the fireplace Was a young hippie couple with packs on their backs. Whitey was taking no chances. He watched them remove their gear and as they did so he reached down and retrieved a machete from a tree stump. From the angle in which the couple was standing, they were unable to see Whitey creeping up behind them. He had an automatic in one hand and the machete in the other. When he was within ten feet of his prey he spoke in a cold commanding voice. "Hold it pal, hold it right there!"

The couple froze in their tracks, not daring to move.

"Turn around slowly," Whitey ordered.

Doing what they were told, and with caution, they turned slowly to face Whitey. They were terrified at the sight of his countenance and the weapons he held.

"Who are you people?" Whitey asked.

"Look, we're from Oregon and. . . ."

"I asked who are you fucking people?" Whitey cut him off raising the machete as if to strike.

"My—my name is William, William P. Mumford, and this is. . . ."

"Let her tell me," Whitey shouted.

"My name if Flo Harrison," the girl said with a nervous smile.

"Just what the hell do you people think you're doing snooping around my camp?"

"I'm sorry we gave you the impression of snooping, but really we weren't . . ."

156

"Bullshit! If you weren't snooping, then what the hell were you doing?"

"Look mister, would you let me explain?" Flo asked.

Whitey turned his attention to the girl, and for the first time realized how attractive she was. "Yeah go ahead."

"You see when we stumbled into your camp we were looking for a place to camp ourselves." Pointing at Longley's tent she continued, "When we saw your tent there we looked inside to see if anyone was o home. No one was . . . "

"My friend lives there," Whitey interrupted. "My tent is over beyond he clearing."

"Oh I'm sorry, we didn't see your tent, we thought no one was ere, so we decided to take off our packs and wait until the owner eturned, that's the truth." She waited for Whitey's reply, but he said othing, just stood staring at her.

"Honest," she began to plead, "we really are looking for a place to amp. We got our own food and the necessities, don't you believe ne?"

"I don't know yet. Where do you come from?"

"Oregon."

"Washington." They both answered simultaneously.

In a cold voice Whitey said, "Make up your minds, which is it? Oregon or Washington?"

"It's Oregon and Washington," William hurriedly answered. "You see I come from Oregon, and Flo comes from Washington, and we're spending the. . . ."

"Just shut the fuck up!" Whitey shouted in hostile rage.

The couple was startled and confused at Whitey's outburst, and stepped backwards.

"I don't know but you guys may be the fuckin' narcs. Toss me your wallet," he ordered Mumford with a motion of the gun.

"I'm no narcotic agent," William protested.

Whitey raised the automatic a trifle, and aimed it point blank at Mumford's head. In a chilling voice he said, "Toss me your fucking wallet, or I can take it off your dead body, it's your choice."

William's hand started for his rear pants pocket.

Whitey stepped forward. Gesturing with the machete he said, Easy Mumford, you better be reaching for your wallet."

William noted the danger sign. He carefully removed his billfold nd tossed it to Whitey's feet. Without taking his attention off the ouple, Whitey drove the machete into the ground, and picked up the wallet. Inside he found an ID card containing the name of William P. Mumford, Portland, Oregon. Inspecting further he found a cash sum f $400, and $1,500 in Travelers checks.

"Well it looks like your name is Mumford, what do they call you?"

"My friends call me Bill."

"Okay Bill," Whitey said in a more friendly tone, "you got a nice wad of money here, more than you need don't you think?"

William was nervous, very nervous and replied, "Yes, yes sure I got more than I need. Go ahead take a hundred or two, I mean it, go ahead."

Whitey looked from Mumford to the money and back again; then without touching a cent, he closed the billfold, and handed it back to him. Then he turned to the girl.

"Your name is Flo Harrison?" he asked.

"Yes it is," she produced her Washington state driver's license. Whitey examined it, and returned it to her. In a more friendly tone he said, "Flo Harrison, a lovely name for a pretty girl."

She smiled and said softly, "Thank you."

Flo was surprised at the change of events. At first she thought this rough-talking man was going to kill them, and now he sounded almost poetic. The tone of his voice was sweet and gentle when he pronounced her name.

Whitey pulled the machete out of the ground, and as he did so he tucked the automatic behind his belt. "I guess you people are okay," he said, "but what's the deal? Are you making it with each other, or are you just traveling buddies?"

"That's what I was trying to tell you before. We are just two friends traveling together," William answered.

"What brings you here?"

"Well we've never been to Lake Tahoe, so we decided to stop here for a few days, then we are off to San Francisco. Have you ever been there?"

"Yeah I've been there once or twice," Whitey replied with an ironic smile.

"Do tell us about it," Flo said, "we have never been there."

"There's nothing really to tell; to me it's just another city. You'll have to see it for yourselves."

"You sound like you don't much care for San Francisco," William said.

"I guess the city is all right if you're a rich tourist, but when you're a nobody it don't mean all that much." Addressing himself to Flo he continued, "To hell with San Francisco, what I want to know is, do you know how to cook?"

"Yes sure, I'm a great cook!" she replied. "But I've never done to much over an open fire."

"That don't matter. You want to try cooking something?"

"I'd love to! Does that mean Bill and I can stay?"

"Yeah why not? I don't own the forest."

William laughed and said, "Just a few minutes ago I thought you did!"

Whitey smiled, "When you live out here in the boonies you can't be too careful."

"How long have you camped here?"

158

"I've been here a few weeks. So what do you say Flo? You want to cook us something. There's meat and stuff in the ice-chest. Also there's canned food and whatever in those boxes over there, help yourself."

Whitey had a variety of food to choose from. But Flo put together a simple meal. She heated up canned beans and hot dogs in a pot. It was consumed as though it was a meal cooked for a king.

Later that evening John returned to camp, and after he was introduced to the new arrivals, Whitey called him aside.

"I hope you don't mind these people bedding down here."

"No Whitey, not at all. What's been happening while I've been gone?"

"Nothing much. Where have you been? Over to your chick's pad? I thought you were gonna move in with her."

"I was, but her fucking parents came up from the City. They are going to be here a whole month. That means I can't move in until the first of August."

"Ah what a tough break, but piss on it man, let's party! You want to get down with us?"

"Na, I'm tired Whitey, I'm gonna crash."

"Come on John, this guy's got some good acid."

"I can dig it man, but I'm beat, I got to get some sleep. Score a couple of hits for later."

John went into his tent, while Whitey opened a fifth of whiskey and the party began!

William had fifty tabs of Purple Haze concealed in his backpack. He offered one to Whitey and Flo, and took one himself. The trio chased the tabs down with whiskey.

It wasn't long before the acid had its effect and they were riding high! William was feeling generous and gave Whitey ten hits of the Purple Haze. Whitey immediately added this to his ever-growing stash. He was accumulating quite a variety of different drugs. Including Purple Haze, he had a gram and a half of hashish, four lids of high-grade marijuana, five hits of windowpane, six tabs of Orange Sunshine, and an ounce of Chocolate Mescaline. With his supply continuously being replenished, Whitey Was constantly loaded throughout the summer, and on this particular night he was feeling no pain!

The party lasted until the wee hours of morning. William was the first to crawl into his sleeping-bag, leaving Flo and Whitey alone by the fire.

Shortly after this Whitey announced, "I don't know about you Flo, but I'm ready to crash."

"Me too. Where shall I put my sleeping-bag?"

Ignoring her question Whitey asked, "Is it true there is really nothing between you and Bill?"

Looking him straight in the eye she replied, "It's true, there is absolutely nothing between us, we're just good friends."

"Well in that case you can throw your sleeping-bag in my tent!"

Flo replied by picking up her backpack and walking into his tent. They were to sleep together for the following two nights.

On the fourth day Flo and William continued their journey to San Francisco. Before leaving, William handed Whitey a hundred dollars, and insisted that he accept it. Then Flo embraced him with a farewell kiss. There was a feeling of sadness. Four days' prior, their meeting with Whitey had been a fearful one, and now seventy-two hours later, they were reluctant to leave.

Flo Harrison and William P. Mumford were the first of many travelers to stay at Whitey's camp. There were a number of campsites throughout Blackwood Canyon, and the nearest one to Whitey was approximately a quarter of a mile away. In time he became acquainted with all of them. Every night without fail, there would be a party in progress, and on most occasions it was held at Whitey's camp.

Young people would come in off the highway driving all types of vehicles. There were cars, vans, pickup trucks, motorcycles, and occasional converted bus. Then there were the unfortunate ones who relied solely on their thumbs. They would come, spend a few days, then be on their way. They came from all over the U.S.A. and as far as Alaska, and Canada. When they would leave, the ones who could afford it, would give Whitey food, drugs, or money. Seldom did he have to purchase anything.

During the summer of '71 Blackwood Canyon became known by the hippies as "Whitey's Canyon." They had heard the word along the road that Whitey's Canyon was a good place to party or crash. At any given night it was not unusual to fine fifteen or twenty traveling hippies in his camp. A number of them would party all night, while others would nod and fall asleep. The next morning the campsite would look like a battlefield with bodies lying all over the ground! The warmth of the morning sun, and the aroma of fresh coffee always brought them to life!

One morning toward the end of July John and Whitey were having their morning coffee.

"I'll be moving in with my chick next week," John announced.

"Shit I got to get my ass to Sacramento next week. I told Ben I was coming down."

"So why don't you head down?"

"I can't, I might not get back until after you've gone. Shit I don't want this camp left alone!"

John finished drinking his coffee and threw the tin cup into a bucket of soapy water. Then reaching toward Whitey he gave him an affectionate slap on the back and said, "Hell, go down to Sac Whitey, I'll stay here until you get back okay?"

"Ah shit John, I don't want to hold you up from moving in with your chick."

"It's okay Whitey, what the hell, I don't mind waiting a few more days, besides I'll be fucking her either way, so go ahead on!"

"Hey thanks John, I really appreciate it man. Say when are you gonna bring your chick around? I never met her. I don't even know her name."

"Her name is Donna, and I'm not going to let you meet her."

"Why?" Whitey was stunned.

"Why? Because for the past five weeks you've been fucking every chick that comes into this camp!" John replied with a laugh.

CHAPTER 27.

Whitey was lucky, he caught a direct ride to Sacramento, and arrived at Ben's home shortly before noon. He was about to knock on the front door when suddenly it opened.

"You finally made it down," Ben greeted him with a bear-hug, and before Whitey could answer he continued, "When did you leave Tahoe? Did you have any trouble coming down?"

"No problems, I left around nine this morning. Where's everybody?"

"They're out in the back yard, come on."

Whitey could hear the stereo blaring out back, and as he entered the yard he received a joyous reception.

"Hey Whitey, how did you get down here? About time you showed up, let's party man!"

"Break out the booze, Whitey's here!"

"How's it going man? Good to see you." They shouted in unison.

They were all here, Chris, W.A., Fuzzface, and many more of his friends. Hands were reaching out from all directions. After the welcome ceremonies were over, someone thrust a bottle of whiskey into his hand. He took a stiff drink, and passed the bottle on. At that moment the back door swung open and Debbie and Sharon came charging through. Whitey hardly had time enough to recover from the previous onslaught of welcoming friends, when the two girls hurled themselves at him, knocking him to the ground.

"Whitey," they shouted, "it's great to see you."

"Yeah me too. Damnit, let me up off the ground. Help!"

"Rape! They're raping Whitey!" W.A. shouted with a laugh.

Joining in, Ben shouted, "Come on girls, compose yourselves! Let that man up!"

Regaining his feet, Whitey gave Sharon a hug and kiss, then taking Debbie by the arm he said, "We'll be right back." Hurriedly he led Debbie around to the side of the clubhouse, and immediately took her in his arms.

"Oooooh you're looking good Deb, real good." Before she could reply, he pressed his lips to hers in a lingering kiss. A few moments later they released each other, and sat down on the grass. They both started to talk at the same time.

"Okay Debbie you go first."

"Okay, I'll go first then. Whitey don't you think it's a little dangerous coming to Sac?"

"No more than being anywhere else. What's happening, how come you're not working?"

"It's my day off, but I work tomorrow."

"Good, then you don't have to rush off home. What's with Valerie? How's she doing?"

"She's doing fine, how come you ran her back from Tahoe? She wanted to stay with you."

"Yeah I know Deb, believe me, I didn't want to send her back, but I had to."

"You had to? I don't understand. Tell me the truth Whitey."

"Damnit all Debbie, you want the truth? Well here it is. I was getting hung up on her, I mean really hung up, so I sent her away."

"That's what I don't understand. If you're falling in love with her, why make her go?"

"Look Deb, don't be so naive, she's your fifteen-year-old sister we're talking about."

"I don't know what you mean. Why do you say I'm naive?"

"Look damnit. You and I, we think a lot of each other, right?"

"Yes we do."

"Okay, you and I could be lovers making it together, and one day I get busted or killed, what would happen then?"

"I'd feel awful about it."

"Sure you would, but by the same token you would pick yourself back up, and go on with your life. But now Valerie, a fifteen-year-old girl, how would it affect her?"

"Pretty bad. When she first came home, she felt awful because you sent her away. She's very much in love with you."

"That's just my point Deb, she's in love with me now, or she thinks she is. Shit, I'm the first guy she made it with. Don't you see, I had to break if off with her to give her a chance to find out that she can receive the same pleasure from another man, a younger man, someone with a future?"

Before replying, Debbie put her arms around Whitey and held him close. "I understand now. I think you're wonderful Whitey, just wonderful. Do you plan to see her?"

"No, I don't think so, I think it would be wise not to let her know I'm in town."

"Yes I think you're right. How long do you plan on staying?"

"Just a few days I guess."

"Well be careful Whitey," Debbie cautioned.

From the front of the clubhouse Ben called, "Hey Whitey, break it up out there, and come here a minute."

"I'll be right there," Whitey answered. He gave Debbie a quick kiss and hurried around the building. Ben, Chris, and W.A. were standing

163

in front of the clubhouse doorway. Ben was the first to speak, "Come on inside Whitey, we have something for you."

"For me? Wait a minute Ben," Whitey hesitated in front of the door. "I don't like this." He was suspicious that something was amiss because of the mischievous looks on their faces.

"Go inside," Ben ordered.

Moving back a step, Whitey said with a laugh, "You're crazy Ben! You guys aren't pulling any shit on me."

Handing him a bottle of whiskey Chris intervened, "It's no joke man. It's something for you."

"That's right," W.A. cut in. "We're not trying to set you up. You know better than that!"

Laughing at W.A.'s remark, Whitey took a long pull on the bottle and said, "Okay to hell with it, let's get this show on the road!" Then boldly walked into the clubhouse.

"Okay Whitey," Ben shouted, "don't bogarde the whiskey, pass it around!" Then he turned to Sharon, "Hey babe, go on to the house and get that box."

Sharon returned with a large box which she handed to Whitey. Not knowing what to expect, he cautiously opened it. He was surprised and happy to find it contained a new pair of leather pants and vest. He was overwhelmed with the gift, and with misty eyes he stood there staring at the present. For Ben and the rest of the group, to see the expression on Whitey's face, was thanks enough.

"Put 'em on! Put 'em on!" everyone shouted.

Whitey pulled off his boots, then with shrieks and shrills from the girls, he removed his clothes and donned the leathers. The fit was perfect.

Whitey felt emotional, his thoughts flashed back to another time when he was on Alcatraz. His friend Johnny House had given him an unexpected birthday present. Now he was choked up and speechless, but they could see gratitude in his eyes.

"This goes with the leathers Whitey, put it on."

The expression on Whitey's face was one of disbelief. Ben handed him a highly polished belt made from a motorcycle primary chain. As he put it around his waist he said, "I don't know what to say other than I appreciate these gifts very much. I'm touched man, I really am."

Thrusting a bottle of Wild Turkey into Whitey's hand W.A. shouted in his ear, "Drink up you old cad, we're gonna get fucked up tonight!"

W.A. was a blond, blue-eyed youngster of eighteen years. At one hundred and forty-five pounds, and five foot six, he stood as tall as any member of the gang. He was a one-man demolition squad when it came to throwing punches! After first meeting Whitey, and learning about his background, W.A. had great admiration and affection for him.

Whitey took a long drink from the bottle, and as soon as he passed

164

it on, W.A. handed him another one, "Drink up Whitey, we're going to a party tonight!" he shouted.

"That's right," Ben affirmed, "we're going to a party, we'll leave right after dark. Are you coming with us Whitey?"

"Does a bear shit in the woods?"

"I'm coming with you," Debbie told Whitey.

"No way!" Ben shouted. "No chicks are coming, that goes for all of you!"

Turning to Debbie Whitey asked, "Will you be here when I come back?"

"Yes I'll probably be here, depends on when you get back. But if I don't see you, I'll be by after work tomorrow night. I get off at eleven, so it will be around eleven-twenty before I get here."

Chris was standing in the clubhouse doorway, and called out to Whitey, "You want to get down? Then come on in here."

They all sat down at the table, Chris produced two grams of hashish wrapped up in aluminum foil.

"This is elephant-ear hash, really good stuff, after a few hits you'll be walking on a cloud!"

The hash pipe was passed around the table, followed by beer, wine and whiskey.

"Where the hell's the Tank? How come he ain't here?" Whitey asked. The noise was so loud no one heard him.

The Tank was a two hundred and seventy-pound, six foot five scooter-tramp. He wore a German swastika ring in his left ear, and had long back hair with a bushy beard. He had the appearance of a formidable eighteenth century sea-pirate.

"Goddamn it where's the Tank?" Whitey shouted again.

"He's in jail," Jay answered. "You were at Tahoe Whitey, so I guess you didn't hear about the Tank. He punched a judge out, a Municipal Court judge."

"You mean he punched a judge in a court room?" Whitey asked.

"No, the Tank and a few other guys were partying with a couple of chicks in Ansel Hoffman Park. They were sprawled out on the grass, you know, drinking a little wine, beer, and smoking a little pot. Anyways this dude tells the Tank and his friends to stop making a spectacle of themselves or he will call the law and have them arrested. You know the Tank, it's a mistake to threaten him!"

"Is that when he hit him?"

"No not just yet. The Tank was on the grass dry-fucking some chick. He jumped up and said to the dude, 'Just who the fuck do you think you are? You redneck bastard!' " That's when the dude told the Tank he was a court judge, and he wanted them to vacate the premises immediately. Like a roaring bear, that's when the Tank punched the judge out. At that moment a squad car was passing by and caught the scene, and radioed for help. It took five pigs to haul the Tank off to the slammer! His buddies got thirty days for disorderly conduct. And the Tank got a year, he'll be out around December if he don't fuck up and lose his good-time."

As Jay recounted the story, Whitey could visualize the whole episode, and see the Tank knocking out the judge!

Sitting there so engrossed in storytelling, drinking, smoking pot and hash, they were unaware of the warm summer afternoon slipping by, until darkness began to settle in.

To freshen up, they all dove into the swimming pool. From the water Ben called out to Sharon, "Hey babe, is the food ready yet?"

"I'm setting the table now, come and get it!" she replied.

Sharon had set the clubhouse table with paper plates, and plastic utensils. In the center of the table she placed a large platter of spaghetti that disappeared within minutes.

With the meal over, the men were ready to go to the party. Whitey, Ben, Chris, and W.A. rode in Jay's car, while the rest of the men rode their motorcycles. When they arrived, the party was already in full-swing. A few members of Ben's gang were already there, the Duck, Jim, Curly, Fuzzface, and many more. Beer, wine, and whiskey were flowing. Marijuana, Reds, Angel Dust, and hashish were being used freely. Several guys in the crowd were getting down with stronger stuff.

Whitey browsed from one room to another, occasionally stopping to chat before moving on. In the living room he saw a pretty young girl sitting alone. He decided to introduce himself. As he walked toward her, she sat there watching him approach.

"Hi there, how come you're sitting here alone?" he asked.

She didn't reply. She sat there looking at him coldly. Whitey wrapped his arms around his chest and said, "Wow, it suddenly got chilly in here! Is that it? Your tongue is frozen, you can't talk?"

Her expression remained the same, if anything it was colder.

"Come on, you're not that cold are you? Won't you even say hello? Wait a minute, I know what's wrong, you don't like my approach? That must be it. Okay, I'll tell you what, I'm gonna make a new approach. It's my famous 'You can't resist me' approach!" Taking a few backward steps from her, he got down on his hands and knees and said, "Hi there, I know why you are sitting here alone. Your tongue is frozen. Here take a swig of this," he held out a bottle of Wild Turkey, "it will thaw you out. Once you're thawed out, I'm sure you will be grateful and want to reward me. So what do you say? Do you want to remain an icicle? Or can I thaw you out so we can become friends?"

Her expression slowly changed and a sparkle appeared in her eyes.

"I see a twinkle in your eyes, you're beginning to warm up, come on now smile—smile!"

She could not contain herself and a smile appeared on her face.

"I knew it! I knew you didn't want to be an icicle! I saved your life, you owe me a reward!"

166

"What kind of reward did you have in mind?" she asked.

"From a gorgeous looking girl like you, there's only one reward!"

"Yes, well you can just forget it Whitey Thompson, I know who you are."

He was surprised at her knowing his name, "How did you know who I was?" he asked.

"You know Mike don't you? Mike Gaines?"

"Yeah sure, he rides with Ben and his gang. What's he to you?"

"I'm his sister, Marsha."

"His sister?" Whitey was surprised. "You're Mike Gaines sister?"

"That's right, I drove him here tonight."

"Yeah I know he's here, but tell me, if you knew who I was, why were you so cold to me?"

"I wasn't just cold with you, I was mad period. I don't like these kind of parties."

"Then what the hell you doing here?"

"My brother made me drive him here because his junky motorcycle broke down, and I have to stay and drive him home."

"Well now that you're here, why not enjoy yourself. Would you like a drink?"

"Yes, but I don't like it straight from a bottle."

"Wait here a moment, I'll get some coke and mix you. . . ."

There was a sudden rush for the door.

"What's happening?" Whitey shouted as everyone charged out of the house. "Stay here Marsha, I'll be right back."

Whitey pushed his way toward the exit. As he neared the doorway, he recognized a voice coming from outside. It was Ben shouting, "Don't let them bastards get away, stop 'em!" The urgency of the cry sent Whitey charging through the doorway. He knocked people aside as he made his way to the front yard. He was just in time to see two guys running. They were pursued by Ben who was brandishing a knife in his hand. Ben saw Whitey rushing out of the house and called to him, "Stop 'em Whitey! Stop 'em, don't let them make it to their car!"

Whitey immediately took off after the fleeing men. They were running toward a parked 1969 Mustang. They arrived at the car a few seconds before Whitey, and quickly jumped into the vehicle locking the doors behind them. The man behind the wheel frantically searched his pockets for the keys, finding them, he hastily sought out the right one for the ignition. Still in hot pursuit, Ben was a short distance from the car screaming at Whitey, "Don't let them get that car started. Don't let 'em!"

In a split second with violent precision, Whitey unwound the primary chain from his waist, and in one swift motion, swung it across the windshield with a splintering crash.

Desperately, the man tried to fit the key into the ignition, and in his haste dropped them to the floorboard, losing them in the darkness. With blinding fury, Whitey swung the chain again and again, and each shattering blow exploded chips of glass in the interior of the car. The victims screamed frantically as they tried to cover their faces with their hands.

Suddenly the door on the right side of the car swung open. A man jumped out attempting to escape, but to no avail. Whitey's talented chain caught him across the shoulder blades ripping his flesh open, and knocking him to the ground. Repeatedly the sound of the cruel chain could be heard as it swished through the night air, followed by it's sickening impact.

Ben was on the other side waiting for the driver to exit the car. When the door opened, he sunk the blade of his buck-knife into the man's shoulder, and sliced him down the back. The crowd watched Ben as he grabbed his victim by the hair. He dragged him around to the other side of the car, and deposited him alongside the other man. Lying there on the ground both of them begged for mercy.

"Ben, please don't kill us man, we were just shooting off our mouth. Just give us a little time, we'll pay up."

"What makes you think you deserve any time? Your debt was due tonight."

"I know Ben, we fucked up and it won't happen again. Just give us three days and we'll pay in full, honest."

"All right you sad sons of bitches I'm giving you three days. Pay up or you'll get more of the same, only next time you won't be so lucky. Now get in your crate, and get the hell out of here."

The two men dragged themselves to their feet, staggered to their car and drove away.

"All right you guys bust it up," Ben shouted, "go back to the party." Turning to Whitey he said, "You were heavy Bro, how can I thank you?"

"You already have Ben, you know that."

Impulsively Ben threw his arms around him and said, "Thanks anyway."

As they walked toward the house to rejoin the party Ben said, "Do you want to know what that was all about Whitey?"

"Not really Ben, you was after them guys, that's all I have to know."

"I been dealing with them guys for six months, I never had no problems, they always paid on time. Last week I fronted some stuff, they were supposed to pay me tonight, but instead they thought they could strong-arm me out of it, you know the rest. But anyway thanks once again bro."

"Hey anytime Ben. Right now I got a chick waiting for me, you know Marsha don't you?"

"Yeah she's a fox, but you won't get nowhere with her, she's down on scooter-tramps."

The two drug dealers were furious as they drove away. Although they were severely injured, they did not seek medical attention. Instead they went straight home where they picked up two twelve-gage shotguns. They were on their way back to gun down Ben and Whitey.

"The sons of bitches," the driver said. "They won't be expecting us to come back Art. We'll blow their fucking heads off! Open me a can of beer."

Art put his hand to the floorboard and fished up a six-pack of beer. Opening a can he handed it to his partner. "Here you go Roger, how you feeling?"

"My back's killing me man, I don't know if I can make it."

"I'm not in much better shape, but I'll drive if you want me to."

At that moment there was the sound of a siren and flashing red lights.

"Shit, it's the law!" Roger exclaimed. "We're dead men with these stolen shotguns!"

Roger pulled the car over and stopped with the police right behind him.

Walking up to the driver's side shining his flashlight on the occupants he exclaimed, "What the hell have we got here?"

One look at the men and the condition of their car, the officer immediately pulled out his service revolver. He aimed it point blank at the driver's head while keeping an eye on the passenger. He ordered them to get out of the car on the left side. Roger obeyed the officer's command, and Art, with a struggle, scooted his body over behind the steering wheel. Then he pivoted himself around and placed both feet on the ground. He did not realize how much blood he had lost until he attempted to stand up. Both legs collapsed under him, causing him to sprawl out on the ground. Roger, who had also lost a considerable amount of blood, collapsed up against the fender of the car.

The officer held his revolver pointed at the fallen men, and took a backward step. He called to his backup in the squad car. "Call an ambulance Pete, these men are hurt."

The injured men were taken to the County Hospital, and admitted for treatment. After a four-day recovery they were transferred to the county jail, and booked. The charges ranged from drunk driving, to stolen property. Once the booking was completed, the two men were taken up to the fourth floor, and placed in Four North Five, a twelve-man cell.

A committee of seven prisoners were facing Art and Roger as they entered the cell. A short stocky greasy-looking man was seated at one of the two tables playing solitaire. Looking up from his game at the new arrivals, he said, "Well looky here! You guys look like you been dragged through a meat grinder."

"They sure do!" someone else agreed

"What happened?" the greasy man asked. "You guys fall off a freight train?"

Both Art and Roger were feeling somewhat apprehensive amongst the rough-looking men, especially the huge one sitting alone in a corner.

"Speak up," the greasy man said again, "what happened to you guys?"

To boost his courage Roger looked to Art. Using a tough voice he said, "We got fucked over by a gang of scooter-tramps. The bastards owed us some money on a deal, when we demanded our bread they jumped us."

The huge man in the corner bellowed. "Did you know these guys?"

"Yeah," Art cut in. "One was a dude called Ben Vakno. When we asked him to pay up he pulled a knife. Then some old blond-headed dude appeared out of nowhere swinging a chain. Before we knew it the whole gang was on us, but you can bet your ass we're gonna get each and every one of them bastards when we get out!"

"How you gonna do that?" the huge bear-like man asked.

Roger spoke in a slick voice, "We'll play it cool, we'll get them one at a time starting with Ben Vakno. Then we'll get that old blond-headed dude. We're gonna cave their fucking heads in!"

"I guess in time you're gonna get every member of that gang, right?"

Roger and Art were now feeling at ease, and felt they had established themselves as tough.

"You can count on it pal," Art replied in a surly voice.

Slowly the big man got to his feet. For a moment he stood there stretching his enormous arms and flexing his gigantic muscles. Simulating the cracking of a head he pounded his ham-like fist into his other hand. Towering over the other prisoners, he resembled a Kodiak bear at bay.

"If you punks want to get each member of that gang, then you can start with me. I'm called the Tank, I'm a member of that gang!"

At the party, Whitey found Marsha waiting for him, and after fixing her a drink, he sat down beside her.

"I don't like these kind of parties," she said, "they always end up in a fight. What happened out there?"

"Just a little mix-up," Whitey replied. "It's all settled now, nothing to worry about."

Marsha looked directly into Whitey's eyes, and said, "I'm curious, just how old are you?"

Without the slightest hesitation he answered, "Forty-eight, how old are you?"

"Forty-eight! I don't believe you're that old! You sure don't look it."

"Forget the flattery, I asked you how old you were."

"I'm twenty-two."

170

"Hey Whitey," Ben interrupted, "we're getting out of here."

Turning from Marsha, Whitey saw Ben standing by the front door. "Give me a minute Ben. I'll be right with you." Turning back to Marsha he said, "Look I have to rush off. I'd like to keep in touch, could I have your phone number?"

"Okay, if you promise not to give it out to anyone."

Reaching into his wallet, Whitey pulled out his address book, handing it to her he said, "Would you write it down for me?"

She complied and handed the book back.

"Thanks Marsha. I'll give you a call." With a quick kiss on the cheek he was gone.

The following morning found Whitey in a restless sleep on Ben's living room couch. Shortly after 9:00 A.M.. Sharon shook him awake.

"Whitey wake up, Debbie's on the phone."

"Ah shit! Tell her to call back, tell her I'm asleep!"

"She can't call back, she's on her way to work. Come on, get up and answer the phone."

Sharon made a hasty retreat to the kitchen. Whitey, mumbling to himself, and in the nude, crawled out from under the covers and made his way to the hall telephone.

"Whitey I'm sorry I couldn't wait for you last night. How did the party go? Did you have a good time?"

"Terrific—terrific. Is that why you called?"

"No, I wanted to find out if you are okay, and to let you know I'll see you after work tonight, I'll be there after five, all right?"

"Okay, I'll see ya then, bye."

After hanging up the phone Whitey washed up, got dressed, and went out to the kitchen. Sharon had made coffee and offered him a cup.

"How about some bacon and eggs to go along with your coffee?" she asked.

"Yeah that would be fine thank you. Where is Ben at? Is he still asleep?"

"No he's out to the clubhouse with Chris and the others."

Whitey finished his breakfast, and after thanking Sharon he went out to the clubhouse. A number of the guys were still asleep, but Ben, Chris and W.A. were sitting at the table nursing a fifth of whiskey.

For the next half hour they sat there smoking marijuana and drinking Wild Turkey. When the rest of the bikers finally woke up, they found Whitey, Ben, Chris, and W.A. well on their way to getting loaded. They too joined in, and the drinking continued throughout the day.

When Debbie arrived she found Whitey drunk lying alongside the swimming pool. With the aid of Sharon, she managed to get him into a clubhouse bed, where he remained for the rest of the night.

CHAPTER 28.

Ten A.M. the following morning when Whitey got up, there was no one else in the club room. He went into the house, and after looking in each room he realized no one was home. He felt hazy from the debauchery of the previous day, and thought some cold water would bring him around. While splashing water on his face he tried to recollect the evening before, but could not remember, and was unaware of Debbie having been there.

He began to feel despondent and angry with himself, "Goddamn it all, where the hell did everyone go? I don't even have a fuckin' cigarette."

With a feeling of animosity, he stomped out of the front door, slamming it behind him, and walked up Eagle Road to San Juan. At the junction he turned right, and walking on the shoulder of the road, he proceeded to the next crosswalk. Above the noise of the heavy morning traffic, his attention was drawn to the sound of a vehicle pulling up behind him. Without looking back his instinct told him it was the law. Subconsciously his right hand went for the automatic, but was dismayed when he suddenly remembered leaving it behind in the clubhouse. Holding his composure, he kept on walking until a commanding voice ordered him to halt. Slowly, ever so slowly, Whitey turned his head and looked over his shoulder. Just beyond the opened door of a patrol car, stood a deputy sheriff aiming his service revolver point blank at him.

"Get your hands above your head and turn around," the officer ordered.

With hands raised, he turned to face the lawman who stepped out from behind the patrol car door. The deputy was a youngster in his early twenties. He wore the look of an eager and impatient man, anxious for advancement.

"Walk in front of the car," he commanded.

Not responding and in the same tone of voice, Whitey asked, "What the hell's your trip? What's the harassment for?"

"Never mind. Just do as I say, and get in front of the car—NOW!"

Reluctantly Whitey complied as he walked to within a foot of the car's grill.

"Okay punk, just place your hands on the hood of the car and

172

spread your legs."

"What the fuck for? What's the beef?"

"Make it easy on yourself and do what you're told."

Driving down the opposite side of San Juan, Ben and Sharon were heading home.

"Watch it Ben there's a patrol car—my God that's Whitey! That pig is busting Whitey!" Sharon cried.

Glancing across the road, Ben saw Whitey spreadeagled in front of the patrol car. Without the slightest hesitation he turned the steering wheel sending the pickup truck careening into a Safeway store parking lot. As he jumped out of the cab he yelled at Sharon, "Get behind the wheel and keep the motor running!"

Without waiting for a reply he dashed across the parking lot to the shoulder of San Juan. With no time to spare, Ben boldly ran across the road dodging speeding vehicles from both directions. Once safely across, he slowed to a fast walk and came up behind the officer. The lawman had returned his gun to his holster before attempting to shake Whitey down.

"Remove your wallet, take everything out of your pockets."

Whitey did not respond to the command, he remained leaning up against the car grill with his hands on the hood.

"Did you hear what I said?" the deputy shouted angrily. "Unload your pockets."

With contempt in his eyes, Whitey looked over his shoulders at the lawman. "If you want my pockets unloaded, do it yourself pig!"

The officer took a step forward, "Why you punk, I'm going to. . . ."

He did not finish for the sound of movement from behind interrupted him. Ben had crept up within striking distance when the deputy glanced round.

Thinking quickly Ben said, "You need some help officer? What's he done?"

The sudden appearance of Ben startled the deputy and he angrily replied, "This is a police matter, just stand clear."

With an apologetic smile Ben said, "I'm sorry officer." He turned around as if to walk away. The deputy focussed his attention back to Whitey, while Ben, in a rotating manner, spun on his heel. Using his fist he struck the young patrolman a sickening blow behind the head. At the precise second of impact, Whitey whirled around, and with full force drove his right elbow into the victim's sola plexus. The officer fell to the ground unconscious. Whitey made a grab for his gun, and once he had it in his possession, he held it to the deputy's head. "Call me a punk will ya? You're gonna die pig!"

"No!" Ben screamed. "Don't kill him, let's get out of here before people realize what's happening."

For a tense moment Whitey held the gun at the officer's head.

"Don't do it. It's not worth it," Ben pleaded.

173

Undecided, Whitey hesitated a moment longer, then savagely kicked the deputy, driving the toe of his boot into the small of his back. He quickly pulled a handkerchief from his pocket, and after wiping the revolver free of fingerprints, he threw it in the brush. Rapidly he wiped off the area on the hood where he had placed his hands.

The traffic on San Juan was moving along briskly. Except for a few, no one seemed to notice the drama taking place. The ones that did, slowed their vehicles down, then without stopping, quickly sped away.

Above the noise of the traffic Ben shouted, "Let's get the hell out of here!"

"Okay, split! I'll see you at home," Whitey yelled.

Again dodging vehicles, Ben ran across to the Safeway parking lot. Whitey dashed into the brush, jumped over a fence and cut through a backyard over to the next street. He paused long enough to cock his ear to listen for the sound of wailing sirens—none could be heard.

CHAPTER 29.

Breathing heavily, Whitey hurried down a side street to another road that took him back to San Juan. He was a mile from where the incident had occurred. Even with the distance of a mile he did not feel safe and thought the wisest thing to do was to get off the streets. Keeping a sharp lookout for patrol cars, he started to walk south on San Juan. Eventually he made his way to a bar and grill called "Blinkies." Once inside he bought a pack of cigarettes, and then sat at a corner table to relax with a beer. Halfway through the second glass he phoned Vakno's home. After the sixth ring he was about to hang up when Ben's sister Jackie answered.

"Hi Jackie, it's me, Whitey. Is Ben there?"

"No, he dropped Sharon off a while ago, and then took off."

"Put Sharon on the phone then."

He sat there impatiently waiting until Sharon came to the phone. "Hello Whitey."

"Hi Sharon. What's happening?" he asked anxiously.

"Nothing so far. Ben went out for a look-see, he should be. . . .wait a minute he's pulling into the yard now, hold on."

While waiting Whitey quickly lit a cigarette. "Come on Ben," he impatiently mumbled to himself.

Whitey's concentration was so intense that Ben's voice startled him. "Whitey, where you calling from?"

"I'm here at Blinkies," Whitey replied.

"Sit tight, order me a beer, I'll be there in five minutes."

In less than five minutes Ben walked into the bar accompanied by Chris, W.A., and Jay. Whitey ordered a round of beer. Nothing was said until they were served.

"What's the plan Whitey?" Ben asked.

"I don't know," he replied, "right now I'm so fucking tired I can't think straight."

"Why don't you go back to my place?" Chris suggested.

"That's a good idea. Then I can head for Tahoe, but I need a ride."

"Don't worry about that, Chris or I will drive you up there," Ben assured him.

"No, I don't think it would be wise to ride with any of you. I think it would be smart if I stood clear of you guys for a while, especially here in town."

"You're right," W.A. agreed, "But you can't hitchhike. How'll you get there?"

"Why did that pig stop you Whitey?" Jay asked.

"I guess I just looked suspicious!"

"Suspicious hell Whitey! That punk was out to bust anyone when he spotted you. The fool almost got himself killed," Ben said with a laugh.

"Hell if I were a cop and seen any of you bums walking down the street I'd stop you too, only I would shoot first before I. . . ."

"Shut up Jay," W.A. interrupted, "your bullshit isn't helping Whitey get out of town."

"Wait a minute," Whitey said, "I think I have it, I'll call Mike's sister, she'll drive me up."

"You're crazy man!" Jay said with contempt. "That stuck-up bitch wouldn't drive you to the hospital if you were bleeding to death!"

Whitey dialed her number. Marsha answered on the second ring, "Hello?"

"Hello Marsha. This is Whitey, you know, Whitey Thompson."

"Hi there. I was wondering if you would call."

"Well to be honest with you I wasn't going to call so soon. What I mean is. . . ."

"Oh no? When were you going to call?"

"I was going to call you sometime next week, but an emergency came up."

Marsha gave a short laugh and said, "I'm curious as to the emergency that prompted you into this call."

"I can't tell you Marsha, but will you do me a favor?"

"Yes, I'll do you a favor, but first I want to know what the emergency is."

"Look I can't tell you over the phone. Right now I need a ride to Auburn. Will you come pick me up?"

"Okay, if that's the favor just tell me where you are, and I'll pick you up."

"I'm at Blinkies. Do you know where it is?"

"Good God Blinkies! I've never been in there, but I know where it is. I'll be there in fifteen minutes."

Whitey hung up the phone and returned to the table.

"Is she gonna take you or not?" Ben asked.

"Yeah, she's on her way over," Whitey replied.

"How the hell did you do it?" Jay asked incredulously. "I never got to first base with that bitch!"

"You couldn't get to first base with an ape!" W.A. chided.

"You'll be needing this," Ben whispered to Whitey as he opened his vest revealing Whitey's automatic.

Ben slipped the weapon to Whitey who quickly concealed it inside his leather vest.

"Well you're all set then, we might just as well take off," Ben announced.

Chris walked toward the exit, and turned to Whitey, "Whitey, tell Libby I'm staying at Ben's tonight. I'll be home sometime tomorrow."

Alone at the table Whitey finished his beer. He ordered a refill, and sat there drinking with an eye on the entrance. Occasionally the door would open, but each time it did, Whitey was disappointed to see a patron coming into the bar. He looked at the Lucky Lager clock hanging on the wall. Twenty minutes had elapsed; he became somewhat worried until he realized it was the peek hour, twelve o'clock. Marsha had probably been delayed in heavy lunchtime traffic. He was just about to order another beer when she came through the doorway. She saw Whitey and walked toward him smiling. He jumped up from the table and hurried across the room.

"Where's your car parked?" he asked.

"Out front," she replied.

He took her by the arm and ushered her out the door. Parked at the curb was a snappy cream colored 1970 Volkswagen. Moments later they were traveling north on Highway 80 with Marsha behind the wheel.

"Okay Whitey, you promised to tell me what the emergency was. I'm waiting."

Turning his head, Whitey looked at her, "Do you really want to know?"

"Yes," she said, "I want to know, and you promised to tell me."

He recounted the events of the morning, and why he must leave town. When he finished explaining, he was surprised at how well Marsha had taken the news. She remained very calm, and showed no signs of surprise at his confrontation with the law.

"What is it with you Marsha? You're taking what I said very calmly, how come?"

"Well, when you said an emergency, and you had to leave town in a hurry, I figured it was something like this."

"Why are you helping me then if you know I'm a fuckup?"

"I don't really know, I guess it's because you're different from the rest. You fascinate me, besides, I like you."

Twenty minutes later they arrived at Chris's place. Whitey got out of the car while Marsha remained behind the wheel. She held her hand out to him and he gripped it warmly, "I want to thank you Marsha, I really appreciate your help. You got me out of a tight spot, and I'll never forget it."

Before she could reply he grasped her by the shoulders, and twisting her around in the seat, he kissed her. As their lips parted, she said, "I better be going Whitey."

She started the car, and as she drove away Whitey called out to her, "I'll see ya Marsha."

She waved her hand out the window and drove out of sight.

177

Whitey walked around the side of the house and was warmly welcomed by the Airedale, Tail.

"Hi there Tail, you haven't forgotten me have you? Where's Libby, is she home?"

"Yes I'm here," a voice called from within the house. Libby had been watching out the window and had seen Whitey's arrival.

Whitey went to the back door, and entered the house. Libby stood waiting for him and said, "Who's the chick? Why didn't she come in?"

"Her name is Marsha Gaines, she's Mike Gaines sister, you know him don't you?"

"Yes I do, but I never knew he had a sister. Don't I get a hug or something? I haven't seen you for a while."

Whitey took her in his arms, and just before kissing her he said, "Are you happy to see me?"

"You know I am, but I wish I knew when Chris was coming back."

"You don't have to worry about Chris, he won't be back till tomorrow sometime. He told me to tell you he's staying over at Ben's. As for me, I'll be staying here tonight, but the first thing in the morning I'll be hitchhiking to Tahoe."

"That's great, I'll fix you a nice spaghetti dinner, would you like that?"

"Sounds good Lib, but right now I'm going to take a bath and get me some sleep. I'm one tired son of a bitch!"

"I'll have dinner ready for you when you wake up."

"Boy that was some spaghetti Lib," Whitey said as he wiped his face on a napkin.

Beaming with pleasure Libby replied, "I'm glad you liked it Whitey. It's nice cooking for someone who appreciates it."

"It was delicious Lib. I wish I had you in camp, you could do all my cooking."

"Is that all, just the cooking? Nothing else?"

With a mischievous look in his eye he returned, "We'll just play that by ear."

"All kidding aside, I wish I could go with you Whitey. I would love to be going any place just to get out of here for a while. I'm bored stiff always being left here alone."

"It's a shame Lib, a chick of your age should be out enjoying life."

"Tell that to Chris!"

Whitey got up from the table, stretched his arms and retrieved a beer from the refrigerator. He went to the front room to drink it while Libby cleared the table.

At eleven o'clock Whitey retired to the bedroom while Libby took a bath. After undressing he turned out the light, and laid across the bed waiting in anticipation for what was to come. A few moments passed before she came into the bedroom and laid her nude body down next to him. The fragrant aroma of her freshly bathed body enhanced his already aroused sexual desires. Breathing deeply he laid there quietly until he felt her hand rest on his chest. His flesh began to quiver delightfully as her fingers brushed gently across his nipples. She turned on her side and extended her leg over his torso At the same time she pressed her face against his chest. Her protruding tongue began to explore his body as it worked its way down to his navel.

Whitey could contain himself no longer. He quickly rolled her over on her back, and let nature take its course.

The next morning shortly after six, Whitey bid farewell. After hitching two successful rides, he was back in Blackwood Canyon at 10:45 A.M.. He walked into camp to find John and a girl sitting beside the fire eating breakfast.

Looking up from his meal, John was surprised to see Whitey, "That was a short trip, I thought you were going to be gone for at least a week."

"Yeah well something came up, I came back early. Who's the foxy dish?"

"This is Donna. Donna I've told you about Whitey. This is him—Whitey Thompson."

Donna stood up and held out her hand, "Hello Whitey, I'm happy to meet you."

Ignoring her hand, Whitey pulled her into his arms and just before kissing her he said, "When it comes to pretty women, handshakes are old fashioned, a hug and a kiss are much better!"

Donna smiled, "John told me about you, but neglected to tell me about your greetings!"

"I'm just being me, I hope I didn't offend you," he said with a shrug.

"No, I thought it was rather pleasant, it's nice meeting you. Would you like me to cook you some bacon and eggs?"

"Yeah that'll be great." Turning to John he said, "What's been happening? Anything exciting?"

"No nothing much, right after you left a couple of hippies came in camp and stayed all night. By their actions I think the law was after them. They kept asking if the cops ever came out here."

"Here you go Whitey, fresh off the fire, bacon and eggs," Donna said as she set the plate next to him on a log.

Thanking her he hungrily began to eat, and in between mouthfuls he spoke to John, "I guess you'll be moving soon, huh?"

"Now you're back I'll move today. By the way how would you like to have a Wolf Hybrid? A friend of mine has one and he has to get rid of him. He would be great company for you out here.
What do you say Whitey do you want him? If you do he's over at Kings Beach."

"Yeah, sure I'd like to have him .I'll go over there right now."

"The guy who owns him is called Mark Olsen. I'll write down his address. The best time to see him is before five, he works nights in one of the casinos."

John wrote down the address, and as he handed it to Whitey he said, "Just tell Mark I sent you over, okay?"

"All right John. I expect you'll be gone by the time I get back."

"Yes, I'm not taking much except for my personal gear. I'll leave everything else behind."

"Thanks John. I'm gonna split now. Drop in once in a while, you too, Donna."

"I'll be by in a week or two, but I'm not bringing Donna."

"How come?"

"I told you the reason before you went to Sacramento!" John said with a grin.

CHAPTER 30.

Kings Beach is on the north shore of Lake Tahoe. Whitey had no difficulty in locating Olsen's residence.

Ringing the door bell, he patiently waited for someone to answer. A moment passed before a young man opened the door. "Yes what can I do for you?" he asked.

"Are you Mark Olsen? A friend of mine, John Longley, said you had a Wolf Hybrid you wanted to get rid of."

"Yes that's right, he's out back, I'll show him to you."

As they walked around the side of the house Mark commented, "I don't want to let the animal go, but my landlord is bitching. I have to get rid of it or move out, also my wife is afraid of it."

The backyard was fenced in. As they walked up to the gate, Whitey heard a deep growl. Just beyond the gate, chained to the corner of the house, was a magnificent Wolf Hybrid.

"You better wait here a moment he gets a little mean, he even growls at me occasionally."

"I'd more than growl if you had me on the end of that goddamn chain!"

Olsen was taken aback, and stood there a moment looking at Whitey, then he explained, "My wife insists I keep him on a chain. She's afraid of him."

"Shit there's nothing to be afraid of," Whitey said as he opened the gate and walked in. "You just got to understand the way of Wolves."

He walked toward the Wolf Dog and sat within distance of the chain.

Staying just beyond the gate Mark said, "I hope you know what you're doing."

Whitey paid no attention to the remark. He held out his hand and began talking to the animal. "Come on big fellow—come on boy, let's be friends."

There was no doubt about the Wolf in this animal, and his size was unbelievable. At nine months old he was well on his way to being 150 lbs.

"Come on fellow," Whitey coaxed.

Cautiously the animal moved toward him, smelled his hand and

181

then took a backward step. This action was repeated several times, then he began to wag his tail.

Mark stood there amazed at what he had seen, then he realized that the man sitting on the ground was as wild-looking as the Wolf Dog!

"Well it looks like you found a friend. Do you want him?"

"Yeah I'll take him, what's his name?"

"The truth of the matter is, I never gave him a name, a friend of mine gave him to me, and he's been out here in the yard ever since."

"How about shots? Has he had any?"

"Yes, he's had all his shots."

Turning to the animal Whitey removed the chain, "Good, I'll just get going then."

"Hold on a second, I'll be right out," Mark said and disappeared into the house. He reappeared with a leather collar and lead which he handed to Whitey.

Whitey slipped the collar over the dog's head. With a nod of thanks he went out the gate, and started walking toward the highway.

The first car to pass by was a Highway Patrol, but he took no notice of the man and dog walking along the road. Three more cars passed in succession. Then a Chevy van stopped to give him a ride as far as Tahoe City, where he once again stuck out his thumb.

It was twenty minutes before he caught the next ride. A young girl driving a Jeep picked him up. Before climbing in Whitey noticed the vehicle had Massachusetts license plates.

Smiling at Whitey the girl said, "Hi there, where are you heading?"

"Are you going anywhere near Blackwood Canyon?" he asked.

"Yes, I live just beyond the turnoff in Homewood."

"Far out! Can you drop me off at the turnoff?"

"Are you camping out there?"

"Yeah," he replied glancing sideways at the girl. She was pleasing to the eye with her long wheaten hair cascading in the breeze.

"I notice your Jeep has Massachusetts plates," Whitey stated.

"Yes I come from Massachusetts, Cape Cod to be exact. I'm spending the summer here."

"Are you vacationing alone, or is someone with you?"

"No, I'm here all by myself, but I work, it's more or less a vacation job. What do you do?"

The unexpected question caught Whitey off guard. "Ah—at the moment I'm between jobs!"

"So you're camping in between jobs, how nice for you. By the way my name is Joan Tyrrell," she said holding out her hand.

"Glad to meet you Joan. My name's Whitey Thompson."

Taking her eyes off the road, she quickly glanced at him, causing the Jeep to sway.

"Hey watch it girl! You're gonna pile us up!"

Her attention immediately went back to the road. "Sorry about

182

nat! But I've heard of you."

"It must have been something bad, you almost drove off the road!"

"No, nothing bad," she said laughing. "I met a few hippies who mentioned something about Whitey's Canyon, and the wild parties they had with you! They said you're a far out guy."

"That's quite a compliment, thank you. You mentioned a job, where do you work?"

"Sunnyside Inn."

"I know the Inn, it's a high class joint ain't it?"

"Yes it is rather exclusive, I don't really need to work, but I do it because I love meeting people. You know your long hair and beard reminds me of a mountain man."

As they traveled along, she often shifted her eyes to observe Whitey.

"My God is that a chain you have around your waist?"

"Yeah, it's a primary chain. You said you don't really have to work, how come?"

"Like I told you, I come from Cape Cod. My family's well-off and don't need to work. But I enjoy working at the resort, to me it's fun."

"What about Cape Cod? When do you have to go back?"

"I leave right after Labor Day, my parents are expecting me by the tenth."

"We're coming to the turnoff, you can let me off just around the corner."

"I'm in no hurry, I'll drive you to your camp if you like."

"That'll be fine, I sure appreciate it."

Approaching the turnoff Joan applied the brakes slowing their speed. She turned off the highway onto Blackwood Canyon Road. As she did so the Wolf Dog lost his balance pressing against Whitey.

"Easy fellow, you'll soon get used to riding."

"That's an impressive looking dog. Hasn't he done much riding?"

"I doubt it, he spent all his life on the end of a chain. He was just given to me. The guy who had him kept him on a chain in the back-yard. He's just a pup."

"Just a pup!" Joan exclaimed, "God he looks like a huge Wolf."

"You guessed it, he's three quarter Wolf."

"What's his name?"

"He hasn't got one yet. You got any ideas?"

"How about Tosh? I've always liked that name."

"Tosh it is! Slow down—slow down, our turnoff's right here."

Joan quickly applied the brakes, causing the Jeep to skid on the gravel right past the turnoff.

"I better pay more attention to my driving," she said as she backed up the vehicle.

"It wasn't your fault, I'm the one that's supposed to be showing you the way."

They both laughed as she turned off the road and drove the short

183

distance to the camp.

"Oh it's just beautiful here, look at those tall pines, and thos
mountains, they are so picturesque. You picked a lovely campsite.

As soon as the Jeep stopped Tosh jumped out and disappeare
into the woods.

"Would you like something to drink Joan? A cup of coffee o
something?"

"A cup of coffee would do just fine."

Whitey picked up a bucket and went to the creek for some watei
As he dipped the bucket into the flowing stream, Tosh came dashin
out of the woods charging through the water, splashing Whitey as h
passed.

Laughing Joan shouted to Whitey, "Looks like he's enjoying hi
new home!"

After the coffee was made, they sat on a log together, and th
conversation continued.

"You must be from the east Whitey, you don't sound like ;
Californian."

"I originally come from New Haven, Connecticut. I haven't beei
back there since the war."

"The war? You mean World War II? How old are you?"

With a smile Whitey replied, "I hope I don't shock you, but I'n
forty-eight."

"Well you could have fooled me, I thought you were in your earl
thirties."

"Thank you, flattery will get you everywhere! How old are you?"

"Seeing as you were honest in telling me your true age, I'll tell yoi
mine, I'm an old lady of twenty-one! How old did you think I wa:
Thirty?"

Whitey laughed, "Shit no! I'd of guessed you were eighteen, thougl
you look a lot younger."

"Why eighteen?"

"That's simple, I figured if you were under eighteen your parent:
would not let you drive across the country by yourself, and numbe
two, you have to be eighteen or older to work in the resort, right?"

"Right on both counts. Oh my God, look at the time!" she ex
claimed glancing at her wrist watch. "I love talking to you, but I mus
rush off."

"I hope you'll drop by again."

"I'd love to, I'll drop by after work some evening, how would tha
be?"

"Sounds great, I'll be looking forward to seeing you."

"Thank you—bye-bye Whitey." She climbed into the Jeep, and wa:
about to drive away when Whitey quickly kissed his fingers ani
touched them to her cheek.

The camp was not the same without John. No road-wear)

hitchhikers or hippies had stopped by since his departure. Except for the companionship of Tosh, the past few days were lonely for Whitey, and even more so when Joan did not appear. To occupy his time, on two different occasions, he and Tosh took long hikes into the mountains. He bonded to the Wolf Hybrid who became his constant companion, and immediately the camp guard. In the days that followed no one could get past the Wolf. Tosh would hold them at bay until Whitey called him off.

It was Monday four days later, Whitey was sitting on a stump in the shade of a pine tree drinking a beer. Tosh, who was lying at his side, suddenly raised his head listening to a sound too distant for Whitey's ears.

"What is it boy? You hear something?" Whitey asked.

Straining his ears, Whitey could hear nothing but the canyon's updraft rustling through the pine needles at the crown of the trees. A moment later he could hear the sound of an approaching vehicle. Listening carefully he heard it slow down, and he knew it had made the turn and was heading toward his camp. Slowly, silently, Tosh eased his powerful body into a crouching position, making himself at the ready for the intruder. Whitey's hand automatically went to the butt of his gun as he stood hidden behind the tree. The vehicle broke into the clearing. He was relieved to see Joan as she climbed out of the Jeep. Before leaving his cover he slid the gun back into his waistband.

Tosh recognized Joan, and with tail wagging, he rushed across the clearing to greet her. She had to brace herself from the onslaught or be knocked to the ground. It took a few moments to get Tosh under control before he settled down.

"I'm not the only one happy to see you," Whitey remarked.

"I'm surprised," Joan commented, "I didn't think he would remember me."

"As pretty as you are there's no way he could forget you!"

"I haven't been here a minute and you are already showering me with compliments!"

She looked beautiful as she walked toward Whitey. She was wearing boots, Jeans, and a T-shirt with Mickey Mouse printed on the front holding his hands over her breasts.

"Oh boy!" Whitey sighed. "Mickey Mouse, I like where he has his hands!"

"Silly, it's only a T-shirt. Oh before I forget, I have something for you." Propped up in the back of the Jeep was a 50 lb. bag of Purina High Protein dog food. "Well it's not really for you, it's for Tosh. You can repay me by giving me one of those." She pointed to the beer in his hand.

Whitey guzzled his drink, hurried to the ice chest, and retrieved two more beers.

"Would you like to take a ride with me?" Joan asked. "I'm going to Tahoe City to do some shopping, do you want to come?"

"Sure, but aren't you supposed to be at work?"

"No this is my day off, I'm off on Monday and Tuesdays, didn't I tell you?"

"No, you didn't, but hey that's okay, I need a few things myself from the store."

"Okay our first stop is the Laundromat, you do have clothes that need washing, don't you?"

"What're you trying to tell me girl?"

"Nothing, but I'm sure you must have some clothes that need washing."

"Well it so happens I do have a few things, I'll gather them up."

Their first stop was the Laundromat, it was then that Whitey realized Joan had no laundry.

"Hey girl what's the deal? Where're your dirty clothes?"

"The place where I stay includes my laundry. We're here to wash your clothes not mine," Joan replied with a smile.

"Okay slick chick, let's throw this stuff in the machine, then go shopping."

They went to the supermarket. Joan had only a few items to get and began supervising Whitey's purchases.

"No Whitey, don't get that! Junk food is no good for you. You need good nourishing food, meat, and plenty of vegetables."

"Okay girl, you pick out the food, but I know what I want to drink!"

At the checkout stand, Whitey paid for the food, plus one case of Pepsi, two cases of beer, two gallons of wine, four bottles of Wild Turkey, and one case of Kal-Can Beef Chunks for Tosh. He also picked up ice for the coolers.

They collected his clothes from the Laundromat, and started back toward camp. As they turned into Blackwood Canyon Road Whitey asked, "What are your plans for this evening Joan? Would you like to spend it with me out at my camp?"

"I was hoping you would ask!"

"Well I'm asking. How about staying all night?"

"Well—I might, that's if you really and truly want me to."

He threw his arms in the air, and as he bounced on the seat he yelled, "Does a bear shit in the woods? You know I want you to stay!" And in his enthusiasm he impetuously took hold of her head and kissed her cheek.

"Hey!" she exclaimed with a laugh, "You're going to get me excited and cause a wreck!"

Whitey unloaded the Jeep while Joan put the groceries away. When everything was secured, he opened a can of dog food, and mixed it with three cups of Purina High Protein. After Tosh had finished the mixture, Joan tossed him a huge knuckle bone.

"Well that ought to take care of him for a half hour or so!" she laughed.

"This high altitude gives you a hell of an appetite, even a wolf! And talking about food, when do we eat?"

"As soon as I wash up a bit I'll fix dinner." With a towel around her neck Joan went to the creek. When she returned Whitey had a fire going, and was stacking wood beside it. Joan peeled potatoes and opened a number of cans in preparation of the meal.

"Do you need some help?" Whitey asked.

"No, you just sit there and relax. I'll get the meal." Joan said as she placed a kettle over the fire. Every so often she looked toward Whitey who was watching her every move.

"What are you staring at?" she asked. "You're going to make me self-conscious and I won't be able to cook."

She turned her attention back to preparing dinner. A moment passed, she glanced at Whitey once again. "What are you looking at now?"

"If you must know I'm looking at your ass!"

Joan burst out laughing. "If you don't behave yourself I'll never get this meal cooked, why don't you take a short walk with Tosh, or better still, go wash your face!"

After dinner Whitey rekindled the fire before they sat down to enjoy a glass of wine. He lit a cigarette, and while smoking it Joan remarked, "Whitey you smoke far too many cigarettes, you light one right after the other. How many packs do you smoke a day?"

"Oh I don't know, five or six, so what?"

"Good God you're going to kill yourself."

Whitey shrugged his shoulders, "Shit, I have to die of something, why not cancer?"

"That's not funny Whitey. You seem to always downgrade yourself. You're very sweet, and sweet to me, but you're hard on yourself. You put yourself down like you're not good enough for me, or something like that. If that is the way you think, well let me tell you something. I don't care who you are, what you are, where you've been, or where you're going. I think a lot of you, and I wouldn't be here now if I didn't think you were good enough for me."

"You just covered a lot of territory there girl! But truthfully with all these young dudes around, I don't know what you see in me."

"Whitey can I be totally honest with you?"

"Sure, if that's what you want, go ahead."

"The truth is, you fascinate me, and I'm sure you realize I have become fond of you. . . ."

"Fond of me!"

"Be quiet will you, let me finish. As I was saying, I'm very fond of you, and I feel that you do care for me. I can sense your feeling's

Whitey, I mean I can pick up the vibes. I know something is wrong and I want you to know you can completely trust me. I have a feeling you're running from something—maybe yourself, but I think your camping trip is more of a hiding trip."

Surprised at her wisdom, Whitey sat there absorbing everything she said. Not only is she pretty, she can read my mind, I can't hide anything from this girl.

"Whitey I know you're carrying a gun," she continued. "Once or twice I caught a glimpse of it. I know something's wrong, if you want to tell me about it I'm a good listener."

He sat there looking at her. He could see the sincerity in her eyes and knew at a glance he could trust this girl.

"Okay," he said with a smile, "You asked for it! Do you want to hear part or all of it?"

"I'm staying the night, so why not tell me all of it."

Whitey walked over to the ice chest, and as he reached for a beer he said, "You might as well have one too Joan, this is gonna take a while."

Sitting next to her, Whitey recounted his story.

"Well that's it girl. You know all about me for whatever it's worth."

"Whatever it's worth, I'll tell you what it's worth. I'm going to spend the summer with you right here in this camp. When summer's over—well I'll just worry about that when summer is over!"

Before Whitey could reply, she walked over to the ice chest and got two cans of beer. Darkness had settled in, and while Joan was getting the beer he replenished the fire. When she sat down, he took her in his arms, and gave her a warm lingering kiss, and then whispered in her ear, "No matter what happens Joan, I'll never forget you , and the summer of '71."

"I'll never forget it either," she said emphatically.

"You know Joan there's something I've been meaning to tell you. You remember the other day you said you didn't have to work because your family was well-off?"

"Yes I remember, look I wasn't bragging, I was just trying to tell you I didn't have to work unless I wanted to."

"I know you weren't bragging, you're not that kind of person. What I wanted to tell you is never give that sort of information to a stranger. You took a chance in telling me."

"Tell what? What did I say that was wrong?"

"Look Joan, you're a sweet innocent looking girl and I want you to listen to me carefully. Number one, don't ever pick up a hitchhiker again. Number two, never tell a stranger your parents are well-off. You don't know who the hell you're talking to and before you know it, you could be kidnaped. Christ you could get hurt or maybe killed, do you understand what I'm saying?"

Whitey was so intent on emphasizing his words he did not realize he was shaking her.

"Whitey," she laughed, "Don't shake my head off! But you know you're right in what you said, and it scares me. This is the first time in my life I ever told anyone my parents were wealthy. I'm glad it was you instead of someone else."

"I'm glad too, always keep your guard up. Never let it down, there are a lot of nuts in the world. Be extra careful, even of your friends. Never trust a stranger and you won't go wrong."

"You're absolutely right Whitey, but it's ironic that you're the one to tell me. You're a wanted man, a fugitive. Who would of expected a person with your background to be concerned about me? I'm touched Whitey, really touched. Regardless of your past, I trust you more than any person I have ever met in my entire life."

"That's quite a compliment, thank you. Would you like another beer?"

As they sat there drinking the beer Joan spoke again, "You remember the first night we met? When I was ready to drive away, you kissed your fingers and then gently touched my cheek. We had just met, why did you do that?"

"That's just it, we'd just met, and we were saying goodbye. I wasn't sure if you'd come back. The gesture with my fingers was my way of saying, I like you."

"Well I like you too, very much."

"Do you like me enough to crash now?" Whitey asked as he put his arm around her.

"Right on, let's go!" she cried enthusiastically.

Whitey lit the Coleman lantern, and then extinguished the fire. Holding it high he led the way to his tent. Once inside he hung the lantern up on a support. As he did so Tosh grunted as he lay down outside the entrance.

Undressing they were unaware of the chill in the air. The night breeze drifted through the canyon, and as it did so they held their warm bodies close together.

Joan snuggled up in his warmth and whispered, "I never thought giving a stranger a ride would end up like this!"

CHAPTER 31.

Joan enjoyed spending her off hours with Whitey, hiking, boating, laughing, joking, and at times, skinny-dipping in the creek. Each evening upon returning from work, she would bring food from the Inn. The Inn specialized in lobster and crab, and regularly after work she would bring back large quantities. Tosh adored shellfish, and each evening he received his equal share!

While eating lobster one evening, in between mouthfuls Whitey blurted out, "I wonder what the poor people are doing!"

"Why do you say that?" Joan asked.

"Shit, just look at me and my Wolf sitting in the middle of the forest eating lobster. It's even delivered to my door by the prettiest waitress of the Sunnyside Inn! Now if that isn't rich, what is?"

"You're only getting what you deserve, and you deserve the best!"

They both laughed.

Toward the end of August on a Wednesday while Joan was at work, Ben and his gang rode in from Sacramento. The visit was unexpected, and Whitey was happy to see his old friends. They were all there, Ben, Chris, Jay, Fuzzface, and many, many more, plus Sharon, Jackie, and several other girls. As usual drugs were plentiful and the booze began to flow.

"Here Whitey I got some good hard acid you can add to your stash," Chris said as he handed him a small packet. "This stuff is dynamite man, it'll blow your mind! Take a hit."

Whitey placed a tab on the end of his tongue. Just before he started to hallucinate he felt lightheaded, and experienced the feeling of floating on air. This time he failed to keep in mind that he was on acid, and the expression on his face began to change. First he began to smile, then laugh, then smiled again. This was followed by a blank look that turned to panic. Emitting a chilling scream, he suddenly tore off his vest. He fell to the ground, with legs kicking and arms flailing he screamed again. He was experiencing the sensation of bugs eating away at the insides of his stomach. They felt as though they were devouring his intestines. The tortuous pain was devastating as his fingers clawed at his stomach. He writhed on the ground as the group stood watching. A few of them shouted, but Whitey could not hear them, nor could he hear his own screams. The pain was so intense, all reason was gone, he had to get the bugs out the only way he knew. He reached for his buck knife and flipped the razor sharp blade open.

"What's he doing? Stop him!" Sharon shouted.

"They're eating me alive!" Whitey screamed as he raised the knife to cut open his stomach.

Lunging forward, Ben grabbed Whitey's wrist just before the blade penetrated his skin.

"Help me, goddamn you fools—help me!" Ben cried in panic as he struggled with Whitey for the knife. Chris, who realized the urgency, jumped in to help Ben wrestle the knife away. W.A. with quick thinking grabbed hold of Whitey's free arm, and as he held it in a vicelike grip he shouted in his ear, "Whitey you're on acid, come on man listen to me, you're on acid, everything's all right."

Subconsciously Whitey began to pick up the message, he could hear a voice from within, "You're on acid Whitey, just relax and enjoy the trip—relax and enjoy the trip."

The party lasted until 8:00 P.M., when Ben announced it was time to leave.

"I'd like to meet this girl friend of yours, what's her name Joan? But we can't wait around. We want to get over to South Shore. You sure you don't want to come with us?"

"I'd like to Ben, but I don't want her to come home to an empty camp."

"Yeah I can dig it, look I gotta be going. Is there anything else before I leave?"

"Yeah, you gonna be back before Labor Day?"

"No, I don't think so, but I can come up the day after, why?"

"It'll be time to pack up and get the hell out here."

"I guess you don't want to freeze your ass this winter!" Ben laughed.

"That's right, tell me the exact day you'll be up so I can plan on it."

"Okay I'll be up the day after Labor Day for sure."

"Fine, but come in your pickup. I'll be packed and ready to haul this shit to your house. If it's safe, I may stay at your home for a week or so."

"Hey bro, you can stay as long as you want. I'll see ya after Labor Day."

Each member of the group, including the girls, embraced Whitey and said their goodbyes. A moment later the motorcycles fired up, and after they were gone you could still hear the echo of the engines throughout the canyon.

That evening after retiring, Joan had a few questions to ask. "From the looks of things you and your friends must have partied here today."

Whitey with eyes closed was lying on his back and did not reply. Joan was sitting next to him and noticed the scratches on his stomach. "My God! Look at those scratches, how did that happen?"

"Ah it's nothing, we were feeling good and had a little free-for-all, that's all."

"You and your friends have to be crazy! Look at those gashes, I'd better clean them up before they get infected."

While Joan administered to the scratches she said, "Whitey what will happen to you after Labor Day? Do you have any plans?"

"I don't know yet, I'll have to find a place to stay for the winter."

Having finished with the medication, Joan laid down cuddling up to Whitey. "Why don't you come back with me?" she asked.

Surprised, Whitey turned his head to face her, "I can't do that."

"Why not? I'd love to have you come to Cape Cod with me."

He took her in his arms, and held her close. "It sure sounds tempting babe, but it would mean trouble for you if I went back there."

"What trouble? The authorities or no one else would know you were there."

"But I'd know it, and it wouldn't work. Eventually it would mean trouble for you, and I don't want that to happen."

"Please Whitey don't just say no, won't you think it over first?"

"Look Joan, I'd love to go with you, I want you to know that, but I have to say no. You said you wanted to spend the rest of the summer with me, and at the time that was all that mattered. Well summer's almost over, and we knew it would have to come to an end. The best thing to do is for me to go back to Sacramento, you head for Cape Cod and forget all about me."

"Just like that? Forget all about you?"

"Well you know what I mean, damn it, you knew it would come to this. Shit, I'd love to go with you, I want to go with you, and if I didn't love you I would go with you. Don't you understand, I'm trying to protect you from really being hurt in the future?"

"I was hoping against hope that it didn't have to end this way, but I guess you're right Whitey," her voice was sad. "It hurts now at the thought of parting, but it would hurt even more so if you came back with me with your uncertain future."

That night, lovemaking was extra special to them.

The last week of August passed quickly, and the morning after Labor Day they were ready for their goodbyes. Joan knelt beside Tosh, threw her arms around him, and buried her face in the thick hair of his neck. "I'm going to miss you Tosh. Take care of Whitey for me." She held her arms around him a moment longer, then stood up and turned to Whitey. A lonely tear trickled down her cheek as she opened her arms to him. Their embrace was full of love and emotion, and their last kiss was a lingering one. When they parted, stepping back to look at each other, there was no need for words, for they could see it all in each other's eyes.

Quickly Joan turned and hurried to her Jeep, and just before she drove away, Whitey kissed his fingers, and pressed them gently against her cheek.

Once more Whitey was alone, he wanted to scream for it broke his heart to see her drive out of his life forever. While he was on the run he could never make a lasting commitment. He would always have to be alone. With Tosh at his heels, he turned and ran toward the boxes that were packed and ready for departure. Lighting a cigarette he hastily took a bottle of whiskey out of one of the boxes, and put it to his lips.

"Fucker—mother fucking son of a bitch—fuckeeeeer!" he screamed. He remembered the heroin in his stash, and slammed the bottle to the ground. His heart was breaking and it would take more than whiskey to numb the pain.

CHAPTER 32.

Ben kept his promise. Shortly after Joan's departure he came to pick Whitey up. Together they loaded the camp supplies and proceeded to Sacramento. Ben no longer lived on Eagle Road; while Whitey was gone he moved to Jerger Street in Rancho Cordova. It was a spacious house with a spare bedroom. Ben and his mother encouraged Whitey to stay with them as there was no indication that the authorities knew of his whereabouts.

The weeks that followed were peaceful until one December morning the doorbell rang.

"Hey Mom, someone's at the door," Ben shouted. "Answer it will you."

Whitey was sitting in the living room watching TV. As Jo walked by, he followed her movements to the front door. She opened it, and standing on the porch with his back to them, was his parole officer, Rosemar.

Gripping the handle of his gun, Whitey sprang from the chair concealing himself behind the open door. If he had been a second slower in his movement, Rosemar would have seen him when he suddenly turned to face Josephine. It wasn't until he turned before she recognized who he was, and was taken aback.

"Oh—Mr. Rosemar, I wasn't expecting you."

"I'm sure you weren't! It took me over two months to find out where you moved."

Using a sarcastic voice Josephine replied, "I wasn't aware I was supposed to notify you when we moved."

"I'm sorry Mrs. Vakno, I didn't quite mean it that way. I realize you have no obligations to me, but I would highly appreciate your cooperation."

"I do cooperate, but I don't know of what help I can be to you."

"As you know, I'm Leon Thompson's parole officer. I'm trying to locate his whereabouts. Have you seen or heard anything from him lately?"

"No, I haven't seen him since last June. I don't know where he may be."

"Well I've reason to believe he's in the Sacramento area. I know he spent the summer at Lake Tahoe. My source told me he left Tahoe in September, and I. . . ."

"Look I don't know where you got your information," Jo interrupted. "He could of been at Tahoe or Timbucktoo for all I care! All I know he's not around here, if I learn of his whereabouts I will gladly let you know."

"Thank you Mrs. Vakno, your cooperation is well appreciated."

Rosemar turned to leave as Jo closed the door behind him.

With a sigh of relief Whitey wiped his brow just as Ben hurried into the room. He threw his arms around his mother, and said in a mimicking voice, "If I learn of his whereabouts, I will gladly let you know!"

Jo smiled, "Well what else could I say to him?"

"Nothing Mom, you were great." Then turning to Whitey, "Well what'll we do now bro?"

"I'd like to know how he found out I was at Tahoe, and how the hell did he know I was back here in Sacramento? One thing I do know, I have to get the hell outa here. That son of a bitch will be back with a search warrant. But where can I go?"

"How about Ophir Road?" Ben suggested.

"I hate to impose on Chris and Libby again."

"Don't worry about imposing on Libby. Tell him what happened Sharon, you like to gossip."

"That's not true Ben! Anyway, Jackie and I went up to see Libby yesterday, but only Chris was there. Chris told us she ran off with a guy from Reno. He said he was moving in with his ex today. So as far as I know the house is empty."

"You know there's another house back in the woods don't you Whitey?" Ben asked.

"Yeah, I know that. The place is a perfect hideout, but it don't have any electricity. Where does Chris get his from?"

"He has a friend that works for PG&E who hooked him up unofficially. You could run a line from Chris's house."

"I'll worry about that later, right now I gotta get out of here, and in a hurry."

Promptly the camp supplies and personal gear were loaded on to the pickup. Shortly after Ben and Whitey were on their way to Ophir Road.

The house was well hidden behind brush and trees. Concealed just below it on the bank of a small creek, stood another building. This structure had been used for a tack room and storage, and inside Whitey found an old brass bed and mattress. There were many other items stored, such as paint, wire, and wood.

The deserted house, though livable, was in dire need of cleaning and repairs. It's only occupants had been insects, mice and other creatures of the forest. The old house had a large kitchen, living room, bath, and three bedrooms with plenty of closet space. The place was empty except for two antique stoves that were in excellent condition, but in need of a thorough cleaning. One was an old cooking range in the kitchen, the other was a potbelly wood burner in the living room.

Upon arrival, Tosh had thoroughly inspected the house, and in short order, established residence. The wooded area was to his liking, and he felt well at home.

On the back porch attached to the wall was a rusty electrical fuse box. Whitey cleaned and restored it to working order. After checking the outlets, he went about stringing heavy-duty electrical wire through the brush and trees to the main source of power. If there were any spirits in the rear house, it must have been quite an occurrence for them when the lights flashed on.

Whitey had no time to be lonely, the first few days were busy ones. It was quite a task making furniture out of old wood that had accumulated over the years. With various cans of different colored paint, he redid the interior of the house. The repairs and cleanup progressed rapidly, and at a glance one could see the historic beauty of the place.

Whitey was so engrossed in his work, he did not realize how much time had gone by. Ben came to visit one day bringing him an old refrigerator. He couldn't believe the improvement and how much Whitey accomplished in two short weeks.

Tuesday morning of the following week Whitey was busy connecting a water pipe. He was interrupted when he heard Tosh growl. Hastily he ran to the door and saw Tosh halfway down the pathway holding a stranger at bay. He grabbed his automatic off the table, and held it behind his back as he walked through the doorway.

"Who the hell are you mister? What do you want?" he shouted in a surly voice.

"Hey I'm just a friend of Chris, his house is empty, do you know where he is?"

"How did you know there was anyone back here?" Whitey asked.

"I didn't, I was about to leave when I heard some banging."

The noise he had heard was Whitey working on the water pipe. Tosh's growls were gathering momentum each time the man spoke.

"Would you call off your dog before he bites me."

"He's his own boss he does what he wants. You got just about one minute to tell me who the hell you are before he does bite you."

Still growling, Tosh stood firm ready to spring.

"Look, I'm a friend of Chris's, my name's Tom Tyson. Hell, I only live down the road a ways."

"That don't tell me shit! Do you know any of his friends?"

"Yeah I sure do. His old lady is called Libby, he runs with a motorcycle gang from Sacramento, Ben, Duck, Fuzzface, W.A., Jay, Chris . . ."

"Okay—okay," Whitey interrupted. "How come you didn't know he moved? He's been gone three weeks."

"I work days in a lumber mill on Grass Valley Road, I stop by here once in a while. Shit I didn't know he was gone."

It wasn't long before they became good friends, and soon Tom was spending most of his off-hours at Whitey's place. Tom was a good-hearted rough, tough, country-boy. On an average of twice a month, from the mill, he would haul in a load of scrap wood for the stoves.

New Year's Eve started out quietly for Whitey. First Tom dropped by, and shortly after that, Ben and the gang arrived to help celebrate the incoming year of 1972. Like so many parties in the past, there were plenty of food, beer, wine, whiskey, and drugs of all description. The party lasted for four days, and when Ben and the others finally departed, the house looked like a disaster area!

On January 23 Ben and a few friends returned to celebrate Whitey's birthday. As they entered the house, Sharon presented him with a gift-wrapped package. He had completely forgotten this was his birthday, and had no idea what the present was for. With great expectation he hurriedly opened it. Under the ribbon was a card that read:

HAPPY FORTY-NINTH BIRTHDAY WHITEY.
YOUR FRIENDS.

It was signed by the gang members. Inside the box was a new pair of leather boots that Whitey was in dire need of.

"Hey man, I completely forgot what day it was, but you guys remembered."

He was really touched by the gift, and after the presentation of the boots, the party got into full swing, lasting all night!

CHAPTER 33.

Except for an occasional party with Ben and the gang it had been quiet on Ophir Road. But as time went by, it began to liven up to the point where hardly a day went by that there wasn't a party. Like the Blackwood Canyon days, hippies started dropping in from all over the country. There were always girls, food, booze, and plenty of drugs. Occasionally one would drop by that had previously been to Blackwood Canyon.

Thumb-tacked on the wall of Whitey's bedrooms, like trophies, were seventeen pairs of girls' panties! Each time he made it with a new girl he would take her panties, and put them on the wall.

Besides using small quantities of heroin, from time to time Whitey would chippy on other types of drugs. It was during this period that his heroin habit increased to a spoon a day. Three times a week he would make a connection run to Sacramento. He would pick up five spoons of heroin at $50 a spoon. He would cut each spoon into four quarters, and sell each one for $25 a hit.

Under these circumstances' Whitey was never pressed for money. A few weeks previously, a transient hippie had stayed three days at the Ophir house. When he was ready to depart, he presented Whitey with eight stolen blank payroll checks, but Whitey declined them. The hippie stated he wanted to pay him something for his stay there, and all he had were these blank checks. He suggested that Whitey could use them in the future if needed. Not planning to use them he accepted the checks. One day toward the end of July Whitey fixed a heavy hit of acid, and while under the influence, he filled out the checks and cashed them. He was not aware of what had happened until the next day when he discovered the checks were gone, and one of his friends told him what he had done. Whitey was furious with the stupidity of his act, but it was too late and he cast it off with the thought, "I've done far more stupid things than that in my life."

The parties continued, and it was during the month of August that Whitey became friends with three local boys from Auburn, Broadman, Mike, and Sid. Drugs were nothing new to these men, for they were users long before becoming acquainted with Whitey.

Two weeks after the check cashing spree, Whitey and his new

friends decided to go to see Ben. A few months earlier Whitey had purchased a 1956 Ford pickup truck for $300. With it's rusty doors and fenders, it was not much to look at, but the running gear was in excellent condition.

It was 7:00 P.M.. when they arrived in Sacramento; Ben and Sharon were about to drive off when they saw Whitey's Ford approaching the house.

"Hi ya Whitey? Who're your friends?" Ben asked as the foursome approached his truck.

"These boys are from Auburn," he told Ben. "Ben, Sharon, this is Broadman, Mike, and Sid."

With the introductions over Ben said, "My old lady and I were just going to a party, do you guys want to go?"

"Hey a party!" Mike exclaimed. "We never turn down a party, right Whitey?"

The party proved to be dull, and at eleven o'clock they departed for Ben's house, where the heavy drinking began.

An hour later W.A. and Jay drove up, both men were already intoxicated. After a few more drinks they were ready to go home, and started to walk out to their pickup.

"Hey where you guys going?" Ben asked.

"We're going home to crash man. It's dead here," W.A. replied.

"You guys are too drunk to go anywhere, why don't you crash in the garage?"

"Ah we gotta couple of chicks waiting for us at the house, who wants to crash here?"

"I don't give a shit where you crash, you guys are too fucking drunk to drive," Ben insisted.

"Well fuck it, why don't you drive us home?" Jay suggested.

"Hey Whitey do me a favor," Ben asked. "You're the soberest guy here, will you drive these fools home?"

"Shit man, they live clean on the other side of town, I don't feel like driving all the way there and back this hour of the morning."

"You don't have to come back for Christ's sake," W.A. said with a slur. "You can crash at my pad, I'll bring you back in the morning, what'd you say?"

"What about us?" Broadman asked. "What're we going to do?" indicating Mike and Sid.

"Crash in the garage. Come on W.A., where's your pickup parked at?"

"Its out front, where the fuck do ya think it'd be?"

"I know where I wished it was! Come on let's go,"

A few minutes later with Whitey driving they headed toward the north area. Using extra caution not to exceed the speed limit Whitey was surprised to see a flashing red light coming up from behind.

"Shit, pigs! They're gonna pull us over," Whitey shouted in anger.

"Goddamn it all, what the hell did you do Whitey? Run a red light or something?" Jay taunted.

"No fucker! I'm gonna get busted on account of you drunks!" Whitey retorted. "Goddamn I'm packing too!"

"Quick kick it under the seat Whitey," W.A. suggested.

Whitey reached for the automatic in his waist band, placing it on the floor, he pushed it under the seat with his foot. As he did so he pulled over to the side of the road stopping the vehicle, and waited for the inevitable.

The patrolman walked up to the side of the pickup and ordered Whitey out of the truck.

"Are you aware your turn signal isn't working?" the officer asked.

Acting nonchalantly Whitey replied, "Thanks for telling me officer, it must of just blown out."

"How much have you had to drink?"

"Just one or two, that's all."

"One or two! You smell like a brewery, let me see your license."

Whitey reached in his back pocket, and with a look of surprise he said, "Gee I'm sorry officer, but I left my wallet at home, my license is in it."

"What's your name?"

"John P. Hewitt," Whitey lied.

"All right Mr. Hewitt, I'm taking you in for drunk driving, get into the squad car."

"Ah come on man, I'm not drunk, give me a break."

"Just get in the squad car," the officer ordered as he opened the rear door. Then he walked back to the pickup. "Do either of you men have a license?"

"Yes I do," W.A. said in a sober-sounding voice.

"Okay you drive, let's move this pickup out of here."

W.A. started it up, and as he put the stick into first, there was a grinding of gears before he drove away. The patrolman paid no attention and returned to the squad car.

Whitey was mad as hell. He was the soberest of the gang, but here he was on his way to jail while W.A. who was the drunkest, was on his way home. It did not make sense.

With its passenger, the patrol car made its way into Sacramento, and a few minutes later was traveling west on F Street. Four blocks from the County Jail, a call came in over the police radio.

"Unit nine—unit nine. Proceed to 16th and I Street. Liquor store holdup in progress."

With squealing brakes the squad car came to an abrupt halt. Quickly the officer unlocked the back door releasing Whitey.

"Hewitt I'm going to give you a break and let you go. Don't *ever* drive under the influence again, and carry your license at all times."

"I sure will officer," Whitey said as he jumped out of the car.

With the squealing of rubber, and sirens wailing, the car sped away, and once it was gone, the street became silent. Whitey made his way to a telephone booth located in a service station. After dialing his number Ben answered the phone, "Yeah who is it?"

"It's me Ben, Whitey."

"Jesus Christ are you in jail?" He was shocked at the sound of Whitey's voice.

"No, what the hell made you think I was in jail?"

"W.A. called me a little while ago, he told me what happened, and said a cop arrested you."

"Yeah that's right, but I got away."

The first thought that flashed into Ben's mind, he must have shot the officer!

"How the hell did you get away?" he asked excitedly.

Whitey explained it to him, and from the other end of the line he could hear Ben laughing, and he was still laughing when he picked Whitey up.

That same morning, Whitey and his three friends returned to Ophir Road. Because of the incident with the police, except for his heroin runs he seldom ventured from the house anymore.

One night September 1, Mike informed Whitey that he had made plans to burglarize a small country store.

"Look man, if you're gonna pull any burglaries don't come back here," Whitey was angry, "I don't want no goddamn heat coming down on this place."

"The job's a cinch, shit I won't bring no heat here man. Besides we can use the food, money, booze, and whatever we can get."

"We're well-heeled here, we don't need any of that shit. You pull this job man and I'm telling you, don't come back here. You understand me?"

Mike reluctantly conceded, "Okay Whitey, if that's the way you want it,"

"Yeah that's the way I want it, that goes for anyone else I let stay here."

The subject was dropped, and Whitey thought no more about it until the morning of September 19. He had to make a run to Sacramento to pick up some stuff from his connection. After his business was accomplished, he remained in town until late that night. It was shortly after midnight when he returned to Ophir Road.

As he walked up to the house he heard the noise of a party in progress.

"Damn it all another bash going on," he grumbled to himself as he opened the door.

The party was in full-swing as he walked into the front room. The floor was cluttered with cartons of cigarettes, and wine bottles, most of them unopened. There were seven cases of beer scattered about. Also laying on the floor, was a large moneybag along with various types of canned goods, and a payroll checkbook.

201

"Where the hell did all this shit come from?" Whitey growled.

No one heard him over the noise of the music. He charged across the room, and turned off the stereo and slammed the cover down. The room immediately became silent and as Whitey turned to the crowd he saw the shocked expression on their faces.

"I asked you sons of bitches where this shit came from."

Still no one answered.

"No one wants to answer huh? Okay we'll see about that," Whitey stormed into the bedroom, and a moment later reappeared with a double-barrel twelve gauge sawed-off shotgun. "All right you mother fuckers, someone speak up or you can all get the hell out of here, and take this shit with you!"

At the sight of the shotgun their faces turned white with fear, for they knew he was dangerous when angered. Holding the weapon waist-high he shouted again, "All of you get the fuck out of here, no one wants to talk then get out!"

Whitey took a menacing step forward, and as he did so Tom Tyson said, "Hold it a minute Whitey," and turned to face the other members staring directly at Mike. "All right you fuckers, you know who you are, and I know who you are, so you better speak up."

"Never mind Tom, I know where the shit came from," Whitey followed the direction of Tom's eyes. Looking directly at Mike he continued, "You pulled that burglary after I told you not to, didn't you?"

"Yeah Whitey we did, but listen, no one seen us, we got away clean," Mike said nervously.

"We—we? Who the hell is we?"

"Me Whitey," Sid answered, "I was in on it with him."

"Me too," Broadman added. "Because of my van, Mike asked us to pull the score with him, what's wrong with that?"

"What's wrong? I'll tell you what's wrong. A couple of weeks ago this chump here told me he was going to pull a burglary, and what did I tell you Mike?"

"You—you said you didn't want to bring no heat down on the place, and if I pulled a burglary I couldn't stay here." Mike answered.

"Then why the hell did you pull it?"

"I don't have no money. I was just trying to help out."

"Have I ever asked you for money? Goddamn it, I didn't want you to pull no burglary."

"I'm sorry Whitey, it won't happen again."

"That goes for us too," Broadman apologized for Sid and himself.

"All right we'll forget about it this time, but the first thing in the morning I want you to get all this crap out of here."

"I'll see that it's done, you can count on that," Broadman said. "By the way Whitey, I'm supposed to pick up a couple of chicks, is it okay to bring 'em here?"

"Yeah I guess so. When and where are you supposed to pick them up?"

"They work in a restaurant below Newcastle. I was supposed to pick them up at one o'clock, and it's almost that now. Do you want to come along?"

"Why not? Let's go."

Newcastle was a mile and a half below the house, and for such an innocent trip Whitey felt there was no need for his gun, and left it behind.

A few minutes later after he and Sid hopped into the van, Broadman drove south toward Newcastle. The burglary incident had been forgotten until Whitey looked across the highway and noticed two squad cars parked in front of a country store and service station.

"Jesus Chris!" he exclaimed. "Is this the place you guys burglarized?"

"Yeah that's it!" Broadman said with a laugh as they drove by.

"You dumb bastard!" Whitey angrily screamed at him. "You dumb mother fucker what're you driving by here for?"

"It's cool Whitey, no one seen us."

Little did they know that a man living across the highway had given a description of a van he had witnessed leaving the scene of the crime.

"They seen us, I think they're coming after us," Sid cried.

Looking to the rear, Whitey saw a patrol car with flashing red lights coming up from behind.

"Shit they got us hemmed in," Sid shouted. "We're running into a road block!"

It happened quickly. After they pulled over to the side of the road, the police arrested the three of them on suspicion of burglary. They were taken and booked into the Auburn County Jail. Broadman and Sid were booked on their given names, but Whitey, who carried a false identification purchased earlier from a hippie, was booked under the name of John P. Hewitt.

At 5:00 A.M. the same morning, armed with a search warrant, the police went to the house on Ophir Road. The party had broken up only minutes earlier. The place was deserted except for Mike who was sound asleep on the couch when the officers entered the room.

"Wake up, come on wake up there!" an officer ordered.

Mike opened his eyes, and was paralyzed with fear at the sight of the uniformed men. At that moment another deputy walked in. "There's no one in the other rooms," he said glancing at the floor. "Well I'll be damned! This must be the stolen stuff."

"Don't touch anything until it's been dusted for prints," the first officer said. Then turning back to Mike he continued, "All right you, up on your feet and turn around."

Mike, shaking nervously complied. The second officer shook him down and said, "He's clean."

203

The first officer looked coldly at Mike and roughly pushed him back on the couch, "All right mister, you better start talking, and I want the goddamn truth. What is your name, where did all this stuff come from?"

Mike was afraid, and it took a few moments before he could speak coherently, "My name is Mike Breen, an—and three friends brought this stuff in, I don't know where they got it."

"What are your friends names? And where are they now?"

"Their names are Whitey Thompson, Broadman, and Sid. I don't know Broadman and Sid's last names."

"What time was this stuff brought in? And what did you see?"

"I'm not sure I think it was around twelve A.M. We were drinking last night and I fell asleep. Around midnight I heard some noise and woke up. That's when my friends carried all this stuff in, and dumped it on the floor. I went back to sleep, and I been sleeping until you officers woke me up."

"All right Breen we're going to take you in for more questioning."

CHAPTER 34.

Unaware of the police having Mike in for questioning, Whitey, and his two friends were taken before the D.A. and officially charged with burglary. They were then taken to the courtroom for a hearing, and directly afterwards bail was set. Brodmann and Sid had no criminal record, and Whitey, under the name of John P. Hewitt had no record either. Subsequently the court ordered them released on their own recognizance. The three men were returned to the county jail booking room for their release.

Brodmann was the first to receive his property and signed the release papers. Sid was next, and once he was finished, Whitey was ready to sign his document. Just as he was about to do so, a detective walked into the booking room. He looked directly at Whitey, and in a gruff voice, said, "Don't bother signing that Thompson, you're not going anywhere."

"Were you addressing me?" Whitey calmly asked.

"That's right Thompson. I know who you are. Pull up your shirt."

Before Whitey could respond the detective grabbed the back of his shirt and pulled it up revealing the electric chair on his back.

"You're Leon Thompson all right," the officer snickered. "You're a parolee out of Folsom, I know all about you mister wise-guy!"

Brodmann and Sid showed disbelief. They didn't understand how the detective had discovered his identity until Whitey said, "Mike Breen, that fucking Mike Breen!"

Addressing Brodmann and Sid, an officer said, "All right you two, you're free to go, follow me." He led them through a door way while Whitey was taken upstairs to the top floor, and placed in an isolated semi-dark cell.

Whitey was very despondent at the thought of being in jail, while the three who had committed the crime were walking the streets.

The afternoon of Whitey's arrest Tom Tyson came to see him. "Is there anything I can do for you Whitey? What do you want to do about Tosh? He's still there, and no one can get near him except me."

"I'd appreciate it very much Tom, if you would take Tosh home with you."

"I was hoping you'd say that Whitey, I'll take damn good care of him, you can count on it."

Whitey motioned Tom to put his ear nearer the screen. "My guns are they still stashed?"

"I picked them up Whitey, don't worry about them."

"Thanks a lot Tom."

While waiting for trial, the first month of incarceration was a living hell for Whitey. He was forced to kick his drug habit cold turkey. After the second day of incarceration he began to vomit continuously, and could keep no food on his stomach. At times he would choke and gag on his own vomit, and in between spasms he would lie there freezing in his own perspiration. He experienced the feeling of his brain frying. He began to hallucinate, and suffer terrifying flashbacks. His father was whipping him with a cat-o-nine-tails, he was fighting for his life on the chain gang, he was in the hole at McNeil Island being beaten by the guards. He was again on Alcatraz, the prison of no return. The flashbacks began to build up speed, one after the other, faster and faster. He was in prison, he was out of prison, his mind was whirling, and his body began screaming with pain. Except for the jailor and trusty who brought him his food, there was no one to hear his pitiful cries.

In time the worst was over. Each day he began to get stronger and stronger. On occasions he would have flashbacks, but nothing compared to the intensity he had already endured. During this period Whitey was allowed no visits.

The police had taken away his boots and he was forced to make a number of court appearances barefooted. When his friend Tom learned of his predicament, on one of his regular visits he brought Whitey a pair of shoes.

Each time he appeared in court, Broardman and Sid told the truth, stating that Leon Whitey Thompson had nothing whatever to do with the burglary. They further stated that Whitey Thompson was out of town during the time the crime was committed. At this turn of events Mike Breen under oath, admitted that he falsely implicated Whitey Thompson.

The three men admitted their guilt thereby vindicating Whitey of any wrong doing. They had no criminal records, and received suspended prison sentences, and placed on probation. As for Leon Whitey Thompson, he was transferred to the Sacramento county jail. There he was charged with cashing unlawful checks, and a detainer was place on him for violation of parole.

The District Attorney offered him a plea bargain. If he pled guilty to the charge, he would receive a sentence of one year in the county jail. He did not decline the deal, but asked the D.A. if he could see his parole officer before giving him his answer. The D.A. agreed.

The following day Mr. Rosemar came to see him.

"Well Thompson it's been a long time since I've seen you eyeball to eyeball! You led me quite a chase." Checking some notes, Rosemar continued, "You are charged with four counts of forgery, and I understand the D.A. offered you a deal. Is that correct? Are you going to accept his terms?"

"I don't know yet, he offered me a year in the county jail if I pled guilty. But before I do anything, I want to know if you're gonna violate my parole."

"According to my notes you go back to court the first Monday in January. I'll come back before you make your appearance, and give you my decision."

Nineteen seventy-two came to an end, followed by the New Year and Whitey's court appearance.

While waiting in the holding cage before entering court, Rosemar talked to him. "All right Thompson," he said, "if you plead guilty to a year in the county jail, I'll go along with it. Also I'll reinstate your parole on one condition, that your time in the county jail must be unblemished. If you get into the slightest trouble, your parole will be revoked, and you will be returned to prison."

"You got a deal, don't worry I won't be getting into no trouble."

Shortly after Rosemar left, Whitey made his court appearance, but the judge would not accept a plea at this time, and postponed his case for two weeks.

January 23 was Whitey's fiftieth birthday. The following morning he returned to court, entered his plea of guilty, and two weeks later he was sentenced to one year in the county jail. The following day he was transferred to the Branch County Jail in Elk Grove. Shortly after his arrival Mr. Rosemar reassured him that he would reinstate his parole after his county jail time was served.

PART 3.

THE MERRY-GO-ROUND

1973—1975

CHAPTER 35.

Incarcerated at the Branch County Jail, the subsequent months were uneventful until the morning of May 29. Whitey was taken by surprise to hear a guard called out his name, "Leon W. Thompson, roll 'em up!"

He was not due for release until September. "Hey screw, I'm not due to get out yet, where the hell am I going?"

"You're going on the Gray Goose, (state prison bus) so let's go."

Whitey exited his cell and started down the corridor toward the guard who was standing behind a grilled gate. As he approached him, he said, "Hey man there must be some mistake, my P.O. didn't violate me, and besides if I. . . ."

"Your name is Leon W. Thompson isn't it?" the guard interrupted.

"I told you it was, goddamn it!" Whitey was angry now.

"Your name is on the list for San Quentin, so get a move on Thompson or we'll drag you out."

"That's the only way you're going to get me out of here fucker!" Whitey shouted amid the cheers of the other prisoners.

"Come and get him copper, you won't take him alive!" A prisoner shouted.

It took four deputy guards to drag the struggling Whitey out of the building. He grappled with the officers all the way across the compound to the control center. Here he was chained and shackled, then guided onto the prison bus, and transported to San Quentin.

After his arrival he was showered, given a shave and a haircut, and once again dressed in prison blues. After dressing-in was completed, he was escorted to the South Block where he was placed in a cell on the second tier.

His first night was a sleepless one, for Rosemar was constantly on his mind. Now he realized that Rosemar never intended to let him go free.

The following day he was taken before Mr. Morson of the California Adult Authority, and it was at this time the violation of parole charges were read to him.

1. Leon W. Thompson violated condition two of the conditions of parole by leaving his residence in Sacramento County without

notifying his Parole Agent or the parole department.

2. Violation of condition 11. Pleading guilty to the charge of forgery.

3. Violation of condition seven. Having a shotgun under his control.

4. Violation of condition seven. The use of narcotic drugs illegally.

At the end of the hearing Whitey pleaded not guilty to all charges, and was returned to his cell.

That noon while Whitey was having lunch in the South Dining Hall, he heard someone call his name. "Hey, Whitey, Whitey Thompson, over here pal!"

Whitey turned quickly and looked in the direction of the steam table where he saw along line of men waiting to be served. At the end of the line with his arms waving in the air, stood Lou Peters.

Whitey's gloomy face turned to a radiant smile at the recognition of Lou.

"Hey Lou, Lou!" he yelled as he stood up from the table. Overcome with excitement he started to hurry toward him.

"Stay there Whitey, you're gonna get yourself busted. I'll be there in a minute," Lou shouted.

The sudden movement of Whitey jumping up from the table caught the gun rail guard's attention. He raised his rifle, but relaxed when he saw Whitey sit back down. Under the watchful eye of the guard, the two friends shook hands and patted each other's back.

"I'll be damned Lou, I thought I'd never see you again. How long you been here?"

"I transferred here a few months ago from Folsom. How about you Whitey? Are you here on a new beef?"

"No, I'm back on a straight violation. Hell Lou I thought you had gotten out."

"No, I haven't been out yet, but I should make parole in September. So what happened to you Whitey? I heard you jumped parole and took it on the run."

"Yeah you heard right Lou, I'll run it down to you later. By the way, I live in the South Block. Where do you live, and where do you work Lou?"

"I'm in the North Block," he replied. "Also I'm a clerk in the Machine Shop. Where do you want to be assigned?"

"To the streets, but I guess they'll assign me to. . . ."

"All right let's eat and move it out," a guard interrupted. "What do you think this is, the Waldorf?"

"You could of fooled me," Whitey said sarcastically.

The two men finished their meal, and as they departed from the Mess Hall Lou said, "Look after you've been assigned to a job you'll be able to go to the lower yard. I go there every day after lunch to wait for work call, I'll see you then."

That evening after lock-down a guard walked up to Whitey's cell. He handed him a jar of instant coffee, one pound box of cubed sugar, one can of Bugler smoking tobacco, a rolling machine, one package of cigarette papers, six postage stamps, six sheets of writing paper, six envelopes, and four paperback books, all the compliments of Lou. Whitey was grateful to have such a good friend.

On the evening of the fourth day he received a ducet (pass) to report to Classification at 9:00 A.M. the next morning where he was placed on close custody.

Later that same morning he went before the Assignment Lieutenant who assigned him as a cook on the afternoon shift. He was to report to the main kitchen the following afternoon. Upon receiving his job assignment he made a cell move to the East Block. After the move he fell into the monotony of the daily routine. Although this was boring, it was nothing like the monotonous killer routine of Alcatraz. After having a taste of the free world, it was hard to dismiss it from his mind. Subsequently it took a number of days before he could mentally and physically accept the fact that he was back in prison.

After his move to the East Block his work days were tiresome and tedious, followed by sleepless nights. His mind kept straying back to the summer of '71. He thought of Joan, and hoped she had made it back to Cape Cod all right. And Valerie, he hoped she had found the right person to fulfill her dreams. His sleepless nights were beginning to tell on him. He realized he must block out Joan, Valerie, all his friends, and that unforgettable summer. He must channel his thoughts on today and tomorrow if he were to survive. To live in the past was a torture to himself, and the only way to end the tedious days, and sleepless nights was to cast these thoughts from his mind.

The week after he moved to the East Block, he received a ducet for a cell move back to the South Block. He couldn't believe it, and thought it must be a mistake.

The next morning after moving back to the South Block, he went to see the Lieutenant. "All right Thompson, what can I do for you?"

"Hey Lieutenant, what's this bullshit? Last week I moved into the East Block, and this morning I got a ducet to move back to the South Block."

"So what are you doing here Thompson? Why aren't you moving then?"

"Goddamn it Lieutenant, I already moved, do you know what it's like carrying a heavy piss-soaked mattress all over the joint?"

"Simmer down," the Lieutenant ordered. "Didn't I assign you to the kitchen last week?"

"Yeah that's right, you also had me transferred to the East Block too. So why the hell did I have to move again?"

"Hold up Thompson, keep your temper down, I'm sure there's been a slight mistake."

212

"Yeah, I bet!"

Most cell moves are very irritating to an inmate. To move from one cell block to another required a prisoner to travel past any number of locked doors and gates. Each door or gate was controlled by a guard, and on most occasions a prisoner would have to wait until the guard decided to unlock the gate or door. While the inmate is waiting for doors to be opened, he is burdened with a mattress, pillow, blankets, and all his personal property. Occasionally, a cell move required more than one trip.

"All right Thompson what is your first name and number?"

"Leon, Leon Thompson, A-92856."

"Oh so you're an old A number," the Lieutenant said as he turned to his filing cabinet and pulled out the cell movement sheet. He looked it over carefully before slamming it on his desk. Then he said, "Damn it all, you're not supposed to transfer to the South Block. The Ducet Clerk made a mistake. You were supposed to move to the North Block."

The Lieutenant pressed the intercom button on his desk.

A voice answered, "Yes Lieutenant?"

"Send the Ducet Clerk in with his daily movement sheet."

A few seconds later the office door opened admitting a neatly dressed, well groomed inmate. "Yes Lieutenant?" he said.

"Carlson you made a mistake on a ducet. Thompson here is A-92856 and he was supposed to move to the North Block this morning, but your ducet sent him to the South Block."

"I'll straighten it out right away Lieutenant," Carlson snapped. "He'll be on the next movement sheet." He turned to Whitey and continued with, "You'll receive another ducet tonight for a cell move to the North Block tomorrow morning."

"Tomorrow morning!" Whitey shouted at the Ducet Clerk. "You son of a bitch, I ought to make you carry my fucking mattress. You ass-kissing pen-pushing bastard!"

Carlson looked from Whitey to the Lieutenant and back at Whitey again; then quickly turned on his heels and left the office.

The following morning Lou obtained permission to help Whitey move to the North Block. He remained there a little over a month, and on the evening of July 11 he received another ducet. The following morning at 9:00 A.M. he was to report to Receiving and Release.

As ordered Whitey reported to R and R. He was told to check in his personal property as he was being transferred the next morning to D.V.I. (Duel Vocational Institute) Tracy for his parole violation hearing, known as a Morricey Hearing.

Later that same day after lunch he met Lou down in the lower yard.

"Well old buddy it looks like we part again," Whitey said. "I'm being sent to Tracy for my Morricey Hearing."

"Hey that's great, you might be out in six months."

"Don't feed me that shit Lou! You know damn well I'm gonna do at least two or three years."

"On a straight violation Whitey? No way!" Lou insisted. "You won't do a day over six months."

"I hope you're right Lou, but I doubt it. Anyways if I don't get a chance to see you before I transfer, I wish you luck pal."

"You too Whitey. Next time you get out, stay out, we're getting a little too old for all this."

"You're right Lou, next time I get out I *have* to make it, I can't do no more time."

It was an emotional moment as the two friends shook hands, and said their farewells.

The following day, July 13 Whitey was transferred to D.V.I. Two days after his arrival he was Classified and assigned to the kitchen as Lead Cook on the morning shift.

It was August 22 when Whitey went up for his Morricey Hearing. Mr. Morson and a representative of the California Adult Authority made up the panel. Mr. Rosemar was also present to press charges of parole violation. Mr. James O. Bues, an attorney, was there to represent Whitey, and to argue the charges. As the hearing progressed Whitey did most of the arguing himself. At an earlier date he previously pled guilty to two charges. Number one, leaving the county without permission. Number two, forgery.

As to the charge of using drugs and having a shotgun in his possession, Whitey claimed it was hearsay and could not be proven, and to these charges he pled not guilty.

The hearing continued for three hours. When it was finally over the Adult Authority found Whitey guilty on three charges, the use of drugs, forgery, and leaving the Sacramento area. The gun charge was dropped as they could not prove that he had a gun without one to show as evidence. Whitey argued that the same should go for the drug charge. Eleven months had gone by and there was no way he could be connected with the use of drugs, it was all hearsay.

Rosemar said this was not true, for Leon Thompson himself had admitted to him in having used such drugs as crank, weed, heroin, and other dangerous substances.

Whitey came up out of his chair and celled Rosemar a liar, and wanted to know why he would ever tell him that he was a user of drugs, as this would incriminate himself. He accused Rosemar of assuming that he had been on drugs, and that he had no evidence to prove it.

At one point Whitey was so furious toward Rosemar he had to be restrained by a guard. All of his arguing was to no avail; he was found guilty of the use of drugs. He was then informed he would appear before the Adult Board in January 1974. The panel recom-

214

mended that he be sent to Vacaville Medical Facility to have tests made to find out if there was any brain damage due to the use of drugs. The hearing was dismissed. As Whitey was being escorted from the room, he shouted, "The only one in this room with bran damage is that fucking pinhead parole officer!"

On that note the guards ushered him from the room.

CHAPTER 36.

On September 24 the transfer was carried out. While under guard Whitey was dressed out in the customary white coveralls. Along with fifteen other prisoners, he boarded the bus, and arrived at Vacaville shortly after 1:00 P.M. Whitey and one other convict were dropped off at the Medical Facility, while the remaining inmates continued to Folsom.

Vacaville had a dual purpose, really two prisons in one. The Medical Center was on one side, while the other side was called the Guidance Center. The Guidance Center was set up for receiving new prisoners from the county jails. Most of these men were first-timers. The Guidance Center is where they received their prison numbers, medical checkup, and a ninety-day evaluation. Then they are sent to such prisons as San Quentin, Folsom, Soledad, etc. etc. The medical side of Vacaville was known as the Time Side where prisoners would undergo various treatments, such as stress, and group therapy. The criminally insane, and inmates with emotional problems were also housed here in separate units.

After Whitey's arrival and dress-in, he was taken to I Wing and placed in a segregated cell. I Wing was one of eight Wings on the third floor of the prison, and each Wing contained single cells. This floor was known as Penel Unit.

The day after his arrival, Whitey was assigned to the kitchen as a cook, and one week later he was moved from I Wing to L Wing, cell 364. It seemed no matter what prison he was sent to there were always some old-timers that he knew. Occasionally he would even meet a guard that knew him from past years, for they too, on rare occasions were transferred for various reasons. Vacaville was not like an ordinary prison, it did not have the cold gray atmosphere of Folsom, or the chilling affect of San Quentin. Compared to all the other prisons security was not quite as strict, and there seemed to be a camaraderie between the inmates and guards.

Three weeks after Whitey's arrival he was given an EEG test to decide whether he had brain damage or not. Once it was completed, he was told it would be two weeks before he could receive the results of the test. It was just two weeks to the day when they came in, and

Whitey was notified. The results showed there were a few damaged cells, but this was normal. Over a course of fifty years most middle-aged people will have brain cells die out or be damaged from hard work, contact sports, or accidents.

"Well Thompson, with the normal wear and tear of a man of fifty, you've got a good brain."

"If I have a good brain, then what am I doing back in prison?" Whitey asked.

"Only you can answer that," the Technician replied. "I sure as hell can't."

"It's because I've been a fool, a goddamn fool! When you think right, you do right, and when you think wrong, you do wrong, and I've been wrong all my fucking life. But from here on out, and for the rest of my life, I'll be playing no more games. I'm gonna be straight with myself."

Christmas was followed by the New Year; it was January 23, 1974, Whitey's fifty-first birthday. For the first time in years, he was thinking positive, and comfortable with himself.

He was scheduled to go before the Adult Board, but it was post-poned until next month. On February 18 Whitey was sitting in the waiting area outside the Board Room door. Presently his name and number were called. He entered the room and felt a sudden change in the atmosphere as he took his seat. Sitting across from him representing the Adult Panel was two familiar faces, Larkin, and Morson.

Leafing through a folder Larkin was the first to speak, "Well Thompson looks like you had a nice little run for yourself!"

Whitey smiled but made no comment.

Larkin turned the page then looked up at Whitey, "It seems you ran a little short of money so you wrote a few checks. This is something new for your Thompson. You always got your money with the use of a gun, but never behind a pen! That's an improvement, you can't shoot anyone with an ink pen, can you?" Larkin laughed.

He turned a page in the folder. "How about this drug charge? How do you plead?"

"The same as I did six months ago—not guilty."

"I have a report here in your jacket from Mr. Rosemar, he states that during an interview in the Sacramento county jail on January 3, 1973 you confessed to him of having used drugs. What have you to say to this?"

"It's a lie, I never told him no such thing."

"Then why would he state you had?" Larkin asked.

"Like I said before at my last hearing, he's just assuming I had used drugs, but he has no proof, he just made up that phoney report."

"That doesn't seem likely Thompson, he had nothing to gain by

217

putting in a false report."

"Mr. Larkin you know of my reputation."

"Yes Thompson I'm afraid I do."

"Then how can you sit there and honestly believe that I would cop out on myself as to using drugs? You stated that Rosemar had nothing to gain by putting in a false report, what the hell would I have to gain by copping out on myself? It's been seventeen months since I was arrested, and no one, I repeat, no one can prove I ever used drugs, including Rosemar."

Still leafing through the folder Larkin again looked up at Whitey and said, "It is stated here that last October you had an EEG test, and the results states that you have traces of brain damage. No doubt caused by the use of drugs."

"That's not so," Whitey contradicted, "I don't know what results you're reading there, but my EEG test report showed that I had a normal amount of brain damage that any man of my age could have. If you people want to believe I told Rosemar I was on drugs that's your privilege."

"Then what you're telling us Mr. Thompson, is that you are not guilty."

"I'm saying no such thing," Whitey said in a surly voice. "I may or may not have been on drugs, all I'm stating is that Rosemar lied when he said I had told him I had been using drugs."

Larkin turned his attention to Morson, "Do you have any further questions for Mr. Thompson?"

Morson looked at Whitey, their eyes locked, and for a fleeting moment Morson smiled. Then turning to Larkin he said, "I think everything was fairly well covered, I have no questions."

"All right Thompson," Larkin said, "this hearing is ended, we'll let you know."

Whitey rose from his seat, thanked the Board members, and vacated the room.

Three days later he received his results—Parole denied, placed on R and R Panel February calendar 1975.

Two days after his denial he had to appear for reclassification. Lieutenant Gribble, Dr. Wilson, a woman psychiatrist, Sergeant Mosely, and Mr. Simmerly, correctional counselor, formed the committee.

Whitey entered the room and was seated in front of them.

Lieutenant Gribble was a typical Department of Corrections officer. With graying hair from years of service, he had a square jaw and stern cold gray eyes that gave the impression of a strict disciplinarian. But as one got to know this man, underneath his armor, he was kind, just and fair.

"Well Thompson," the Lieutenant said, "As you know you were denied parole, and I'm sorry about that."

"Thank you sir."

"It's up to the committee to decide what to do with you. As you know this is a medical facility, there is nothing wrong with you, so therefore you will be transferred. You have your choice, you can go back to San Quentin or Folsom."

Locking eyes with the Lieutenant, Whitey sat there a moment. Then with a laugh he said, "That's not much of a choice, I guess Folsom."

"All right Thompson, so be it, you'll be sent back to Folsom."

"How long will it be before I leave sir?"

"You will leave within the next three days."

"Thank you sir."

The next day Whitey was walking down the Wing corridor, by chance, he bumped into Mr. Simmerly. Simmerly had been with the Department for many years, and in the near future was due for retirement. During his early years he was a guard at Soledad Prison, and rose to the rank of Lieutenant. Due to his interest in helping inmates, he resigned, and became a Correctional Counselor.

"Hello Mr. Simmerly," Whitey greeted. "Can I speak to you for a moment?"

"Why sure," he replied, "what's on your mind?"

"Do you think there's any chance I could stay here on a work crew or something? To be truthful I don't want to get back to the rat race. I mean the rat race of Folsom and Quentin, you know what I'm talking about."

"I believe so. Look Thompson I'm on my way to my office, if you got a moment I'll take a look at your record."

At the counselor's office Simmerly removed Whitey's record from the file cabinet.

"Well let's see what we have here," he said as he thumbed through the folder. "Technically Thompson, according to my records, I see quite an improvement in you since you left Alcatraz. Other than the crimes that brought you to state prison, you've been conducting yourself well. Maybe I can do something for you. Look, I can't answer now, but give me a chance to go over your records with a fine tooth comb, if possible I'll have you brought back before the committee. In the meantime, I'll put a hold on your transfer."

"Thank you very much sir," Whitey said as he stood up reaching for Simmerly's hand.

The following afternoon the counselor summoned Whitey to his office. He was talking on the phone when Whitey entered. "Take a seat Thompson, I'll be with you in a moment."

After hanging up the phone, smiling at Whitey he said, "I went through your record completely. I was surprised, all the years you served in state prison you never had a disciplinary report. That's really hard to believe. I think that in itself is worth some consideration. Next Wednesday I'm going to have you brought back before the committee. At that time I'll recommend your desire to stay here

219

at Vacaville."

"That's great Mr. Simmerly. I appreciate what you're doing for me, I won't let you down."

"Don't thank me yet, it might not be approved. When you go for reclassification, you'll have to convince the rest of the committee to let you stay here."

"Well I want to thank you anyway Mr. Simmerly. Thank you very much."

On the following Wednesday morning Whitey went before the Reclassification Committee. He sat there with his arms folded across his chest. Lieutenant Gribble and Dr. Wilson were giving him hard stern looks. The Lieutenant was the first to speak, "Well Thompson it looks like you're trying to pull a string!"

"In all honesty, yes sir!" Whitey said returning the stern look.

For a fraction of a second the Lieutenant's armored face almost smiled. "You have requested to stay here as a worker. You are just looking for a cushion," he accused.

Whitey jerked forward in his chair, and did not try to conceal his anger, "That's right Lieutenant," he said in a sarcastic voice, "I'm looking for a cushion! I broke my goddamn. . . ."

"What makes you think you deserve a cushion?" the Lieutenant interrupted.

Half rising out of his chair, Whitey flared back, "I broke my ass for years cooking behind the walls of Folsom, you're damn right I'm looking for a cushion. For over five years I cooked for twenty-eight to twenty-nine hundred men. I never had a single day off. There were times . . . ."

"Hold it Thompson, hold it, simmer down," the Lieutenant interrupted again. "You needn't say anymore, I have your records right in front of me."

"You asked me if I was looking for a cushion, I was just telling you damn it!"

"And I'm telling you to simmer down!"

Whitey settled back in his chair. With a challenging expression he looked from one member to the other, then back to the Lieutenant who was now smiling.

"I have to hand it to you Thompson, for a man of your age you still show spunk." He turned to the other members, "Are there any more questions?"

Dr. Wilson's cold piercing eyes focussed on Whitey's face and for a moment held him in her hypnotic gaze. She was a woman of wisdom who could not easily be fooled. She had been a psychiatrist at Vacaville for a number of years, and was wise to the ways of a convict. Behind her mask was a warmhearted woman.

"I think you've just about covered everything," she said.

220

Both Simmerly and the Sergeant replied with, "No questions."

"Very well then," turning to Whitey he continued, "Would you step out into the corridor Thompson, we'll let you know our decision in a minute."

Whitey had a five minute wait before being summoned back into the room.

"Thompson, the panel has agreed to your request to remain here at Vacaville, and shortly we will be in need of a Screening Clerk, do you think you can handle the job?"

"I've never been a Screening Clerk, but I'm willing to learn."

"It's not difficult Thompson, you'll soon pick it up. Our present clerk is leaving on parole in a few days, he will teach you the ropes before he leaves."

"Thank you sir, thank you very much." Turning to the other members of the committee he thanked them also.

CHAPTER 37.

Whitey found the duties of the Penel Screening Clerk quite simple but it required a man of wisdom and experienced in the ways o prison life. On the evening prior to screening, he would receive a lis bearing the names and prison numbers of inmates who were t appear before the committee. The following morning at 7:30 A.M Whitey would pick up the medical record of each inmate on the list These records would be taken to the screening room. In preparatior for the committee, he made coffee, set ashtrays, pens, pencils, an paper pads on the table in front of each committee member's chair Whitey's office and the screening room were divided by a glass panel Through this panel he had clear view of the committee, and at a giver signal Whitey would send in the next inmate.

Before screening started he would have the inmates line u according to their prison numbers. Some of the inmates were firs termers, just kids of twenty-one recently incarcerated. Thes youngsters didn't know what to expect and were afraid. Occasionall one or two of them would try to cover up their fright by acting tough None of them could fool Whitey for he knew the pros and the con: He would take time to talk to each inmate and prepare him in th right fashion in representing themselves before the committee.

"Look," he would say to them, "when you go before the committee don't sit down until you're told to be seated. And when you do si don't slouch, sit up straight in the chair. Don't say a word unt you're spoken to, and above all don't get mad and lose your tempe: On your first appearance you may be denied whatever it is you'r after, but a good appearance is very important. Then you will have better chance of getting good results on the second or third time yo go in front of them. The important thing is to stay out of trouble, an have a good attitude. A good attitude goes a long way, and one mor thing, when you're doing time you got to learn to hav patience—plenty of it, and you're going to need it."

Working with these young men was a new and gainful experienc for Whitey. Each inmate represented a new challenge, and after session or two it was rewarding to see change in the attitude of thes young men.

During Whitey's stay at Vacaville he had many visitors, a good many of them were female. Ben Vakno and his motorcycle gang came to see him on a regular basis. It was a rare occasion when a day went by without a visit.

One afternoon while Ben was there he asked Whitey what his plans were for the future.

"I don't know yet," he replied, "but I don't think I'll be coming back to Sacramento."

"What?" Ben was surprised. "Where else would you go?"

"I don't know, but I do know I spent half my life in prison and I'm tired of it. I believe the only way I can stay out is to cut my friends and Sacramento loose."

Ben stood there a moment, then he spoke softly, "Maybe you're right Whitey, I guess that's the wise thing to do, but as long as I have a home you're always welcome. Whatever I've got is yours man, you know that, even my old lady if you want her!" he laughed.

"Thanks Ben I'm glad you understand, I didn't want you to think I was turning my back on you and my friends."

"Shit we know better than that. I know what you're doing and I'm all for it. I respect you and any decisions you make. No matter where you go, we can keep in touch."

As the two men embraced Whitey said, "You can count on it Ben."

One day a notice caught Whitey's attention, it read, "AMANDA BLAIR'S FRIENDSHIP CLUB." The sole purpose of this club was to encourage people to write to prisoners. Whitey wrote to Amanda Blair, giving her a brief outline of himself, and expressing his desire to correspond with someone in the Bay Area. He signed the letter Leon instead of Whitey.

A week later Langley, the Cell House officer, was passing out the mail, and slid a letter under Whitey's cell door. As he picked up the envelope he noticed the Oakland address in the upper left-hand corner. It read:

Helen Thompson
580 Capell St.
Oakland, CA 94302

    Dear Leon,

    My friend Amanda Blair asked me to write to you, which I am happy to do. By coincidence my maiden name is Thompson too.

    Now let me tell you a bit about myself. I'm fifty-two years old, born in England, and after a marriage of twenty-four years to a World War Two GI, I was divorced. We had four children, two girls and two boys, who of course are now grown and on their own. As for me, I'm a retired professional show dog handler

223

and trainer. I had my own kennels for many years. I now live quietly alone with two Whippet dogs, Diver and Richard. I'm an easygoing person, and I have a good sense of humor.

Amanda told me a bit about you, I would like to know more if you would care to write and tell me. You sound like a very interesting person, and if you do decide to write, I promise to answer promptly, and I hope to hear from you soon.

Yours Sincerely
Helen Thompson

Whitey wrote by return telling more about himself. After an exchange of photographs, in a very short time they were writing to each other every day. Although they came from vastly different backgrounds, they seemed to have a lot of interests in common, and through correspondence they became very close friends.

In October Helen visited Whitey for the first time, and as she entered the visiting room they had no trouble recognizing each other. Helen was a pleasant and typical English woman. It was her first time to ever visit an incarcerated person. Whitey immediately took a liking to her, and decided he would tell her the truth about himself leaving nothing out. Helen liked his honesty, and the visit turned out to be a joyful experience for both of them. She began visiting Whitey twice a week.

There were times while Helen was visiting Whitey some of his scooter tramp friends would come to see him. At first it was embarrassing for her, but as she got to know each one of them she began to feel more at ease, and in time, quite friendly.

"I didn't realize you had so many friends," Helen said at one of her visits.

"Yeah, but did you notice how young they are?"

"Yes that's what I was thinking, and the girls, they are all so beautiful, I don't think I can compete with them!"

"Don't worry about the competition Helen, they're not ready to settle down. And if they did it wouldn't last long."

Helen and Whitey developed a warm affection for each other that in time turned to love.

The second Monday in January 1975 Whitey was called to Mr. Simmerly's office.

"Good morning Thompson have a seat," Simmerly greeted him. "As you may know, you were called in here today for your pre-board report. Next month you are due for a parole hearing. I have to get your report in, and I must know what your parole plans are," Simmerly leafed through a folder, then continued, "I see you have

224

been corresponding and visiting with a Helen Thompson for the past seven months. Her name is the same as yours is there a connection?"

"No Mr. Simmerly, it's just a coincidence her name is the same as mine."

"Yes it is. I assume she is included in your parole plans."

"Yes sir, if I make parole we hope to get married."

"Well let's assume you do make parole and get married, what about your drinking problem? And also your drug problem?"

"Look Mr. Simmerly, whether you believe it or not, I don't have a drinking problem, and like I told the Adult Board last year, no one can prove I ever used drugs. I have no problems."

Simmerly sat there a moment studying Whitey's records, then looking across his desk he said, "Just between you and me Thompson, and this will be off the record, did you, or did you not, ever use drugs?"

"You must be kidding Mr. Simmerly, nothing's off the record!"

"When I say off the record Thompson, you can believe me."

For a brief moment their eyes locked, then Whitey replied, "Off the record, yes sir I did drugs when I was on the run in '71 and '72, but they are no longer a problem to me now."

Simmerly smiled and said, "All right Thompson I believe you, drugs are no problem to you. But what about the drinking? The Adult Authority feels you have a problem with alcohol, they might want you to go to Alcoholics Anonymous as part of your parole plans."

"AA is okay for those that need it, Mr. Simmerly, but I'm not a drunkard."

"I agree with you Thompson, I don't believe you are an alcoholic either, but you should go along with whatever program the Adult Board sets up."

"I know, I know, don't worry I'll go along with them."

"Fine, I'm glad to hear you say that. I guess that'll be all Thompson, I'll do the best I can for you at the board."

It was 8:30 A.M. the first Thursday in February. Whitey was seated outside the Board Room door waiting his turn. As he sat there, many thoughts were running through his mind. He wanted desperately to make parole, and he knew he was ready. His name was called, but he was so deep in concentration he did not hear the guard.

"Hey Thompson, you want to go up this year, or wait for next?"

With a sudden start he returned to reality; he jumped out of the chair, and replied emphatically, "Hell no let's go!"

The officer opened the door, and as Whitey passed through he saw the same familiar faces staring at him. He was told to be seated.

"Well, well, Mr. Thompson," Larking greeted him. "We'll get right to the point, what are your plans for the future?"

For a moment Whitey remained silent. He was firmly seated in the chair with both hands on the arm rests. Finally he replied, "My future

225

depends on what happens here today."

"Let me put it to you another way Thompson. If you are granted a parole, what are your plans?"

"My plans are with Helen and. . . .My plans are to follow the conditions of my parole as set down by the Adult Board to the letter. As for any other plans, I believe they are sitting right there in front of you!"

Flushing slightly, Larkin looked down to the Pre-Board report lying in front of him. It was submitted by Whitey's counselor, Mr. Simmerly.

"Yes, I have his report. Let's see, does anyone have any questions for Mr. Thompson?"

There were no further questions.

"All right Thompson, we'll let you know."

Ten days passed. Whitey was seated at his desk in the outer office going over the days screening list. Suddenly the phone rang. He picked up the receiver, and in a level tone said, "Penel Screening Unit, Inmate Thompson speaking."

From the other end he heard a cheerful voice say, "Hello Thompson, this is Officer Langley. I have your Board results lying here on my desk. You're going out on May 5!"

"You're kidding, that's less than ninety days," Whitey shouted with joy.

"That's the day Thompson, you're going on parole May fifth."

That evening he asked the Sergeant if he could make a call to Oakland to let Helen know the good news. The Sergeant gave his permission for a collect call and escorted him to a phone with an outside connection.

Helen was pleased to hear the news and asked if there was anything she could do to hurry the release date.

"Yes," Whitey replied. "Just as soon as I find out who my Oakland P.O. is, I'll send you his name, and you can go see him. With any luck you might get me an earlier release date, but don't count on it."

Two days later Simmerly summoned Whitey to his office and told him who his parole officer would be.

"Herman Simon, and I must warn you," Simmerly said, "he is strict, very strict, and goes by the book."

That evening Whitey wrote a letter to Helen, informing her of the name and address of his new parole officer, and suggested that she go see him as soon as possible.

Upon receiving the letter Helen immediately set up an appointment with Mr. Simon for 1:00 P.M. the following day.

As Helen entered his office the parole office got up from his desk to shake hands. "Hello Mrs. Thompson, I'm Herman Simon," he said, "Won't you have a seat?"

"Thank you," Helen replied.

"As you know Whitey Thompson has been assigned to my case load, I must say I may have my hands full with him!"

Herman Simon was seated behind his desk, and with a surly smile, he picked up a large folder. "This folder I'm holding Mrs. Thompson, is Whitey Thompson's record, and I must say it's not a pretty one. By the way, you both have the name of Thompson, what a coincidence."

Helen was uncomfortable as she sat there clasping her hands, "Yes it is a coincidence."

"I understand you want to marry this man," Simon continued. "Do you realize what you're getting yourself into?"

"Yes I believe I do."

"Well I don't believe you do! How well do you know this man?"

"Well enough to know that I love him!"

The words were barely out of her mouth when suddenly he pounded his desk top, pushed his chair back and stood up. "You love him!" Simon exclaimed in an angry voice. "Don't you realize that Leon W. Thompson is a hardened criminal? He's been in and out of prison all his life."

"I know about his prison life, he's told me everything, and he also. . . ."

"He's told you everything?" Simon interrupted. "I don't think he did, we believe him to be institutionalized."

"That's not so," Helen protested.

"I beg to differ, he's on a merry-go-round. With his violent temper he'll always come back. And one other thing, did you know he has served time on Alcatraz?"

"Yes he told me, he told me everything."

"Everything Mrs. Thompson? Or only what he thought he had to tell you? In such a short time you can't know all that much about him."

"I know more than you realize, I've been visiting him twice a week for the past seven months, a total of fourteen hours a week. What do you think we did for seven hours each visiting day? We talked and talked, and there's not very much that Leon hasn't told me."

"Well it looks like you have made up your mind then, but there's one more thing, did he tell you he's a heavy drinker, and that he has used drugs?"

"Look Mr. Simon I've told you there's nothing you can tell me about Leon. I know him personally, and you don't. All you know about him is in that record you have on your desk."

Simon sat there looking at Helen in amazement; he leafed through a few more pages of the record, then closed the folder. He looked toward a calendar hanging on the wall. He stared at it momentarily, then once again he looked at Helen, and said, "How would you like to see him released on April 10 instead of May 5?"

His sudden change of attitude, and the surprise of his question was

227

almost too much for Helen. She did not expect this sudden change, above all an early parole date. It took a moment or two before she felt the impact of what was said. The excitement was electrifying and she wanted to shout for joy, but her English reserve prevented her from doing so. Very calmly she said, "Thank you Mr. Simon, thank you very much."

The parole officer smiled and said, "You're welcome Mrs.Thompson, you can break the news to him at your next visit."

Helen thanked him again, and on her way home she realized why Simon was so harsh toward Leon at the beginning of the interview. He wanted to see her reaction, but she must have passed the test because Leon would be home in a few weeks. She was happy, and her first impression of Simon changed considerably.

In the visiting room the following Wednesday morning, Helen's face was all aglow. She threw her arms around Whitey, and in a happy level voice she said, "Your parole officer is releasing you early. You'll be coming home on the tenth."

At 11:00 A.M. April 10, 1975. Leon W. Thompson was released from prison for the last time. Helen was waiting for him in the front office with open arms. The drive to Oakland was a memorable one, and after coffee and a light lunch, accompanied by Helen, Whitey went to downtown Oakland to report in to the parole office.

After a formal introduction, Simon's first words were short and to the point.

"Mr. Thompson you are now a part of my case load, you are under my jurisdiction. Just so there is no misunderstanding, I want you to know I go by the book. If you step out of line in the least way, I won't hesitate to send you back to prison. You are not to drink any alcoholic beverages, and if I come to your home and find any sign that you have been drinking, that will be a violation. If you carry anything that could be considered a weapon, such as a penknife, or if you get into a fight, right or wrong, without any hesitation I will send you straight back to prison. Like I said before, I go by the book. I have a large case load, and if you can't go by the rules, I don't have time to fool around with the likes of you. You screw up, you get no second chance with me. In other words' Thompson, don't step out of line."

Whitey sat there listening to his parole officer lay down the ground rules.

"You are to report to me twice a week, once by phone, and once in person, and you will mail in a monthly report to me no later than the fifth of each month. Do I make myself clear?"

"Yes sir," Whitey replied. "Very clear, and thank you sir."

CHAPTER 38

April 14, four days after his release from prison Whitey and Helen were married. During the second week after the ceremony Helen had some afterthoughts. She wondered if she had made a mistake. A few of Whitey's scooter tramp friends showed up one day to celebrate his release from prison. Of course he got drunk, and Helen was afraid he would fall back in his old ways. On two different occasions Whitey went to Sacramento and wound up partying with his old gang. He was there for a number of days, while Helen was home at her wit's end with worry. She was undecided as what to do. Should she notify his parole officer? Or should she wait to see what would happen? She knew if she notified his parole officer he would be violated and sent back to prison. She gave the matter deep thought, and tried to put herself in Whitey's shoes. He had been in prison a long time, and felt entitled to these drinking parties. But hopefully he would realize that this was not the way for him. Helen had faith in Whitey, and decided she would help him and give him every opportunity to bring his life together.

Helen never said anything to Whitey about the drinking parties. One morning he surprised her when he announced that he would never drink again. Whitey did not lie to her, and true to his word he never drank anymore. As for Helen, she was thankful for the faith she had in him. In the end it paid off, and their love grew stronger.

The months flew by. On December 1, Helen and Whitey received an invitation from her married daughter Chris. She invited them to spend the Christmas holidays in Lakewood, near Los Angeles with her and her husband.

The following day, December 2. Whitey accompanied by Helen, went to see his parole officer to obtain permission to leave the county for the holidays.

"Please have a seat," Simon said, "I'll be with you in a moment." He turned and walked to his outer office, and in a moment reappeared carrying a manila envelope. "Well Thompson, what brings you here today? No trouble I hope."

Smiling Whitey replied, "No sir nothing like that. You see Helen's daughter has invited us to come to the Los Angeles area for the holidays. I'd like to get permission to leave the county."

"You don't need my permission to leave the county, as of one minute past midnight last night you were officially discharged."

Whitey and Helen sat there astounded and speechless. Simon continued, "You've been out on parole a little over seven months. You've done well on your job, and your conduct has been excellent. Last month I sent in a request to the Department of Corrections recommending you for a discharge. I was happy to see you and Helen walk into my office today, it saved me the trouble of calling you. Like I said a moment ago, last night one minute past midnight, you were officially discharged from the Department of Corrections."

As Simon handed Whitey the envelope containing the discharge, he smiled and said, "You don't need my permission for anything Thompson. It looks like you're getting off the merry-go-round."

Whitey laughed as he held up the envelope, "What do you mean it looks like I'm getting off the merry-go-round? I *am* off the merry-go-round! I'm free man, this is the brass ring!"

EPILOGUE

After Whitey's release from prison it was still an uphill battle. He had spent a total of twenty-five years in the penitentiary, and felt shame and regrets. He had a feeling of guilt which was too much for him, and he was a lonely man. Despite his marriage to Helen, and his freedom from prison, depression set in, and he was unable to communicate with people. The only person he felt he could talk to was Helen. If anyone knew the feelings of this man it was she. She knew what he was going through. She felt he had paid his debt to society and need not suffer in this way. So in 1980 she suggested that Whitey write his autobiography as a way to clean the soul.

For the next six months Whitey and Helen spent endless hours working on the book. Whitey would do the writing, and Helen would correct the spelling and grammar, and type it up. Writing the book meant reliving his past. It tore at him to the point where he could not go on with the writing. He was ready to throw the book idea out the window.

Helen was very understanding, and sympathized with the man she loved. She knew how hard it was for him to write about the terrible things he had done. She also knew he must get it out of his system before he could have peace with himself. She suggested that if he tried writing the book in the third person he might be able to get outside of himself.

The idea worked, and Whitey plunged into writing with a new and vigorous energy. It became an obsession with him as if time was running out. This almost became a reality for in March 1982, Whitey, who thought he was in fairly good health, was struck down by a series of terrifying angina attacks. He was rushed to St. Joseph's Hospital in Stockton, California where he was given an angiogram. The results showed a 99% blockage to the heart, and to the arteries of both legs. He was given thirty days to live. This condition was caused by excessive abuse to the body by the use of drugs, cigarettes, and alcohol during his earlier years.

Dr. Liem, his cardiologist informed Whitey that he needed three major operations. Number One, a triple heart bypass operation. Number Two, replace the artery in the right leg with an artificial one. Number Three, remove the artery from left leg. Have it reversed inside out, cleaned and replaced in the leg.

Dr. Liem informed Helen that Whitey's chance of survival was practically nil.

Leon Whitey Thompson was a survivor, but this time, it would be the fight of his life. With the support of God, and the love of his wife, he knew he would make it, and survive he did.

Recovering from his ordeal, he dove into his writing with renewed energy. Once more God had spared him, and he was prepared for the biggest role he must play in life.

While writing his books LAST TRAIN TO ALCATRAZ, now published by Pocket Books, and re-titled ROCK HARD, Helen felt that he had a lot to offer young people. She suggested that he give testimony to schools, Juvenile Halls, Continuation schools, California Youth Authority, and several prisons.

For years Whitey has given endless hours to these causes, and now in his seventies he still works at it today.

In writing his books, ROCK HARD and ALCATRAZ MERRY-GO-ROUND both Helen and Whitey decided it was best to leave out most of his crimes. He was not trying to hide anything, he just did not want youngsters to fantasize on all the crimes he had committed. So he just wrote enough about his crimes to let the readers know he deserved to be sent to prison.

During this period Whitey and Helen acquired an Arctic Wolf Hybrid puppy which they named Winter. When they had had her two weeks, she contracted Parvo which, although she survived, it stunted her growth. Otherwise she was normal in every respect, and was loved dearly. She became Whitey's shadow, going everywhere with him, and sleeping beside him on the bed.

She died at the age of six years, and it broke their hearts.

When they published their books, in remembrance of this beautiful Wolf Dog, they had her name printed on the spine of each book, and called it A WINTER BOOK.

After completion of their first book, Whitey and Helen borrowed money from friends they had acquired over the past few years, and managed to raise enough to have five hundred copies printed. Since then Whitey has sold over seventy-six thousand copies on Alcatraz Island. Thousands of tourists from all over the world who have purchased this book have written to Whitey. They all wanted to know what happened to him after Alcatraz. This encouraged him to write the sequel, ALCATRAZ MERRY-GO-ROUND which continues from his release from Alcatraz to the present day.

Today Whitey is at peace with himself. He enjoys talking to people, and tries to help troubled youngsters. No longer does he feel shame, or regret, for a man who feels sorry for himself is a man with cancer. Although he would like to, he realizes he cannot change the past. All he can do today is be 100 percent honest with himself, and that is the key to success. He continuously praises his wife Helen. For without her love and understanding, he might never have made it.

When not autographing his books, or away at a speaking

engagement, Whitey is at his home in the mountains enjoying the companionship of his wife, their dogs, and Wolf Hybrids.

He is very grateful to the many friends who have come to know and love him. Especially to the Rangers of Alcatraz. Whitey appears on the Island once or twice a week to autograph his books, and to talk to the tourists. Each time he returns to the Island he is greeted by Naomi Torres Supervisory Park Ranger, and her staff.

Whitey has made friends including Terry Koenig of the Red and White Fleet, and Frank Heaney, and ex-Correctional Officer of Alcatraz. Frank and Whitey have teamed up together, and have made many appearances at high schools, grade schools, juvenile hall, and many prisons. They have become quite popular, and today they continue their campaign in hopes of saving some youngster from going down a similar road that Whitey has traveled. They have also appeared on several TV shows.

For the past eight years Whitey, once a month, has been attending the Pre-Release classes at Mule Creek State Penitentiary. For his volunteer service he has been awarded The warden's appreciation plaque presented to him by Warden Ivalee Henry of Mule Creek State Penitentiary.

He also goes to Folsom Prison once a month to volunteer his services where he speaks to Dr. Harvey Shrum's Pre-Release program. He is quite popular with the inmates, and the Correctional Officers. Whitey and Helen always receive a warm greeting from Officer S. Houston when they arrive at the Folsom prison gate.

Leon Whitey Thompson is nothing like the Whitey of yesterday. The anger and hate are long gone now, and have been replaced with nothing but love. He has worked very hard to turn his life around, and today he is one of the most honest men you will ever meet.

For the good work he has done for the past twenty years he would have no problem in receiving a full Presidential Pardon. Speaking for himself only, he does not believe in pardons. A pardon does not change the fact that the crimes were committed. He thinks about his victims, the people he has hurt a long time ago, and he is truly sorry for interrupting their lives. A Presidential Pardon will never clear his conscience and for that reason he would never accept a pardon.

Today Alcatraz Island is a National Park, and from all over the world it draws more than a million tourists a year. On almost any given day you can find Leon Whitey Thompson on Alcatraz answering the many questions of the tourists. As for Whitey, he never dreamed that one day he would be sitting on the Rock autographing his books. He had no idea that he would even be alive today, and he is thankful.

LEON WHITEY THOMPSON, ONE OF SIX MEN EVER TO BE RELEASED DIRECTLY FROM ALCATRAZ. PHOTO TAKEN THREE DAYS PRIOR TO HIS RELEASE FROM ALCATRAZ, OCTOBER 25, 1962.

STATE PRISON MUGSHOT OF WHITEY BEFORE ENTERING FOLSOM STATE PRISON ON A 15 YEAR SENTENCE.

THE MAIN GATE, PHOTO TAKEN JUST OUTSIDE THE WALLS OF FOLSOM PRISON.

FOLSOM PRISON. WHITEY AND CORRECTIONAL OFFICER S. HOUSTON WHO GREETS WHITEY ON HIS MONTHLY VISIT TO SPEAK TO THE PRE-RELEASE CLASSES. PHOTO TAKEN JANUARY 1995.

PHOTO TAKEN OF WHITEY WHILE SERVING TIME AT FOLSOM PRISON.

THE REMAINS OF WHITEY'S HIDEOUT ON OPHIR ROAD, AUBURN, CALIFORNIA.

PHOTO OF OVEN DISCOVERED BY WHITEY WHERE HE DID ALL HIS COOKING IN BLACKWOOD CANYON. LAKE TAHOE AREA.

RECENT PHOTO OF WHITEY POINTING TO A TREE WHERE HE CARVED HIS NAME IN BLACKWOOD CANYON 1971.

PHOTO OF HELEN VISITING WHITEY IN PRISON.

WINTER, THE ARCTIC WOLF HYBRID THAT BECAME SPECIAL TO WHITEY. HER DEATH LEFT A VOID IN WHITEY'S HEART.

WHITEY AND TWO OF HIS BELOVED WOLF HYBRIDS. TIMBER COUGAR WOLF, AND TERWIN.

WHITEY AND HIS WIFE HELEN RELAXING AT HOME.

A PHOTO OF WHITEY ON ALCATRAZ AUTOGRAPHING HIS BOOK PREVIOUSLY TITLED LAST TRAIN TO ALCATRAZ, NOW TITLED ROCK HARD.

RECENT PHOTO OF WHITEY WITH HIS WOLF HYBRID NAMED AMORAK. THE WORD AMORAK MEANS THE SPIRIT OF THE WOLF.

RECENT PHOTO OF WHITEY SPEAKING AT THE JACKSON ROTARY CLUB, JACKSON, CALIFORNIA.

PHOTO OF NAOMI L.TORRES, SUPERVISORY PARK RANGER ON ALCATRAZ.
COURTESY OF GOLDEN GATE NATIONAL RECREATION AREA.

NATIONAL PARK SERVICE RANGERS ALCATRAZ 1994. TOP ROW LEFT TO RIGHT: BRETT WOODS, DONNA STRAND, JAMES OSBORNE, BENNY BATON, NAOMI TORRES. BOTTOM ROW LEFT TO RIGHT: ARMANDO QUINTERO, PHIL BUTLER, CHRIS EVANS, FERMIN SALAS, ALLEN BLASDALE, KEVIN TURNER, DONNA MIDDLEMIST, JOHN CANTWELL, RAQUEL LOPEZ, CRAIG GLASSNER.
PHOTO BY CRAIG GLASSNER.

PHOTO OF EX-ALCATRAZ CORRECTION OFFICER FRANK HEANEY. NOW WITH THE RED AND FLEET, PUBLIC RELATIONS. TODAY FRANK AND WHITEY ARE THE BEST OF FRIENDS, AND DO A LOT OF SPEAKING ENGAGEMENTS TOGETHER AT VARIOUS SCHOOLS , PRISONS, AND ROTARY CLUBS.

PHOTO OF TERRY KOENIG, MARKETING MANAGER, RED AND WHITE FLEET. TERRY IS A WONDERFUL FRIEND WHO CONTINUOUSLY TRIES TO PROMOTE WHITEY TO HIGHER LEVELS OF RECOGNITION.

HELEN SITTING WITH HER ARM AROUND TIMBER COUGAR WOLF.

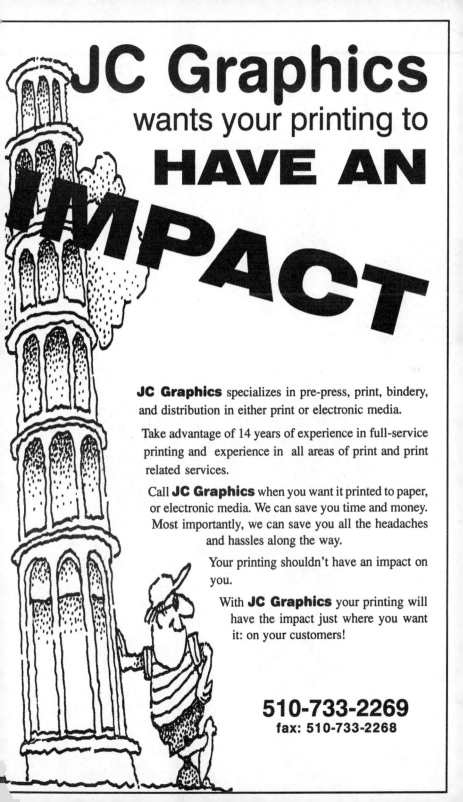